Imperial America
American Foreign Policy Since 1898

THE HARBRACE HISTORY OF THE UNITED STATES

Imperial America

American Foreign Policy

Since 1898

Lloyd C. Gardner

Rutgers University

Under the General Editorship of

John Morton Blum, Yale University

HARCOURT BRACE JOVANOVICH, INC.

New York   Chicago   San Francisco   Atlanta

Frontispiece: 1904 Cartoon, The American
Imperial Eagle by Joseph Keppler, The Granger
Collection

ISBN: 0-15-540896-8

Library of Congress Catalog Card Number: 75-35326

Printed in the United States of America

Copyrights and Acknowledgments

FABER AND FABER LTD for a selection from "Burnt
Norton" in *Four Quartets* by T. S. Eliot, copyright,
1943, by T. S. Eliot, copyright, 1971, by Esme
Valerie Eliot. Reprinted by permission of Faber
and Faber, Ltd.
HARCOURT BRACE JOVANOVICH, INC. for a
selection from "Burnt Norton" in *Four Quartets*
by T. S. Eliot, copyright, 1943, by T. S. Eliot,
copyright, 1971, by Esme Valerie Eliot. Reprinted
by permission of Harcourt Brace Jovanovich, Inc.

Page 289 constitutes a continuation of the copyright
page.

Preface

Time present and time past
Are both perhaps present in time future,
And time future contained in time past.
If all time is eternally present
All time is unredeemable.
What might have been is an abstraction
Remaining a perpetual possibility
Only in a world of speculation.
What might have been and what has been
Point to one end, which is always present.

T. S. Eliot
"Burnt Norton"

Historians do debate the might-have-beens, sometimes with their protagonists and sometimes with each other. And if they are considering as controversial a subject as "Imperial America," the temptation to indulge in a running argument with the past becomes all but irresistible. What is more important to a reader, however, is the historian's endeavor to draw distinctions and make connections. The most difficult of these concern relationships between description and analysis, explanation and justification, and exposition and interpretation.

The historian resolves these often subtle tensions by reference to specific materials and with the aid of a general framework. But the reader is by no means obliged to accept the result as the final word on any subject. Indeed, if the dialogue between historian and reader fails to encourage serious debate, both will lose.

This book focuses on the relationship between policymakers, their ideas, and their institutions. My premise is that history is not a summary of statistical findings, however useful those may be as tools. Perceptions of reality may depend as much on a special (even mythical) view of the past as on current facts. It is the policymaker's task to seek some rational integration of the two that will do violence to neither and keep society intact. Thus a nation's leaders may decide a given issue purely in terms of ideology, but their decision must be explainable in terms of practical advantage. For good or ill, this process helps to shape what is possible in the future.

People interact with the past continuously; they are affected by it; and their perceptions of it change. This could hardly be otherwise. History is taught in schools to make that interaction socially useful. Revolutionary societies are usually the most adamant about imposing limits on what is taught about the past. The old order's history is often not only unsuitable to the present, but a dangerous counterrevolutionary weapon. Teaching about the American Revolution has not been an exception, but the liberal-democratic society that evolved from that revolution has managed better than its rivals to keep open the possibility of coming to terms with its past, a not unimportant accomplishment.

Finally, this book is concerned with American leaders' perceptions of this nation's international role in the twentieth century, the origins of their views, and the way they have grappled with domestic social and political imperatives in an effort to make sense out of the world and to preserve what they believe to be essential institutions. In one sense, it is about the quest to make the world safe for democracy, but it is also about international competition and rivalry.

I am indebted to several friends and scholars who read the manuscript and pointed out where I was more than usually cryptic or just plain wrong. John Morton Blum of Yale University, the General Editor of this series, Diane Shaver Clemens of the University of California at Berkeley, George C. Herring of the University of Kentucky, Walter LaFeber of Cornell University, and Joan Hoff Wilson of Sacramento State College read the original draft and made perceptive comments, most of which I have tried to incorporate into the final version. I would also like to thank William J. Wisneski of Harcourt Brace Jovanovich, who kept after me to get the book written, and three super editors, Irene Pavitt, Alexandra Roosevelt, and Kay Reinhart Ziff, who took over from there. I alone am responsible, of course, for any and all errors as well as for the interpretation.

LLOYD C. GARDNER

To my students at Rutgers

Contents

Imperial America
American Foreign Policy Since 1898

The Paradox of 1
American Imperialism

For more than three hundred years Americans have participated in the construction of an empire, drawn benefits from it, and sought to extend its influence. Yet until Vietnam, a majority of Americans still understood *imperialism* to mean something Europeans did to other people centuries ago. Confronted by critics of the war, the nation's leaders denied the accusation that the United States had become an empire. This country—as it had always been—was antiempire. The only issue in Southeast Asia was the survival of freedom. Our willingness to stay the course in Vietnam could well determine the outcome of the long struggle between two opposed ways of life—and thus the future of humankind.

1

I WANT YOU
FOR U.S.ARMY
NEAREST RECRUITING STATION

As the war dragged on, the number of critics grew larger, and charges that Cold War rhetoric masked an ugly imperial reality grew louder. Eventually, the public debate became unintelligible. This was unfortunate, not only because of the harm being done by the war but also because an opportunity for serious inquiry into the origins of America's position in the world was being missed. Was there a connection between the Founding Fathers' vision of an "Empire of Liberty" and the "Free World" rhetoric of Cold War presidents? This was not the only question to be asked, or perhaps even the most important, but it was a good place to begin.

Near the end of the long war in Vietnam, the official answer to critics developed along a new line: Suppose one agrees that Vietnam was a mistake—even an unmitigated disaster, as Secretary of State Henry Kissinger would say once American involvement came to an end. What follows? A retreat into isolationism

1 and 2 Disenchantment with the war in Vietnam produced some second thoughts about symbols and substance.

would compound the original error and might well topple the collective-security system so carefully put together since the Second World War. Despite what had happened in Vietnam, indeed *because* of what had happened there, it was essential to sustain (or restore) American credibility. Even in a post-Cold War era, world stability would depend on American leadership. And we would scarcely enhance that leadership by debating ourselves into a new quagmire of self-doubt and recrimination in what could only be an ultimately futile effort to discover the lessons of Vietnam.

Not everyone was satisfied with this warning. To many, it was not easy to shrug off Vietnam as a mistake. Surely the presidents who had listened to arguments for intervention were not fools, nor conspirators concerned only with presenting the American people with another glorious military triumph. They acted from the conviction that the United States did have a real interest in preventing

3

a communist takeover in Southeast Asia. To others, the admonition against reexamining the origins of American involvement seemed self-serving, an excuse for the continuation of similar policies elsewhere.

For the dissatisfied, textbooks were not much help. Their approach was outdated, and their focus remained fixed on the battle against isolationism. Imperialism took up only a few pages—a brief episode about an unwanted and unexpected burden in the Philippines. If anything, that small dose of colonialism had immunized Americans against the disease of European imperialism. Moreover, the record of the United States in granting independence to Cuba and in fulfilling a pledge to give the Philippines its independence when it was ready contrasted so sharply with European practice that there was really no question of an American imperialism worthy of discussion.

While it was plain that by tradition and by practice America was anticolonial, it was not so certain that textbook versions of diplomatic history that equated imperialism and colonialism supplied an adequate explanation of American expansion. In an effort to explain what was unique about American expansion, John McDermott, a political theorist and Vietnam expert, settled on the phrase "welfare imperialism."[1] All great powers, he began, have sought to influence the diplomacy of other states, but some go on to seek a guiding influence *within* the other states. Those that succeed are the true empires. Of these, America has become the largest and most powerful in the modern world. But empires are started for different reasons.

Markets and raw materials, McDermott continued, had not been motivating factors in the establishment of America's empire. First created as a byproduct of the postwar alliance system, the American empire was sustained, and then expanded, through foreign aid programs. "[O]ur empire is ostensibly committed to the value of national independence for others, as well as humane and orderly development and social reconstruction."

What went wrong? McDermott wrote:

> We have tried to use our governmental bureaucracy as an instrument of social progress, trying to establish a welfare empire there as we

have established a welfare state here. . . . The nub of the Vietnamese problem was not, as Senator Fulbright would have it, that we were trying to be the world's policeman. It was instead that we were trying to be the world's social worker. Only when that failed did we turn the coin over and call in the police.

At that point, McDermott concludes, we finally began to see that our goals and means were contradictory. By then we were too embarrassed to admit the mistake and plunged ahead without heeding the warnings of those who reported the dangers awaiting the unwary. McDermott's account of the frustrated social worker become imperialist has the advantage of removing the discussion from the level of traditional diplomatic history and thus broadening the inquiry. It also suggests the importance of considering social structure and political behavior, domestic and foreign policy, as originating from the same sources: "a welfare empire there as we have established a welfare state here."

In the end, however, McDermott's thesis leads away from this promising territory and back onto familiar ground, where we recognize that the imperialist social worker is really naive Uncle Sam, still getting himself in trouble overseas because he cannot cope with the wiles and ways of foreigners. Mary McCarthy, another Vietnam observer, approached the same problem from a different

3 Mary McCarthy with Bernard Fall in Vietnam, February 1967.

direction by asking difficult questions about the connection between high-level policy and the search-and-destroy missions carried out on the lowest level by foot soldiers.[2] Her conclusion was that the goal was not simply to deprive the enemy of cover and sustenance. "The ultimate (or residual) aim of the Search-and-Destroy operations was to eradicate an entire rural way of life, based on a monoculture—rice—and closed off to modernization. This accounts for the systematic brick-by-brick destruction of the dwellings. The desired sequel was forced urbanization, usually an irreversible process."

In the new cities the former peasants would "acquire cravings for consumer goods, enter light industry and commerce, acquire a service point of view. Even, some of them, get rich." The Viet Cong, a precapitalist phenomenon that had its roots in fields and village communes, would finally fade away. Out of the ruins of European imperialism and communist-inspired civil war would rise a "modern" society. And if it could happen in Indochina, then why not elsewhere?

Where McDermott saw an ambitious, if overly idealistic, effort to export the Great Society to Vietnam, McCarthy identified a more purposeful attempt to establish basic institutions that would permit decisions to be made by the Vietnamese themselves on the same basis as they are made elsewhere in the "Free World." The distinction may seem to be only a matter of emphasis or angle of vision, but it is in fact fundamental. In 1974 Assistant Secretary of State Robert Ingersoll was challenged by a sarcastic comment from a member of Congress to demonstrate that South Vietnam President Thieu was any less dictatorial than Ho Chi Minh—just less efficient. Said Ingersoll in response: "No, I think he [Thieu] has deliberately chosen, at least from the standpoint of economics, a free market system rather than a completely controlled system."

Deeply ingrained in American political thought is the belief that a "free-market system" will, *must*, produce an open society. The origins of this faith go back to seventeenth-century England. The "liberal" state arose there, wrote political scientist C. B. Macpherson, in response to the needs of the society that emerged after

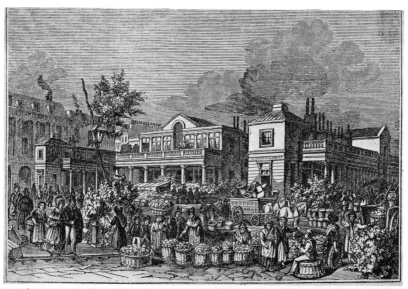

4 The seventeenth-century market society in London: a new way of life and of thinking about life.

the English civil war.[3] It did not begin as a democratic system. For a century the men who had wrested control of the state from the monarch successfully ruled this new, market-oriented society through a closed party system. As the exchange of goods and services on a national level replaced local self-sufficiency, and as new attitudes developed on all levels of society, the men of the directing classes realized that liberty could not be limited to a small elite. They faced the choice of attempting to preserve all their special privileges and risking revolution or of yielding something in the hope of preserving domestic tranquillity.

Whatever risks might attend the enfranchisement of all men of property had to be faced. There was no other way. Eventually this broadening process produced the liberal-democratic society and the justly famous "rights of Englishmen." Certain groups, however, were automatically excluded; slaves, for instance, existed only as a form of property. American Indians were also left outside; their existence even on the fringes of the liberal state became intolerable as soon as whites found it necessary to expand their marketplace area geographically to make room for newcomers of their own kind.

The liberal-democratic state was never fully realized in England before the American Revolution, in part because of the influence of a titled class that impeded mobility. So, ironically, it was the Americans who eagerly seized on the "rights of Englishmen" as their due and who founded the first true liberal-democratic state at the end of the War of Independence. When they looked back at old England, the Founding Fathers saw a powerful lesson in the corruption of the British political system. They agreed that they needed a written guarantee, or constitution, to prevent future distortions and perversions of the rights they should have enjoyed as Englishmen within the empire. What had happened to the mother country under George III must not be allowed to happen to America. The first constitution, the Articles of Confederation, sought to insure liberty by severely limiting the powers of the central government.

Yet the Founding Fathers spoke unashamedly of an American Empire, an Empire of Liberty they called it. Unlike past empires, this American Empire would fulfill the unrealized vision set forth in the writings of the great political philosophers. "American imperialism," the editors of *Fortune* magazine would declare in 1942, "can afford to complete the work the British started; instead of salesmen and planters, its representatives can be brains and bulldozers, technicians and machine tools. American imperialism . . . can get along better in Asia if the tuans and sahibs stay home. . . ." Thus was the vision proclaimed and repeated throughout the first two centuries of American independence.

The success and growth of the liberal-democratic state, noted Macpherson, turned on two essentials: access to the marketplace and an ever larger marketplace to accommodate newcomers. America seemed perfectly suited to realize both conditions. Confident that their vision *was* revolutionary in the history of states and empires, the Americans took possession not only of the rights of Englishmen but also of every bit of the old empires they could lay their hands on before the Revolution ended. In addition to seeking independence for the thirteen colonies, American leaders generated movements to "conquer or absorb all of the British Empire's holdings in North America, meaning Canada, Nova Scotia, Cape Breton Isle, Newfoundland and the Floridas. . . ." They also sought "expansion of the merchant marine, the capture of trade outlets in western Europe, and the creation of a navy able to dominate the waters of the western Atlantic."[4]

Wartime exigencies forced a downward revision, temporarily, of that somewhat grandiose set of expectations. But in the Ordinances of 1784 and 1787, the leaders of the new nation served notice that they did not intend to suffer the loss of the west—an empire of vast proportions that European nations had contested on the North American continent for decades prior to the firing of the shot heard round the world. In addition to the ever present danger that the settlers beyond the Appalachians might establish a rival state and ally it with a European power, there was some concern about the possibility of the west's becoming an area of permanent revolution, thereby threatening the stability of the United States.

These matters were discussed along with other pressing issues at the Philadelphia Convention of 1787, which was called to consider a revision of the Articles of Confederation. Several delegates expressed the belief that the situation developing on the frontier was symptomatic of an excess of democracy in the thirteen states. Discontent in one state triggered mob action in another. Not all of the delegates agreed that the symptoms portended anything so dangerous or that the proper remedy was stronger governmental control at the center. If that were the only issue, perhaps the proposed constitution would not have been adopted. But its sponsors raised another point. The United States had to secure its position in the world—especially if it wanted to remain isolated from European influences. The first decade of independence had demonstrated beyond doubt that the nation could not deal with foreign powers commercially, or militarily if it came to that, under the Articles of Confederation.

But how, asked skeptics, could the individual states surrender

9

power to the central government without sacrificing the liberties they had wrenched free from George III and his scheming ministers in a war that had lasted seven years? Surely it was axiomatic, protested opponents of stronger centralization, that the revenues to support this new government, its army and navy, its court and legislature, and its "princely president," would be drawn chiefly from taxes on commerce. Down that path lay only a new despotism.

It was well known, continued the anticonstitution argument, that republics could exist only in small areas where every citizen could put down work to answer a summons to attend whatever meetings were necessary for governing the state properly. Conservative opponents of change developed this argument with warnings against factionalism and democratic excesses, concluding with the prediction that mobs would seize control of the government to destroy property rights and end "liberty." Liberal critics of the pro-

5 Charles Pinckney was one of several Founding Fathers to state the case for American uniqueness in the history of empires.

posed constitution developed the same argument in a different direction, asserting that the movement for a new government was nothing more than a clever maneuver to put the reins of power into the hands of men with aristocratic and monarchical principles.

At the height of the debate, South Carolina's Charles Pinckney rose to dispute these various critics and to offer the proposition that the "vast extent of unpeopled territory which opens to the frugal & industrious a sure road to competency & independence will effectually prevent for a considerable time the increase of the poor or discontented, and be the means of preserving that equality of condition which so eminently distinguishes us."

It was a familiar proposition, especially to those who had read Tom Paine's *Common Sense* carefully. Paine had dwelled on England's small size in contrast to America, implying that what was not possible within the confines of that island kingdom could be achieved in America. The author of *Common Sense* argued that unlike the old empires that required gold and silver to compensate for natural shortages of raw materials and for equally serious political shortcomings, America had no need of precious metals, and, therefore, no need to rule its Empire of Liberty by tyrannical methods.

That Paine and Pinckney could arrive at such similar conclusions suggests another, more difficult, aspect of this (and later) critical moments in the history of the liberal-democratic state. The ideology that guided its managers could be turned against them or used in conjunction with a radical program for a different society. If America offered a seemingly unlimited field for a planter-merchant society, why not for another kind of society as well? Americans have dreamed of utopias as well as of empires. This may help to explain the puzzlement Americans experience when twentieth-century revolutionary leaders honor American prophets and reject American values.

The Philadelphia Convention of 1787 was such a critical moment, and there *were* fears that a movement to "steal" the revolution was developing. While not a conspiracy in that direction, 11

Abigail Adams's gentle reminder that the convention should consider women as citizens in this new society was a good example as well as a warning that the ideas these men discussed were not private property. "Remember that arbitrary power is like most things which are very hard," she wrote her husband, "very liable to be broken."

Abigail was ignored, but James Madison and Alexander Hamilton took up Pinckney's reply to the anticonstitution delegates. "In all civilized countries," began Madison, "the people fall into different classes having a real or supposed difference of interests. There will be creditors and debtors, farmers, merchants & manufacturers. There will be particularly the distinction of rich & poor." And Hamilton continued: "It was certainly true that nothing like an equality of property existed: that an inequality would exist as long as liberty existed, and that it would unavoidably result from that very liberty itself. This inequality of property constituted the great & fundamental distinction in Society."

But the people of this country, Hamilton asserted in *The Federalist* No. 1, had it in their power, by adopting the new constitution, to determine "the fate of an empire in many respects the most interesting in the world." What made the American empire so interesting, Madison explained in *The Federalist* No. 10, was that "in the extent and proper structure of the Union . . . we behold a republican remedy for the diseases most incident to republican government." It was not true that a republic could exist only in a small area. Quite the reverse. "Extend the sphere," said the Virginian,

> and you take in a greater variety of parties and interests; you make it less probable that a majority of the whole will have a common motive to invade the rights of other citizens; or if such a common motive exists, it will be more difficult for all who feel it to discover their own strength, and to act in unison with each other.

Some clarification of Madison's central theme may be useful at this point. By extending the sphere, Madison meant extending the power of the central government over and within *all* the states. In effect, he admits that the constitution defended in *The Federalist*

12

might endanger liberty in *one* state. The apparent paradox is solved because power is balanced between the states and the national government. Contrary to certain popular fears, therefore, expanding the power of the central government guaranteed the liberties of individual citizens against local infringements. And, of course, citizens would be protected against the central government by the counterbalancing authority of state governments.

Another way of reading *The Federalist* No. 10 is to see it as a blueprint for an ever expanding Empire of Liberty, each new part strengthening the whole and drawing strength from the union. It should be remembered that at the time Madison wrote, a major concern of the political elite was how to manage the territory between the thirteen states and the Mississippi River in the old northwest, not the incorporation of an entire continent into the republic. But no territorial limits were put on expansion in *The Federalist* No. 51:

> It is no less certain than it is important, notwithstanding the contrary opinions which have been entertained, that the larger the society, provided it lie within a practical sphere, the more duly capable it will be of self-government. And happily for the *republican cause,* the practicable sphere may be carried to a very great extent, by a judicious modification and mixture of the *federal principle.*

6   New Orleans, 1803. Thomas Jefferson believed that America would prosper now that it possessed France's empire in the Mississippi.

UNDER MY WINGS EVERY THING PROSPERS

7 The Monroe Doctrine was an attempt to establish a barrier between the colonial powers and America.

This statement comes very close to saying that the "republican cause" requires territorial enlargement, not simply to accommodate the growing number of Americans but to establish ideological boundaries against reactionary social systems. It is almost a recommendation for a policy of controlled "permanent revolution." Jefferson seems never to have doubted it. His fear that the "republican cause" might fail if bottled up by a foreign state controlling the Mississippi outlet and subverted from within by promonarchists did not abate until the Louisiana Purchase assured the removal of Spanish and French power from the lower Mississippi, allowing the expansion of republican authority into the fertile area.

A concern similar to Jefferson's helped to motivate the Monroe Doctrine two decades later. Henceforth, said Monroe, Europe could not colonize the American continents, extend the monarchical system to the Western Hemisphere, or intervene to suppress revolution. Although stated in negatives, this sweeping pronouncement implied a United States protectorate, ideologically as well as politically, over the entire hemisphere.

An early effort to establish closer relations with other hemisphere nations resulted in two disappointments. In 1826 the first Pan American Conference was held. President John Quincy Adams was anxious to use the opportunity thus provided to obtain commercial treaties, an agreement on freedom of the seas, and a collective statement in support of the noncolonization principle. Unfortunately, the new nations to the south did not consider themselves politically and economically bound to a single republican "cause." Adams's desire to use the conference to further American foreign-policy goals was not only offensive to those countries, but it also disturbed southern congressmen, to whom the president's plan smacked of economic sectionalism and posed an ideological threat. They feared that the trade treaties would open the way for the importation of competitive goods; more important, participation in a conference that might condemn the slave trade could help to force a change in the national government's attitude toward the south's "peculiar institution."

Long convinced that slavery was a dying remnant of preliberal society, Adams was chagrined to find it looming up as a serious threat to republican expansion. For their part, southern leaders could see only one solution—to create an empire within the Empire of Liberty. Hence they demanded the annexation of Texas, and, in the name of "Young America," Mexico, and even the Caribbean. This parody on republican themes was deeply offensive to their northern countrymen.

As Adams put it, slavery was the antithesis of the American system, the last vestige of British colonial rule. World opinion opposed human slavery; how long could Americans tolerate its existence within their borders? Did the south really suppose, asked the founders of the Republican party, that the nation would allow itself to be left behind the Old World? Judgments differ as to whether the south really hindered the development of the north, but there is little doubt that those who voted for Abraham Lincoln had strong feelings on the subject. Slavery, Lincoln said, deprived "our republican example of its just influence in the world." He insisted, consequently, that compromise proposals for allowing the south a limited area below a specified line for expansion of their slave-based society could not be countenanced—even to avoid a civil war. Any such plan would only "put us again on the high road to a slave empire."

It is worth noting that the word *empire* vanished from the American vocabulary, except in a pejorative sense, after the Civil War. Republicanism ruled America, the world was given to know, not a slavocracy. Ironically, the most prominent eighteenth-century thinkers and leaders of the south had, in taking part in the American Revolution, set in motion forces that led, a century later, to the destruction of an entire way of life. The ideology of the liberal-democratic state had developed a momentum all its own that brooked no opposition, even in the name of private property. True, many northerners would have allowed slavery to exist in those states where it already existed. Lincoln made promises to that effect. But he assumed, and southerners believed fervently, that to contain slavery meant its early extinction.

Slavery and empire also became closely associated in American thought because of the new outburst of European expansion in the late nineteenth century. Discoveries of ore and precious metals on the American continent practically eliminated the temptation to launch an American neocolonialism in search of raw materials to fuel the booming industrial revolution, although President Ulysses S. Grant did call for the annexation of Santo Domingo for its tropical products and, interestingly, to take up the slack in the first postbellum depression by providing an outlet for exports.

Once again ideology was more important than immediate advantage. Most Republican leaders disagreed with the Santo Domingo plan, urging that the best policy was to see that all remnants of European colonialism were eliminated from the hemisphere. There were several considerations behind this decision. Having attempted to "reconstruct" the south, Republicans were chary of raising the racial question again in connection with annexation. Also, the growing sectional complaint against eastern "capitalism" prevented a leadership consensus on extracontinental expansion in the 1870s and 1880s.

16

8 A confrontation in the making? Farmers protest control of the marketplace by eastern capital.

However much hard-pressed farmers might desire new markets, they opposed a formal colonial policy that, it was feared, would only stengthen metropolitan control at home. William Jennings Bryan would make this point with great eloquence in the election campaign of 1900. But meanwhile, several western legislators began to support recognition for Cuban rebels in 1870, demonstrating that they took seriously the "traditional ideal of expanding freedom as they expanded the marketplace."[5]

Hard times were just ahead. In 1882 Alabama Senator John T. Morgan warned: "Our home market is not equal to the demands of our producing and manufacturing classes and to the capital which is seeking employment. . . . We must either enlarge the field of our traffic, or stop the business of manufacturing just where it is." At a much more critical moment during the depression of the 1890s, Secretary of State Walter Quintin Gresham wrote: "I am

17

9 John T. Morgan's interests were wide-ranging. He was an advocate of the intercontinental railroad and looked to the Far East for markets for the cotton of the "new south."

not a pessimist, but I think I see danger in existing conditions in this country. What is transpiring in Pennsylvania, Ohio, Indiana, Illinois, and in regions west of there, may fairly be viewed as symptoms of revolution."

As Gresham saw it, the basic problem was simple (but fundamental): "We can not afford constant employment for our labor. . . . Our mills and factories can supply the demand by running seven or eight months out of twelve." The solution was self-evident: the government must take immediate steps to "enable our people to compete in foreign markets with Great Britain."[6]

Across the Atlantic, English leaders were considering their own predicament. Cecil Rhodes, for example: "My cherished idea is a solution for the social problem, i.e., in order to save the 40,000,000 inhabitants of the United Kingdom from a bloody civil war, we colonial statesmen must acquire new lands to settle the surplus population, to provide new markets for the goods produced by them in the factories and mines." Rhodes's declaration, and similar statements, heralded the advent of "social imperialism" contends

18 Bernard Semmel, who regards it as a movement "designed to draw

all classes together in defence of the nation and empire and [that] aimed to prove to the least well-to-do class that its interests were inseparable from those of the nation."[7]

Social imperialism actually worked better in the United States than in England—under the rubric of anticolonialism—because it did not have to be manufactured; Americans still took seriously the assumptions inherent in a phrase like "Empire of Liberty," although the term had been abandoned. Where Rhodes advocated the founding of new colonies as a solution for England's problems, many American leaders thought the solution to their country's social problems could be found in decolonizing the world. Wonders could be worked even by a symbolic stand against European imperialism. Thus a Texas congressman wrote to Secretary of State Richard Olney during the Venezuelan crisis:

> Why, Mr. Secretary, just think of how angry the anarchistic, socialistic, and populistic boil appears on our political surface and who knows how deep its roots extend or ramify? One cannon shot across the bow of a British boat in defense of this principle will knock more *pus* [sic] out of it than would suffice to inoculate and corrupt our people for the next two centuries.

Reformer Henry Demarest Lloyd agreed, for different reasons. Great Britain's encroachment on Venezuelan-claimed territory represented to him "the same forces as those which in the past have stood against liberty and progress."

When a new revolution erupted in Cuba everything finally came together: concern for expanded markets, anti-European feelings, the struggle for "liberty." The hysterical efforts of the Yellow Press to take advantage of the crisis to expand their readership simply cannot account for American obsession with Cuba. Support for the rebel government came from Samuel Gompers, president of the American Federation of Labor, who declared that Cuban freedom was essential to the freedom of the American workingman. Those with investments on the island wanted the revolution brought to an end, and if independence was the only way to stop the burning and pillage of their properties, then Spain must go.

Business on the whole was ambivalent. Probably a majority of   19

American business leaders were at first opposed to a war with Spain to free Cuba. Along with Secretary of State Richard Olney they were not overly impressed with the complaints of sugar planters whose property was being destroyed. They feared what a war might do to hopes for a return to prosperity, and, with one eye on western radicals, to the contagion of revolutionary sentiments. It did not help matters, from a business point of view, that prorebel spokesmen "for the people" pilloried as "soulless sordid ones" all businessmen who opposed intervention.

President Cleveland had not hesitated to intervene in a Brazilian revolution on behalf of American export interests, but a war with Spain was a far more serious proposition. Olney may also have been convinced that American investors and exporters would have less to fear under Spanish rule than might be the case if the rebels won. Recognition of rebel belligerency would lead Spain to retaliate by refusing to protect American investments. As a consequence, Cleveland and Olney attempted to shut off the swelling sentiment for intervention by secret offers of mediation.

Despite the failure of these attempts at a solution, Cleveland did not opt for war. Defeated in the 1896 election by Republican William McKinley, Cleveland considered giving Spain a time limit to settle the revolution and then thought better of it. His last annual message to Congress suggested he was moving, albeit reluctantly, toward intervention. He began by warning Spain that the United States could not maintain forever its "hitherto expectant attitude." "The spectacle of the utter ruin of an adjoining country, by nature one of the most fertile and charming on the globe, would engage the serious attention of the Government and people of the United States in any circumstances." After detailing America's large and growing economic interests in Cuba, the president turned to other matters. "Besides this large pecuniary stake in the fortune of Cuba, the United States finds itself inextricably involved in the present contest in other ways, both vexatious and costly." The Cuban insurgents, he complained, had stirred up "the more adventurous and restless elements of our population."

McKinley also protested that the "chronic condition of trouble" in Cuba disturbed the "social and political conditions of our own peoples. . . ." He completed the thought in instructions to the new American minister to Madrid: "A continuous irritation within our own borders injuriously affects the normal functions of business, and tends to delay the condition of prosperity to which this country is entitled." A few months later "liberal" America was at war with "imperial" Spain.

McKinley had put it about as broadly as one could: American well-being and prosperity were now to be defined in terms of Cuban tranquillity. One can find the impetus for an expansionist foreign policy in the less desirable consequences of industrialization: overproduction, unemployment, depression, political radicalism. Had there been no Cuban revolution in the 1890s, it might have been easier for later generations of Americans to come to terms with these forces for what they were and at least to acknowledge the existence of their "new" empire. As it was, they came to believe even more confidently in their own uniqueness, in the purity of their antiempire.

It can also be argued, however, that Americans made of the Cuban revolution exactly what *they* wanted in order to achieve a given set of ends. But whether from self-deception or from rationalization, there arose the most dangerous myth of all—as long as the "Free World" area expanded against the Indians, slavery, European imperialism, fascism, and communism, the liberal-democratic state would flourish at home. What began as a "splendid little war" against Spain thus reached a terrible climax in America's longest war in Vietnam.

The problem of American imperialism cannot be reduced to "economics" or "ideology" as separate considerations. Nor was the antiempire built and controlled by "businessmen" or a small clique of "power-seekers" acting behind the scenes in some conspiratorial fashion to shape policy to their desires. As Madison and his friends argued so eloquently, the liberal-democratic state encompasses a number of competing interest groups. It becomes the duty of policymakers to harmonize these diverse voices and to harness their power for the well-being of the state. Security and national defense

21

shape foreign policy as often in the liberal-democratic state as they do in other societies. There is plenty of room, too, for miscalculation and the irrational. Having thought about the complexity of the problem, consider now how it appeared to American leaders as the Spanish-American War began.

Notes

[1] John McDermott, "Welfare Imperialism in Vietnam," *The Nation* 203 (July 25, 1966): 76–88.

[2] Mary McCarthy, *Medina* (London: Weidenfield & Nicolson, 1973), pp. 89–90.

[3] C. B. Macpherson, *The Real World of Democracy* (Oxford: Clarendon, 1966), p. 9.

[4] Richard W. Van Alstyne, *The Rising American Empire* (New York: Oxford University Press, 1960), p. 29.

[5] William Appleman Williams, *The Roots of the Modern American Empire* (New York: Random House, 1969), p. 144.

[6] Quoted in Walter LaFeber, *The New Empire* (Ithaca, N.Y.: Cornell University Press, 1963), p. 200.

[7] Bernard Semmel, *Imperialism and Social Reform: English Social-Imperial Thought, 1895–1914* (New York: Doubleday, 1968), p. 12.

Bibliography

Adams, Brooks. *The Law of Civilization and Decay.* New York: Vintage Books, 1959. The first, and in some ways still the best, study of the American place in the history of empires.

Hartz, Louis. *The Liberal Tradition in America.* New York: Harcourt Brace Jovanovich, 1955. A "consensus" survey of liberalism and what the author calls absolute liberalism in American thought. The final chapter, on foreign policy, is particularly suggestive.

Hobson, J. A. *Imperialism: A Study.* London: Allen & Unwin, 1938. The classic interpretation, which views imperialism as a correctable malfunction of capitalism.

Lenin, N. *Imperialism: The Highest Stage of Capitalism.* New York: International Publishers, 1939. Hobson made over into inevitability.

Macpherson, C. B. *The Political Theory of Possessive Individualism.* Oxford: Oxford University Press, 1962. A difficult, but extremely rewarding, elaboration of points raised in other works about the origins of the liberal state.

Schumpeter, Joseph. *Imperialism and Social Classes.* New York: Meridian Books, 1955. A brilliant reexamination of easy assumptions about capitalism and imperialism.

Williams, William Appleman. *The Great Evasion: Karl Marx and America's Future.* Chicago: Quadrangle Books, 1964. An effort to apply Marx's insights to the development of American society on broader terms than Lenin's *Imperialism.*

America Goes Abroad: 2
1898–1908

For more than half a century we had in Cuba
a disturbing question lying at our very
door—ten years of continuous revolution
during the administration of President Grant,
followed by a three years' revolution of recent date. That, too, has been settled, and
that which disturbed so long the peace and
tranquility of the American government, and
interfered with our legitimate trade, has now
been ended.

William McKinley

William McKinley was not a man to go looking for trouble. He
had won the election of 1896 by staying home on the "frontporch"
in Canton, Ohio, while his opponent roamed the country preaching
the gospel of "Free Silver." But McKinley was neither cowardly nor
indolent. He waited as long as he dared, given the state of public
agitation, before forcing the issue with Spain. There was much on
his mind besides Cuba, but clearly that would have to be settled
first.

23

THE EDUCATION OF A CONFIRMED PROTECTIONIST

McKinley entered Congress in 1877 a dedicated "protectionist," and he no doubt expected to remain so. His proudest achievement was the 1890 bill that was dubbed the "McKinley Tariff" in his honor. But not everyone, not even every Republican, was happy with this legislation. An irate Secretary of State James G. Blaine protested that the proposed tariff increases were "a slap in the face to the South Americans with whom we are trying to enlarge our trade."[1]

For several weeks during the summer of 1890 Blaine and McKinley wrestled for the soul of the Republican party. Blaine urged Congress to consider the advantages of reciprocity treaties. If the United States could negotiate mutually advantageous tariff reductions, said the secretary of state, new markets would open up for American goods not only in Latin America but also in Europe. He did not ask Republicans to abandon protectionism, only to reconsider and adapt. Until 1890 Republicans thought mainly of protection *from* something, but with the stimulus provided by Blaine, they began to think of protection *for* something—although most remained highly skeptical about this new doctrine.

In the end, a somewhat more outward-looking tariff bill emerged from Congress. Interestingly, Blaine's most promising convert was McKinley himself. Whatever doubts McKinley had about the importance of increased foreign trade disappeared in the first months of the depression of the 1890s. Elected governor of Ohio in the depth of the "hard times," McKinley made a strong statement to the first convention of the National Association of Manufacturers:

> We want our own markets for our manufactures and agricultural products; we want a tariff for our surplus products which will not surrender our markets and will not degrade our labor to hold our markets. We want a reciprocity which will give us a foreign market for our surplus products and in turn that will open our markets to foreigners for those products which they produce and which we do not.

These were still the words and sentiments of an economic nationalist, but McKinley placed almost equal emphasis on

10 President William McKinley and his war cabinet.

overseas economic expansion. Over the next six years, his commitment to the latter policy grew stronger. The very last speech he made, the day before his assassination, was a plea to fellow Republicans. "The period of exclusiveness is past. The expansion of our trade and commerce is the pressing problem. . . ." His "greatest ambition," McKinley confided to Senator Robert LaFollette, "was to round out his career by gaining American supremacy in world markets."

As these public and private remarks suggest, reciprocity is a much more active policy than simple protectionism. It involves, to begin with, treatymaking. Often it also involves the sort of hard bargaining that excites the jealousy of diplomatic rivals who quite naturally fear the loss of their own foreign markets. Thus reciprocity cannot be pursued successfully by a nation that is not prepared to play a large role in world affairs. Finally, it announces to the world that a nation has become a mature industrial power and a strategic problem for others in the Great Power league.

25

There was a strong relationship, then, between this new interest in reciprocity and proposed legislation to enlarge and modernize the navy, and between trade expansion and three diplomatic "crises" of the 1890s. The revolution in Brazil, the proposed annexation of Hawaii, and the Venezuelan crisis all indicated to the outside world that America was stirring again in preparation for—what?

At this point Cuba became the all-absorbing issue in both Europe and America. "The South dearly loves a fighter," an anonymous Georgian wrote to President Cleveland, "& if you will now show yourself strong and courageous in the defense of Cuba, you will have a solid South at your call. . . . Strengthen the Army and Navy of this country & in this way give employment to the thousands of idle men who need it."[2] William "Major Bill" McKinley had once been cited for bravery by President Lincoln, but he was a much greater success at politics, and that was how he would have preferred to deal with Cuba and unemployment.

THE DECISION TO INTERVENE

War scares are tricky. On the one hand, presidents can ask for and hope to receive broad legislative authority to do a number of things that have been stalled. On the other hand, they may be pushed into precipitate action before everything is ready.

Consequently, some historians have interpreted McKinley's inaugural address and the program he outlined therein as clever strokes designed to keep Congress busy with less important questions while he took his diplomats and the Spanish minister off into some private corner of the White House to solve the only really important matter: war or peace. No doubt McKinley wanted to be left alone, but the program he outlined had evolved in his mind and was, over the long run, far more expansionist and consequential than the *fact* of intervention in Cuba, although as a *symbol*, Cuba and the war with Spain, as we have seen, continued to shape the American outlook on the world.

The president asked Congress to consider a new reciprocity proposal, like the one included in the 1890 tariff, "under which so great a stimulus was given to our foreign trade in new and advantageous markets for our surplus agricultural and manufactured products." In addition, the legislators were invited to consider revitalization of the merchant marine, an even bigger naval fleet, ways to secure a Nicaraguan canal, and a new Hawaii annexation treaty. Under Cleveland, the nation had abandoned reciprocity and Hawaii but intervened in Brazil and Venezuela. McKinley's "large policy" included issues that antedated Cuba's latest revolution and that would continue to need attention for almost twenty years.

Nevertheless, as he informed the American minister in Madrid, the United States could not remain idle if things continued as they were. The American people, McKinley advised his representative, expected that all campaigns against the rebels would be carried out according to civilized military codes. A continuation of Spanish *reconcentrado* tactics would not be tolerated. These cruel efforts to drive the Cuban people from the countryside into urban areas must come to a halt, said the president, as must the use of "fire and famine to accomplish by uncertain direction what the military arm seems powerless to directly accomplish."[3]

11 *Reconcentrado:* an American view of Spanish rule in Cuba.

One squirms a bit at those strictures. They have an eerie ring about them. But other words McKinley used in reviewing the situation for Congress came back to haunt Americans much sooner. After listing options, the president came to the one choice not open—forcible annexation. "That, by our code of morality, would be criminal aggression." At that point McKinley only knew what he did not want: he did not want a Cuba left to fend for itself, easy prey for some other European power, nor did he relish the thought of an ongoing revolution, a constant bad example to other Caribbean islands and, as Grover Cleveland had warned, to "restless elements of our population."

Most European observers thought McKinley's decision to send the battleship *Maine* to Havana was unnecessarily provocative. But he had no other choice if Congress were not to do something worse. The president took this step in late January 1898 to give himself more time, although even he was beginning to realize that chances for a peaceful settlement were slim. About this time he learned that Spain's "reform" program for Cuba did not allow for autonomy—as existed for Canada in the British Commonwealth—or anything near it. He discovered Madrid's true intentions from reports the State Department received that Spain would not permit Cuba to negotiate trade treaties with other countries, surely a matter of interest to a reciprocity convert like McKinley.

Had Spain been willing to grant autonomy to Cuba, McKinley might have hesitated, but the question of war or peace would still have remained with the rebels. It was their ability to influence American public opinion that so troubled Cleveland and McKinley, both of them "conservative" men. What McKinley had to decide was how to keep the Cuban issue from getting out of control *inside* the United States. McKinley had little time to ruminate about these problems or to react to publication of the Spanish minister's private correspondence, in which McKinley saw himself described as a weak and venal politician, before he received a cable saying that the *Maine* had been sunk. No one could ever prove what happened in Havana harbor, but 250 Americans had lost their lives.

That was enough.

Ship sinkings and similar incidents were a common occurrence in these "imperial" years. It was not that the industrial powers planned each one, but every time a nation showed the flag in a tropical harbor the potential for trouble was there. Entire countries lost their independence that way. Only three months before the *Maine* went to the bottom of Havana harbor, Germany had demanded a ninety-nine-year lease on the Chinese port of Kiaochow and special rights in Shantung province as proper compensation for the gang murder of two German missionaries. Berlin had been seeking a convenient reason for demanding a coaling-station on the China coast. The unfortunate clergymen provided it.

The same press that had denounced the "piratical" Germans demanded that McKinley do his duty. "Remember the *Maine!*" was the cry. But McKinley still refused to budge. Aware of recent events in the Far East and that war with Spain meant a likely naval campaign against the Spanish fleet in the Philippines, the president held back yet a time to see if the enterprising war propagandists understood what was at stake. "Who knows where this war will lead us," McKinley cautioned House leader Joe Cannon. "It may be more than war with Spain."[4] Cannon solemnly agreed and went back to Congress with the president's request for a $50 million emergency military appropriation.

On March 25, 1898, the president received another important telegram, this time from a trusted adviser in New York City. It read: "Big corporations here now believe we will have war. Believe all would welcome it as relief to suspense."[5] If what the adviser said was true, the message marked a significant advance in the opinions of the economic community. It agreed with Mark Hanna's advice. Hanna, McKinley's most pacifistic adviser, thought that the time had come to settle affairs with Spain.

After the long buildup, the war was a disappointment. A few veterans of the Civil War complained that not a single military campaign was worthy of the name. Meanwhile, interesting things *were* happening in Washington. When on April 11, 1898, McKinley asked Congress to declare war, he told the legislators that it would be neither "wise" nor "prudent" for the United States to recognize

$50,000 REWARD.—WHO DESTROYED THE MAINE?—$50,000 REWARD.

EDITION FOR GREATER NEW YORK.

NEW YORK JOURNAL

AND ADVERTISER.

The Journal will give $50,000 for information, furnished to it exclusively, that will convict the person or persons who sank the Maine.

The Journal will give $50,000 for information, furnished to it exclusively, that will convict the person or persons who sank the Maine.

NO. 5,572.   Copyright, 1898, by W. R. Hearst—NEW YORK, THURSDAY, FEBRUARY 17, 1898.—16 PAGES.   PRICE ONE CENT in Greater New York. Elsewhere, and Jersey City. TWO CENTS.

DESTRUCTION OF THE WAR SHIP MAINE WAS THE WORK OF AN ENEMY.

$50,000!

$50,000 REWARD!
For the Detection of the Perpetrator of the Maine Outrage!

The New York Journal hereby offers a reward of $50,000 CASH for information, FURNISHED TO IT EXCLUSIVELY, which shall lead to the detection and conviction of the person, persons or government criminally responsible for the explosion which resulted in the destruction, in Havana, of the United States war ship Maine and the loss of 258 lives of American sailors.

The $50,000 CASH offered for the above information is on deposit with Wells, Fargo & Co.

No one is barred, be he the humble but misguided seaman eking out a few miserable dollars by acting as a spy, or the attache of a government secret service, plotting, by any devilish means, to avenge financial insults or cripple menacing countries.

This offer has been cabled to Europe and will be made public in every capital of the Continent and in London this morning.

The Journal believes that any man who can be bought to commit murder can also be bought to betray his confederates. FOR THE PERPETRATOR OF THIS OUTRAGE HAD ACCOMPLICES.

W. R. HEARST.

Assistant Secretary Roosevelt Convinced the Explosion of the War Ship Was Not an Accident.

The Journal Offers $50,000 Reward for the Conviction of the Criminals Who Sent 258 American Sailors to Their Death. Naval Officers Unanimous That the Ship Was Destroyed on Purpose.

$50,000!

$50,000 REWARD!
For the Detection of the Perpetrator of the Maine Outrage!

The New York Journal hereby offers a reward of $50,000 CASH for information, FURNISHED TO IT EXCLUSIVELY, which shall lead to the detection and conviction of the person, persons or government criminally responsible for the explosion which resulted in the destruction, at Havana, of the United States war ship Maine and the loss of 258 lives of American sailors.

The $50,000 CASH offered for the above information is on deposit with Wells, Fargo & Co.

No one is barred, be he the humble, but misguided, seaman, eking out a few miserable dollars by acting as a spy, or the attache of a government secret service, plotting, by any devilish means, to avenge fancied insults or cripple menacing countries.

This offer has been cabled to Europe and will be made public in every capital of the Continent and in London this morning.

The Journal believes that any man who can be bought to commit murder can also be bought to betray his comrades. FOR THE PERPETRATOR OF THIS OUTRAGE HAD ACCOMPLICES.

W. R. HEARST.

NAVAL OFFICERS THINK THE MAINE WAS DESTROYED BY A SPANISH MINE.

George Eugene Bryson, the Journal's special correspondent at Havana, cables that it is the secret opinion of many Spaniards in the Cuban capital that the Maine was destroyed and 258 of her men killed by means of a submarine mine, or fixed torpedo. This is the opinion of several American naval authorities. The Spaniards, it is believed, arranged to have the Maine anchored over one of the harbor mines. Wires connected the mine with a powder magazine, and it is thought the explosion was caused by sending an electric current through the wire. If this can be proven, the brutal nature of the Spaniards will be shown by the fact that they waited to spring the mine until after all the men had retired for the night. The Maltese cross in the picture shows where the mine may have been fired.

Hidden Mine or a Sunken Torpedo Believed to Have Been the Weapon Used Against the American Man-of-War---Officers and Men Tell Thrilling Stories of Being Blown Into the Air Amid a Mass of Shattered Steel and Exploding Shells---Survivors Brought to Key West Scout the Idea of Accident---Spanish Officials Protest Too Much---Our Cabinet Orders a Searching Inquiry---Journal Sends Divers to Havana to Report Upon the Condition of the Wreck. Was the Vessel Anchored Over a Mine?

BY CAPTAIN E. L. ZALINSKI, U. S. A.

(Captain Zalinski is the inventor of the famous dynamite gun, which would be the principal factor in our coast defence in case of war.)

Assistant Secretary of the Navy Theodore Roosevelt says he is convinced that the destruction of the Maine in Havana Harbor was not an accident. The Journal offers a reward of $50,000 for exclusive evidence that will convict the person, persons or Government criminally responsible for the death of the American battle ship and the death of 258 of its crew.

The suspicion that the Maine was deliberately blown up grows stronger every hour. Not a single fact to the contrary has been produced.

Captain Sigsbee, of the Maine, and Consul-General Lee both urge that public opinion be suspended until they have completed their investigation, taking the course of tactful men who are convinced that there has been treachery.

Washington reports very late that Captain Sigsbee had feared some such event as a hidden mine. The English cipher code was used all day yesterday by the officers in cabling instead of the usual American code.

the independence of the so-called Cuban Republic. "Such recognition is not necessary in order to enable the United States to intervene and pacify the island." More than one legislator wondered what that meant.

THE FIRST AMERICAN PROTECTORATE

Following McKinley's instructions, the American military authorities in Cuba avoided formal cooperation with the rebels and denied them participation in surrender ceremonies. Perplexed by the president's seeming about-face, the Senate had proceeded to pass an amendment to the declaration of war. This amendment provided that the United States would—before any military intervention—recognize the Republic of Cuba. And it was presumed that then the United States would be guided by that government's wishes once Spain had surrendered.

Slow to ask for war, McKinley now fairly raced into battle against Congress. Using presidential power to the fullest, McKinley ordered his lieutenants to put together another self-denying ordinance, the Teller Amendment, which received unanimous approval. It still seemed a strong statement: "The United States hereby disclaims any disposition or intention to exercise sovereignty, jurisdiction, or control over said Island except for the pacification thereof, and asserts its determination, when that is accomplished, to leave the government and control of the Island to its people."

The Teller Amendment to the declaration of war was acceptable to McKinley, however, because its promise of eventual independence was to some future Cuban government (one yet to be constructed) and depended on completion of the pacification process. Having secured this breathing space, McKinley turned the details over to the War Department. General Leonard Wood, Military Governor of Cuba, defined the problem succinctly: "The people ask me what we mean by a stable government in Cuba. I tell them that when money can be borrowed at a reasonable rate of interest and when capital is willing to invest in the Island, a condition of stability will have been reached."[6]

31

Secretary of War Elihu Root then formulated a plan that eventually became the Platt Amendment to the treaty by which the United States gave Cuba its independence. Cubans were not happy about the Platt Amendment, which Washington required they write into their own constitution, but their advice and consent were not deemed necessary. Under the Platt Amendment, Cuba could not enter into any treaty impairing its independence; it could not contract a public debt that might require special revenues; the United States could intervene to preserve independence and maintain law and order; and the United States navy could maintain coaling stations, one of which, at Guantanamo Bay, is still in its possession. General Wood had it right: "There is, of course, little or no independence left Cuba under the Platt Amendment."[7]

Good authorities, Root advised his colleagues in the Cabinet, were of the opinion that a similar reservation had permitted Great Britain to retire from Egypt physically yet retain moral control. Like the British minister-resident in Cairo, the American minister in Havana soon became—in fact, if not in name—a viceroy whose blessing had to be obtained before the native government undertook any major departures.

Whatever questions remained about the limits of Cuban independence cleared up quickly when the American minister intervened to prevent Cuba from signing a treaty with Great Britain that impinged on the special privileges enjoyed by United States exporters. Despite protests from Cuban President Tomás Estrada Palma that what was demanded amounted to monopoly control of the island's foreign trade, the American minister insisted that the British could not be given equal rights as indicated by the proposed treaty. The 1903 reciprocity agreement between the United States and Cuba came as close to being perfect, from a McKinley point of view, as anything could be. In exchange for a 20 percent tariff break on sugar, Cuba gave the United States an equal reduction on all manufactures and an additional 20 percent on selected items.

In 1898 Spain had accepted war with the United States rather than allow Cuba its full independence, and America had gone to war to free Cuba from Europe. It can be argued that, given the alternative of Spanish rule or the Platt Amendment, Cuba fared exceedingly well. Moreover, had America not intervened, how long would it have been before another power moved in to replace Spain? In an age of colonial acquisition, the Teller Amendment was certainly more enlightened than the heavy-handed practices employed in Southeast Asia and Africa, and Cuba benefited most from the difference.

Measured by other standards, however, American policy fell short of its pretensions. Cuba had not gained true independence or even self-determination. Concerned about stability in the Caribbean, absorbed in a wide new range of foreign-policy problems, and under much less pressure from Congress and the public, policymakers did not hesitate to use American troops to restore order when a new revolution erupted in 1906. Yet many admitted to disappointment that Cuba's new government had collapsed like a house of cards. But instead of self-questioning, this disappointment took the form of blaming Cuban officials for not really giving their new constitution a fair chance. American policymakers were finding out, however, that once started it was difficult if not impossible to call a halt to intervention.

President Theodore Roosevelt had his own answer to what had gone wrong: the Cuban trouble proved the incredible folly of the anti-imperialists who also would have applied the Teller Amendment to the Philippine Islands.

THE GREAT CHINA DREAM

McKinley obviously had not regarded the Teller Amendment as applying to the Philippines. There was once a popular legend, fostered by his offhand remark that he could not have told "where those darned islands were within 2,000 miles," that McKinley had very little knowledge of, or interest in, what was happening in the Pacific west of Hawaii. Accordingly, American acquisition of the Philippines came about solely by accident: the fortunes of war.

Sometimes it seems as if historians conceive of American foreign policy as a legend wrapped within a legend ad infinitum, with

33

nothing in the center. McKinley had no desire, we may be sure, to establish an American orphanage for Spain's little lost islands. Whether or not he knew much about Pacific area geography, the president had been fully briefed on the strategic value of the Philippines. For centuries, since Marco Polo, Europeans had dreamed of the "Great China Market." A powerful motive for the acquisition of California had been the port of San Francisco because it would obviously help America realize that ancient (and continuing) dream of the first explorer-merchants.

Senator Teller himself had no moral qualms about annexing Hawaii: "We want those islands. We want them because they are the stepping way across the sea. . . . Necessary to our safety, they are necessary to our commerce."[8] Since 1895 the men across the street from the White House in the Department of State had studied reports of the steady encroachment of European and Japanese concession-seekers on China's independence. Not content with economic contracts, the foreigners were beginning to demand territorial concessions as well. Soon America's claim to share in the commerce of the Celestial Empire would be in jeopardy. And, if that happened, Hawaii would be of little value to anyone except pineapple growers.

Especially disturbing were detailed reports of Russian tactics in Manchuria, an area that American businessmen were beginning to find attractive. Combined with Anglo-American press reports of German designs on Kiaochow and the entire Shantung peninsula, diplomatic dispatches out of China left policymakers with a deep sense of foreboding.

The Cleveland administration had responded by instructing its representative at the court of the Manchus to be more aggressive in supporting American entrepreneurs who sought railroad concessions or other contracts. Faint heart ne'er won fair hand, but what were the importunities of Mr. Charles Denby compared to the booming voices of Their Excellencies, the representatives of the Great Powers? Where was the American navy? What strongpoint did the United States hold that compared in any way to British Hong Kong?

In January 1898, businessmen, economic theorists, intellectuals, and others interested in keeping China out of the clutches of the "imperialist" conspiracy founded the American Asiatic Association. This hearty group of China-defenders wanted more action out of Washington, although exactly what they expected McKinley to do beyond supporting Great Britain's suggestion for an Anglo-American front against the other powers was difficult to say.

The British initiative for a joint protest against discriminations by foreign lessees in China arrived in Washington on March 8, 1898, when McKinley was absorbed in the many tasks of getting ready to go to war. Spain might be a third-rate opponent, but, as McKinley himself asked, who could say with certainty where the war would lead? It was no time to add such a political complication, even had there been the inclination to agree to London's plan. Once the war began, and it became clear that Spain would get no help from its friends, perhaps the president would reconsider.

But he did not. Instead McKinley struck out on his own. On May 2, 1898, before full reports of Dewey's great victory over the

12 A clever comment on American assumptons about what it could do for China.

35

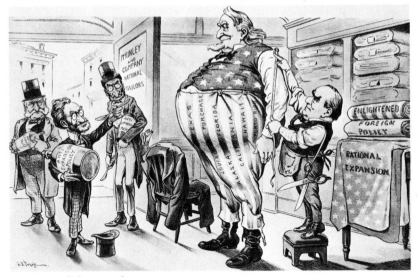

13 An English view of American expansion.

Spanish fleet in the Philippines had reached Washington, the president summoned a war council at the White House. It was decided at that meeting to send an army of twenty thousand men to occupy the Philippines. This step raised some eyebrows in Europe. London asked if it could be advised of American war objectives and received only a short reply that the Philippines could remain Spanish, but the United States would retain "a port and necessary appurtenances." Second thoughts caused the president to enlarge his demands on Madrid. Ideologically, for example, he would not be consistent (or satisfy moralists) if he left the Philippines under the power of the reactionary Spaniards.

But the key considerations were put by McKinley to the American peace commissioners when he met with them on September 16, 1898. First he reviewed the consequences of shirking the previously unforeseen responsibility of possession of the Philippines. Then he turned to a positive assertion. The Philippines offered America an opportunity to maintain the Open Door policy throughout the Orient. "Asking only the open door for ourselves," he coached the peace commissioners, "we are ready to accord the open door to others."

Acquisition of these islands, he assured them, was not one more step on a jingoist journey to the far ends of the earth—only a means to another end. "The commerical opportunity . . . associated with this opening depends less on large territorial possessions than upon an adequate commercial basis and upon broad and equal privileges."[9] McKinley was true to his word. Hawaii was annexed in the summer of 1898, as were Guam and the Wake Islands, to provide steppingstones across the Pacific. But when Spain offered all the Carolines and Marianas in exchange for certain economic advantages in Puerto Rico and Cuba, McKinley refused.

Meanwhile, the American Asiatic Association's campaign for a stronger China policy was about to be rewarded along lines approved by imperialists and anti-imperialists alike. On September 6, 1899, John Hay sent the first of his famous Open Door notes to the

14 The "white peril": America becomes an Oriental power.

15 Philippine insurrectionists in a prison camp.

European powers and Japan. Historians dispute just about everything connected with Hay's action: the stimulus, the authorship of the document, and (more than anything else) its importance. Hay himself had doubts and was dissuaded only by strong representations from the American minister in China not to abandon the policy in favor of seeking (European-fashion) a leasehold on the coast. Ironically, had American policy shifted in that direction, another myth about the predominance of abstract legalism in American foreign affairs might never have arisen.

Be that as it may, this first note called on those who claimed spheres of influence in China to allow the United States and each other equal trading rights. As the secretary of state expected, the replies were evasive, but for his purposes they were enough. The United States had demonstrated an "interest" in Chinese affairs and had laid the groundwork for future action. But not even Hay anticipated the pace of events. Within a few months American troops still engaged in "pacifying" the Philippines received orders to go to China to relieve the beseiged legations in the Boxer Rebellion.

16 American troops dwarfed by a Chinese temple: the first encounter with Asian nationalism.

The Boxers were a secret society dedicated to the destruction of the foreigner and all his disciples, the Christian converts. They enjoyed the clandestine support of the empress dowager, Tzu Hsi, who had her own reasons for wishing to check the influence of the West in China. As an expedition of allied soldiers prepared to march on Peking, Secretary Hay sent a second Open Door note. Dated July 3, 1900, this message went far beyond his recent appeal for mutual respect and equal rights. No longer did American policy admit the right or existence of spheres of influence. Instead, Hay defined it as nothing less than the preservation of "Chinese territorial and administrative" integrity, the protection of "all rights guaranteed to friendly powers by treaty and international law," and the safeguarding "for the world [of] the principle of equal and impartial trade with all parts of the Chinese Empire. . . ."

Did Hay and McKinley really have any idea what all this meant—and what they were letting themselves, and their successors, in for? Probably not. But premonitions and prophecies abounded. Hay's close friend, Henry Adams, an amateur Cassandra in a land of professional optimists, wrote that with Hay's second   39

Open Door note "history broke in halves." Cuba policy was, quite literally, small stuff compared to this extravagant declaration of intent.

THE *DEUS EX MACHINA* THAT FAILED

The worst offender against Chinese territory at this time was Imperial Russia. The Boxer Rebellion had provided the tsar's janizaries with an excuse to seal off Manchuria completely. Their idea was to preserve this natural feeder area for the Trans-Siberian Railroad, a costly project from which great things were expected—indeed, demanded. A "splendid little war" (this had been Hay's description of the Spanish-American tiff) was out of the question so far as Russia was concerned. On January 30, 1902, however, Great Britain and Japan signed an alliance obviously directed against Russia. Two days later Hay dispatched a third Open Door missive, expressing "gravest concern" at any agreement between China and a third power that might exclude others from participating in the development of the former's natural resources. This veiled warning against closing Manchuria to everyone but Russian exploiters riled the diplomatic waters, but aside from extreme irritation at American connivance with London and Tokyo, Russia did not react. Comte Cassini, the Russian ambassador in Washington, a masterful diplomatic fencer adept at turning aside American protests, expressed contempt for almost any combination of adversaries. It was obvious, he boasted, that neither Great Britain nor the United States could undertake a military offensive in that part of the world. As for Japan, declared Cassini, "what can the Japanese do? As usual, sit on their heels and pray to Buddha!"

They must have prayed for the right thing! On February 8, 1904, without a declaration of war, the Japanese fleet destroyed the Russian naval squadron at Port Arthur. In the White House, Theodore Roosevelt was fairly jumping up and down with the news. "Japan is playing our game," he wrote his son. Almost at once Roosevelt was at work on a peace settlement that would guarantee a favorable balance of power in the Far East. He did not want Russia eliminated from the scene, just put in place. As for Japan, he was

17 Imperialism in China after the Boxer Rebellion: but American policymakers did not like to think of the United States as just another imperial power.

willing that Japan's desire for Korea be satisfied if, in return, Tokyo agreed to respect America's position in the Philippines. He was also prepared to agree to many of Japan's special desiderata, such as Port Arthur, Dairen, and (most especially) the South Manchurian Railway. For these, he expected a Japanese promise to respect the Open Door throughout China.

American and British financiers played a role in determining the outcome of the Russo-Japanese War by enabling Japan to obtain necessary funds. Exhausted by a war that made tremendous logistical demands on the one-track Trans-Siberian Railroad, and confronted by a revolution at the palace gates, the tsar's government had little choice but to accept Roosevelt's terms. Less apparent to the outside world, Japan's exhaustion bore down relentlessly on its leaders driving them to the peace table Roosevelt had prepared at Portsmouth, New Hampshire. Russia managed to leave that table without having to pay Japan an indemnity, but it lost a great deal. 41

Roosevelt received the Nobel Peace Prize. But he was pursuing something much bigger in private negotiations behind the scenes at Portsmouth. In 1898, after a long series of appeals and presentations to the throne, a group of American investors had obtained a concession to construct a railroad line between Hankow and Canton. It had been stipulated that the America China Development Company would sell its stock only to Americans, thus preventing Europeans from gaining a dangerous monopoly over central China's railroad connections. Almost at once the company's directors began violating this section of the contract by permitting (indeed encouraging) European interests to buy a controlling share of its stock. By 1903 only 10½ miles of a 710-mile line had been constructed. The Chinese became disgusted and on December 23, 1904, announced they were canceling the contract.

A series of manuevers followed, from which the banker J. P. Morgan emerged as the leading shareholder and spokesman for the company. It did not take him long to realize that under no circumstances would the Chinese Government permit the company to redeem itself and continue to build the line. Hence, he pointed out, the urgent need to sell—while the Chinese were still willing to pay $7 million just to be rid of the contract. Roosevelt thought the sale was bad business, bad from every point of view except the narrow interests of the shareholders. "It seems to me that in the interest of American commerce in the Orient," he wrote Morgan, "it is of consequence for you not to give up your concession." He asked if the company would delay action on its decision. "If so, I'll call a halt, in emphatic terms, to the Chinese Government."[10]

Perhaps it was fortunate that no one asked Roosevelt to comply with this promise. The sale went through, leaving America without a major investment company in China. The seriousness of the loss began to be realized almost immediately, especially when E. H. Harriman failed to secure financial control of the South Manchurian Railway. As Harriman had once explained his plan to the American minister in Japan, he expected to buy out the Japanese interest in that line and take over the Chinese Eastern Railway from Russia. "It'll be the most marvelous transportation system in the world. We'll girdle the earth."[11]

A contract was actually signed for the sale, but there it ended. Second thoughts (and the availability of British financing) convinced the Japanese that they would not have to relinquish a chance to control Manchuria for a junior partnership in someone else's global system. Roosevelt's "retrenchment" in the Pacific, the Taft-Katsura Memorandum of 1905, may have reflected these disappointments or may have been simply a personal reassessment of the Asian situation. Roosevelt hated looking foolish, especially before the "backward" nation he assumed China to be.

In any event, the Taft-Katsura understanding implied that the United States would not challenge Japanese control of the Korean peninsula in exchange for noninterference in the Philippines. The State Department did not give up the effort to establish the Open Door in Manchuria. But the setbacks that investors had suffered in the aftermath of the Russo-Japanese War, China's continuing internal strife, and other problems dampened the enthusiasm of some old China hands in the State Department. It was not a propitious moment for bold new initiatives.

Without a railroad development company similar to those of its rivals, one capable of branching off like domestic lines into mining and related enterprises, the United States simply lacked the necessary leverage to accomplish anything big in China. So Roosevelt concentrated on a limited effort to secure a commercial Open Door in Manchuria. The United States still enjoyed, in early 1906, more than 20 percent of the province's foreign trade.

But even here the situation was ambiguous. American exporters voiced loud complaints that Japanese regulations effectively prohibited them from access to the Manchurian market. Despite Tokyo's soothing assurances that whatever difficulties American traders might be experiencing were only temporary—for example, the unpleasant side effects of necessary military restrictions during the evacuation—Secretary of State Elihu Root, who had succeeded John Hay, expressed a deep concern that "China will find herself—after the Japanese occupancy has ceased—the merely nominal sovereign of a territory the material advantages of which have been appropriated by the temporary occupants."[12]

In less polite language, one of Root's associates in the State De-

18 Secretary of State Elihu Root.

partment complained of China's failure to stand up to Japan; "What can you expect of a jelly fish?" Meanwhile, however, America was experiencing the first fears of Japan and the "yellow peril." In the post-Civil War era Japanese laborers had begun moving into the United States in increasing numbers. In October 1906, the San Francisco Board of Education ordered all Japanese and Chinese children sent to special segregated classes. The board gave two reasons: overcrowding and the need to see that white children would not have "their youthful impressions" affected by exposure to the Orientals.

Word of San Francisco's action reached Washington via Tokyo, where it had been amplified into a formal protest. Roosevelt was not happy with this developing diplomatic crossfire and moved to reach a "Gentleman's Agreement" with Japan, by which the latter agreed to restrict emigration in exchange for a withdrawal of the segregation order. For the first time, nevertheless, an American administration gave serious thought to a future war with Japan. No one imagined that Japan would go to war to push unwanted immigrants into the Pacific coast states. What did occur to various policy-makers was the possibility that Japan might well attempt to shut America out of Asia, citing this nation's immigration policy as one justification. In fact, that happened within three decades. In January 1907, the army and navy undertook preliminary studies of how such a war would be conducted. Six months later Roosevelt gave orders to move the fleet to the Pacific. What began as a "training operation" soon became a grand tour to show off the "Great White Fleet" America had been building for almost twenty years.

The sixteen battleships reached Tokyo about a year later. They received an enthusiastic welcome; but behind all the talk of Japanese-American friendship was the undisguisable reality of the battleships. Once again, as when Admiral Perry had "opened" Japan to the world, American men-of-war were anchored in Tokyo harbor well within gunshot of the national capital. Not surprisingly, Japanese journalists began writing of the "white peril."

THE MANCHURIAN MEETING PLACE

For some Americans Manchuria approximated a new Minnesota, supplied with raw materials and peopled with a hardy race more capable of receiving proper instructions and guidance than their Chinese countrymen. Others looked at Manchuria and saw only a deep Black Forest, a place to avoid at all costs. For fifty years Manchuria was a meeting place of national and international rivalries. From 1895 until the end of the Second World War, Manchuria was the scene of a succession of crises. Perhaps they were all just part of a single crisis that originated in China's weakness and ended only when a Peking regime was able to demonstrate its right to rule Manchuria. If so, the proper date for marking an end to the crisis would be December 1950, when Red Chinese troops drove General MacArthur's United Nations force back from the Yalu River.

What an ironic ending that was to American efforts to help China assert its power in Manchuria against the "evil" forces of Russia and Japan! Young nationalists who opposed the decadent

Manchu regime in its last days deliberately encouraged American interest in this Far Eastern "Minnesota." Actually, Americans needed little encouragement, although they thought the first steps had to be taken in Peking. W. W. Rockhill, the drafter of the actual Open Door notes, wrote in *Colliers* that the needed reform movement must "come from without . . . under direct pressure from abroad."[13]

In later years Rockhill became discouraged, but not so the young consul in Mukden, Willard Straight. Even before his arrival there, Straight had been in contact with E. H. Harriman, who had assured him that he was interested in the possibility of an American-financed line to compete with the Japanese-owned South Manchurian Railway. Straight also felt that he could count on British support. In 1908 what had seemed impossible when the America China Development Company slinked out of China with its $7 million, seemed about to happen. The viceroy for Manchuria had approved a preliminary contract for a Sino-American bank to finance large development projects. At Harriman's suggestion, Straight was recalled to Washington for consultations.

Even skeptics had been impressed by Straight's brilliant performance, not the least part of which had been his ability to keep Harriman intrigued. "Wall Street is feeling confident again," declared one official in a note of explanation to Rockhill, "and is looking for the investment of capital in foreign lands."[14] As events would demonstrate, the State Department was looking for much more in China than investment opportunities for Wall Street. Close behind Straight came Tang Shao-yi, the man with whom the consul had begun the negotiations. Tang's mission was ostensibly a good will visit, a story the Japanese (and others) never accepted. His real purpose was to encourage American investors to go into Manchuria with both feet.

Sensing this danger to their own position, the Japanese asked for a new bilateral understanding. A number of reasons have been given for the Administration's receptiveness to this proposed exchange, which appeared to give the Japanese a free hand in Manchuria just for renewing their promise not to intervene in the Philippines. Roosevelt may well have been suspicious of the men who sent Tang to lure Americans into Manchuria. His previous disappointments in China no doubt played a role. But there were other considerations. Secretary of State Root believed that a new Japanese-American accord guaranteeing the status quo might actually enhance the Open Door policy by undermining a 1907 Russo-Japanese pact dividing Manchuria.

It seems clear that the Root-Takahira Agreement, signed on November 30, 1908, represented a compromise between those who wanted to proceed alone in China and Manchuria, and those who saw a better (and safer) way in cooperation among industrial nations. Moreover, while Straight fretted about Root's seeming indifference to Chinese sensibilities, the secretary had played a subtle game. According to the wording of the Chinese Boxer Indemnity Agreement, the funds China paid the United States as compensation for the outrages done to American citizens and property were to be used for the education of Chinese students in America. Following the visit from Tang, Root and Roosevelt gave the Chinese permission to use a large portion of these funds to establish the Manchurian bank.

So while Root officially warned the special emissary that the American government could not itself sponsor investments in China, he permitted the Chinese government, if it wished, to use its obligations for such a purpose. Who could object to that simple act of benevolence? But the bank never materialized. Roosevelt's successor had to forsake such subtleties and push Wall Street ahead of him as he tried to open a way for American commerce in China.

CANAL ZONE DIPLOMACY

Everyone knows that Roosevelt preferred clear-cut situations. Oriental affairs left him frustrated and unsure of himself. In the Western Hemisphere he could be the man of action. "I took the Canal Zone and let Congress debate," he boasted. Roosevelt relished wielding the Big Stick in the Caribbean and Central America. He loved power.

19 During the Venezuelan crisis of 1902, Uncle Sam warns Great Britain and Germany, "That's a live wire, gentlemen!"

Yet not long after McKinley's assassination, the new president wrote the German ambassador, Speck von Sternberg, an interesting letter in which he stated that he regarded the Monroe Doctrine as equivalent to the Open Door in South America. The China parallel impressed Roosevelt; he feared that Speck's master, the German kaiser, might decide to "seize some Venezuelan harbor and turn it into a strongly fortified place of arms, on the model of Kiaochow, with a view to exercising some measure of control over the future Isthmian Canal, and over South American affairs generally."[15] These statements imply that Roosevelt foresaw the need for a general understanding, such as Hay had promoted by the Open Door notes, as well as a special acknowledgment of American supremacy in the hemisphere.

Roosevelt justified his own intervention in the Panamanian Revolution of 1903 on grounds that the "Bogotá lot of jack rabbits" had refused his cash offer for the Canal Zone and were barring "one of the future highways of civilization." But the sequence of events also suggests that he was trying to keep one step ahead of what he assumed to be the kaiser's secret desire to seize some "strongly fortified place of arms" to exercise control over South America. However fortuitous, the Panamanian intervention came only a few months after the president had warned Germany against going into Venezuela to collect a bad debt. Canal zone diplomacy thus involved an extension of the American protectorate system and not simply a future highway for civilization. It also opened the way for the Roosevelt Corollary to the Monroe Doctrine.

"If we intend to say 'Hands off' to the powers of Europe," Roosevelt instructed Root, "then sooner or later we must keep order ourselves."[16] The secretary agreed: "The inevitable effect of our building the Canal must be to require us to police the surrounding premises. In the nature of things, trade and control, and the obligation to keep order which go with them, must come our way."[17] In December 1904, Roosevelt announced this policy to the world in a message to Congress. When flagrant cases of wrongdoing occurred in the Western Hemisphere, he would, however reluctantly, be forced to act. "If every country washed by the Caribbean Sea would show the progress in stable and just civilization which with the aid of the Platt amendment Cuba has shown since our troops left the island, . . . all questions of interference by this Nation with their affairs would be at an end."

Cuba would hardly prove to be a good advertisement for the benefits of the Platt Amendment nor a model of a nation pulling itself up to civilization the "American Way." But even before the renewed trouble there caused Roosevelt to send in troops, the president had become involved in setting things right in Santo Domingo. American investments in Santo Domingo totaled about $20 million at this time. The most vocal group of property owners were, as in Cuba, the sugar planters, whose holdings worth $6 million were threatened by the continual revolutionary activities in the countryside. There were also constant rumors of European intervention. In short, it was Cuba all over again.*

* This sequence was repeated some sixty years later, when Cuba's 1959 revolution stimulated fears of similar developments in the Dominican Republic and led to the Johnson doctrine of preventative intervention.

20   President Theodore Roosevelt on the site of the Panama Canal, 1906.

The American minister, William F. Powell, had been trying for some time to interest Washington in a Santo Dominican protectorate. With the announcement of the Roosevelt Corollary, Powell's chance for glory had come. His greatest problem was how to keep a government in power long enough to convince it of the benefits of American financial supervision. Powell came to believe that a succession of Dominican strong men were trifling with him, a reasonable assumption under the circumstances. At last, the United States navy managed to arrange matters so that a certain Carlos Morales won a key battle and thus the presidency.

Morales was informed that the United States would not grant diplomatic recognition to him until he turned over control of the country's finances to Washington, along with signed leases to naval bases at Samana and Manzanilla bays. "I have about the same desire to annex it," Roosevelt said of Santo Domingo, "as a gorged boa constrictor might have to swallow a porcupine wrong-end to."[18] Contacted by Roosevelt's special agent, who had been sent to survey the scene, one of the sugar planters, J. L. Robertson, offered a suggestion later adopted almost in its entirety by Woodrow Wilson in dealing with the Caribbean area and Mexico. The Dominicans should be told: All right, you have made your choice. You have elected your president. Now we will not permit revolutions against this government. "This policy will insure lasting peace and will not require the landing of a marine or soldier on that Island."[19]

The marines went in anyway, under Roosevelt, Taft, *and* Wilson. The point is not that some unknown sugar planter predicted the course of events, or that presidents were at the service of special interests, but that the range of alternatives was limited by American objectives, whether defined by General Leonard Wood in regard to Cuba, a sugar planter in regard to Santo Domingo, or Woodrow Wilson trying to find an alternative to military intervention in Mexico.

Congress balked for a time at the treaty Morales signed, which gave the United States the right to collect and distribute Dominican customs, but Roosevelt ignored the rebuff. Claiming the

51

Constitution gave him the power he needed, he instructed the Secretary of the Navy "to stop any revolution. I intend to keep the island in statu quo until the Senate has had time to act on the treaty, and I shall treat any revolutionary movement as an effort to upset the modus vivendi."[20] Eventually, in 1907, the Senate accepted a modified version of the treaty, which paid more attention to Dominican sensibilities.

Even as Congress debated the Dominican protectorate, Roosevelt was looking ahead to greater things. Using a Costa Rican proposition as his example, Roosevelt urged the Secretary of State to expand his horizons even further. It was to America's advantage, he said, to gain "by the free offer of these republics" power over their finances, the lack of which had caused the United States such trouble in Venezuela and Santo Domingo.[21] Without doubt, Roosevelt's determination to keep order in the Canal Zone area reassured (and stimulated) potential investors. Frank Gardner, Secretary of the New York Board of Trade, forwarded to Root the conclusions of his committee on foreign trade in regard to the Dominican treaty:

> If the relations of this country with the republics to the south of us insured the maintenance of their internal peace and order, that would contribute greatly to the development of our trade with those countries, every one of which possess [sic] remarkably fertile soils, on which valuable products are and can be grown, and mines and forests replete with wealth. They present untold possibilities and resources awaiting development, and they would be a highly advantageous outlet for a large portion of the overproduction of our fields and factories, provided they were assured of stable governments. To this we could greatly contribute by properly making our influence felt among them, especially when they appeal to us as Santo Domingo has done.[22]

Enthusiasm for the Roosevelt Corollary quickly spread to San Francisco, where bankers undertook negotiations with Guatemala for a series of loans totaling $12 million. These contracts stipulated that the bankers would have the right to call on their government to ensure fulfillment of all obligations. In 1900 American investments in the Caribbean area amounted to little more than $100 million. In two years the figure rose to $500 million. A decade later it reached $1.5 billion. And by 1929 United States investors had holdings that totaled $3.3 billion.

Foreign trade figures kept pace as United States exporters to the Caribbean rapidly replaced their European competitors. By 1913 Americans had captured 50 percent or more of the trade of Costa Rica, Cuba, Guatemala, Haiti, Honduras, Nicaragua, Panama, and Santo Domingo. "Gradually we are coming to a condition which will insure permanent peace in the Western Hemisphere," Roosevelt wrote Andrew Carnegie on August 6, 1906. The president's approach to Canal Zone diplomacy assured the United States control of a vital sea lane, a fortified place of arms, and a growing network of "Platt Amendment" protectorates.

An eager "imperialist" in 1898, Roosevelt sometimes admitted to being faintly embarrassed by his accomplishments as a peacemaker. A martial man, Roosevelt did his best to eliminate the potential for war in the Far East by encouraging a stable balance of power among nations and Chinese internal reforms. He also tried to sustain the European balance of power in the 1906 Algeciras Conference when Germany called on him to intervene with Great Britain and France on behalf of the Open Door policy for Morocco. Although the United States lacked any substantial interest in Morocco, or the immediate likelihood of any, Roosevelt responded to the kaiser's request. His main concern was to contribute to peaceful settlement of a crisis that might lead to war. But on the Open Door principle, Secretary Root insisted in instructions to the American delegate that "while it is to the advantage of the powers to secure the 'open door,' it is equally vital to their interests and no less so to the advantage of Morocco that the door, being open, shall lead to something. . . ."[23]

America had gone abroad to search for that "something," not to satisfy the psychological needs of a few rambunctious "imperialists."

Notes

[1] Quoted in Ray Ginger, *Age of Excess: The United States from 1877 to 1914* (New York: Macmillan, 1965), p. 118.

[2] Quoted in Ernest R. May, *Imperial Democracy* (New York: Harper, 1961), p. 68.

[3] Quoted in John A. S. Grenville and George Berkely Young, *Politics, Strategy, and American Diplomacy: Studies in Foreign Policy, 1873–1917* (New Haven, Conn.: Yale University Press, 1966), p. 248.

[4] Quoted in Walter LaFeber, *The New Empire: An Interpretation of American Expansion, 1860–1898* (Ithaca, N.Y.: Cornell University Press, 1963), p. 349.

[5] Quoted in Ibid., p. 392.

[6] Quoted in David F. Healy, *The United States in Cuba, 1898–1902* (Madison, Wis.: University of Wisconsin Press, 1963), p. 133.

[7] Quoted in Lloyd C. Gardner, Walter LaFeber, and Thomas McCormick, *Creation of the American Empire* (Chicago: Rand-McNally, 1973), p. 274.

[8] Quoted in William Appleman Williams, *The Roots of the Modern American Empire* (New York: Random House, 1969), p. 436.

[9] The record of McKinley's discussions with his peace commissioners can be found in Thomas McCormick, *China Market: America's Quest for Informal Empire, 1893–1901* (Chicago: Quadrangle Books, 1967), pp. 122ff.

[10] Quoted in Howard K. Beale, *Theodore Roosevelt and the Rise of America to World Power* (Baltimore: Johns Hopkins Press, 1956), p. 209.

[11] Quoted in Charles Vevier, *The United States and China, 1906–1913* (New Brunswick, N.J.: Rutgers University Press, 1955), p. 22.

[12] Root to American Embassy in Tokyo, March 30, 1906, Papers of the Department of State, National Archives, Washington, D.C.

[13] Quoted in Jerry Israel, *Progressivism and the Open Door* (Pittsburgh: University of Pittsburgh Press, 1971), p. 16.

[14] Quoted in Vevier, *United States and China*, p. 72.

[15] Quoted in Beale, *Theodore Roosevelt*, pp. 399–401.

[16] Roosevelt to Root, June 7, 1904, Papers of Elihu Root, Library of Congress, Washington, D.C.

[17] Quoted in Dana G. Munro, *Intervention and Dollar Diplomacy in the Caribbean Area* (Princeton, N.J.: Princeton University Press, 1964), p. 113.

[18] Quoted in Howard C. Hill, *Roosevelt and the Caribbean* (Chicago: University of Chicago Press, 1927), p. 157.

[19] Robertson to Hay, April 12, 1904, Papers of the Department of State, National Archives, Washington, D.C.

[20] Quoted in Wilfrid Hardy Callcott, *The Caribbean Policy of the United States, 1890–1920* (Baltimore: Johns Hopkins Press, 1942), pp. 195–96.

[21] Roosevelt to Hay, January 14, 1905, Papers of Theodore Roosevelt, Library of Congress, Washington, D.C.

[22] Gardner to Root, April 5, 1906, Papers of the Department of State, National Archives, Washington, D.C.

[23] U.S., Department of State, *Papers Relating to the Foreign Relations of the United States, 1905* (Washington, D.C: Government Printing Office, 1906), pp. 678–80.

Bibliography

Campbell, Charles S., Jr. *Special Business Interests and the Open Door Policy.* New Haven, Conn.: Yale University Press, 1951. An excellent discussion of the formation of the American Asiatic Association and the influence of private groups on China policies.

Healy, David F. *U.S. Expansionism: The Imperialist Urge in the 1890s.* Madison, Wis.: University of Wisconsin Press, 1970. A stimulating discussion of all aspects of America's outward thrust with special attention to the relationship of ideas and institutions.

Hunt, Michael H. *Frontier Defense and the Open Door: Manchuria in Chinese-American Relations, 1895–1911.* New Haven, Conn.: Yale University Press, 1973. A new monograph that straightens out much that was confusing to historians about this key area and the problem of internal Chinese politics.

Kennan, George F. *American Foreign Policy, 1900–1950.* New York: New American Library, 1951. The now classic "realist" interpretation of the origin of the Open Door notes.

Morgan, H. Wayne. *America's Road to Empire: The War with Spain and Overseas Expansion.* New York: John Wiley, 1965. A reassessment of the imperial thrust, concentrating on the Cuban revolution and internal politics.

Pratt, Julius W. *Expansionists of 1898.* Baltimore: Johns Hopkins Press, 1936. The first influential study of the acquisition of Hawaii and the Philippines.

Varg, Paul A. *The Making of a Myth: The United States and China, 1897–1912.* East Lansing, Mich.: Michigan State University Press, 1968. How the Great China Market bubble began.

Young, Marilyn Blatt. *The Rhetoric of Empire: American China Policy, 1895–1901.* Cambridge, Mass.: Harvard University Press, 1968. An effort to reconcile various interpretations, leaning toward an independent "realist" position.

Zabriskie, Edward. *American-Russian Rivalry in the Far East, 1895–1914.* Philadelphia: University of Pennsylvania Press, 1946. Still the best book on this crucially important subject.

Progressivism, War, and Revolution: 1909–1919

3

I apprehend that a too emphatic denial might possibly destroy the sobering effect of the idea that intervention in certain circumstances could not be avoided. . . . Accordingly, with your full knowledge of the local situation, it is left to you to deal with this whole matter of keeping Mexican opinion, both official and unofficial, in a salutary equilibrium between a dangerous and exaggerated apprehension and a proper degree of wholesome fear.

Philander C. Knox to Henry Lane Wilson, ambassador to Mexico February 17, 1913

Taft's presidency soon became a burden. Progressives yearned to be free from the disappointment and sheer boredom of those ponderous years; political professionals were amazed and then appalled, by the man's clumsy ineptitude. Who would have thought that Roosevelt's handpicked successor would prove so unsuited for the White House? He was renominated with great unenthusiasm by Republicans who feared a Roosevelt insurgency more than they feared loss of an election. That left the way open for the Democratic governor of New Jersey, Woodrow Wilson, to walk into the presidential mansion.

This brief retelling of the misfortunes that befell William Howard Taft obscures, as do some longer accounts, his efforts to devise a strategy to deal with the foreign policy imperatives and ambitions he had inherited from Roosevelt. Wilson successfully made "dollar diplomacy" a major campaign issue. True to the low-tariff tradition he represented, Wilson also succeeded in leveling a powerful attack on Republican finagling, which aimed to produce a tariff satisfactory only to the special interests who financed the party. He placed equal stress, however, on the high tariff as a national "straitjacket" that constricted the American producer and denied him a proper (and needed) share of the world's market. In this instance, as in others, Taft's predicament in responding to the charge was more the result of Roosevelt's studied avoidance of a dangerous issue than his own bungling, although that put him deeper into the hole.

THE FIRST IMPERATIVE

McKinley had served warning on his Republican colleagues that protectionism no longer satisfied American needs. But Roosevelt adroitly sidestepped the tariff question for almost eight years. Whenever the question of reciprocity was brought up, Roosevelt ducked behind a warning that meddling with the tariff was sure to split the party. Who wanted that? And who thought the Democrats could do any better with their abominable free-trade ideas?

Not Taft, certainly. But he did think that despite Roosevelt's gloomy predictions, McKinley's course was the right way and that a "scientific" investigation was needed to determine a tariff and reciprocity policy suited to a mature industrial power. Taft seemed to have strong support in the business community. In 1907 the National Association of Manufacturers had called for a tariff commission with powers to investigate world tariff schedules. Out of 1260 members polled, 1040 favored reciprocity treaties. "We are the greatest manufacturing nation on earth," concluded the NAM report. "The Protective Policy has vastly helped us to this situation. It must not now be turned against us, but must be adapted to present-day conditions."[1]

Almost twenty years had passed since McKinley had reached that same conclusion. Not much had been accomplished since that time. In theory, the issue was decided. Practice was a different matter. Serious tariff reform involved Congressional politics and was a matter of faith and morals in thousands of election districts. It was still possible for a member of the House of Representatives to assure the "folks back home" that he had saved them from disaster in the form of cheap foreign goods on one day, and on the next to condemn the monopolists who kept prices at whatever level they wanted to impose on the people; just as it was possible to keep the works of William Jennings Bryan and Robert Ingersoll side by side on the same shelf as in many midwestern homes.

Moreover, tariff reformers came in two varieties. The low-tariff men, whose natural home was in the Democratic party, and the reciprocity advocates, who often turned up in the Republican party. The former tended to regard the latter as cunning plotters seeking to ensnare the uninformed in a cruel deception. Taft was caught in between. The 1909 Payne-Aldrich Tariff satisfied neither group and split the Republican party, with midwestern insurgents crying betrayal. The only lower rates, they charged, were on raw materials for the manufacturer. The bill did provide for a "scientific" tariff board to investigate foreign discrimination against American products, and it did grant the president discretionary powers to charge higher rates against those who discriminated, but these were small compensation for the effort and political capital Taft had invested in tariff "reform."

The need for an effective mechanism of this sort was undoubted. The century of relatively free trade was fast coming to an end; nations with large colonial holdings were using a myriad of tariff schedules and quotas to keep out foreign competitors. Unfortunately, when the Payne-Aldrich bill finally emerged from Congress, the minimum rates were so high that the president's discretionary powers had, in effect, been nullified.

Taft swallowed his disappointment. And when he next spoke of the act it was with words of praise for the "best tariff act" ever passed. To some dedicated Progressives, Taft began to resemble a huge boulder that had to be pushed aside before any headway could

21 Woodrow Wilson explains the "New Freedom."

be made in either domestic or foreign policy. What the nation required was a comprehensive foreign economic policy, perhaps modeled on Germany's recent experiments in government–business cooperation.

The Progressive party's 1912 platform set forth that very proposal:

> It is imperative to the welfare of our people that we enlarge and extend our foreign commerce. In every way possible our federal government should cooperate in this important matter. Germany's policy of cooperation between government and business has in a comparatively few years made that nation a leading competitor for the commerce of the world. . . .

At first sight Wilson's "New Freedom" platform seemed the antithesis of such a plan. Certainly he thought so. But Wilson's determination to curb the power of the special interests obviously formed a common bond with Progressive theory. Moreover, his promise to seek a ship subsidy bill and a modernized national banking act from Congress eased the concern of those who feared the New Jersey governor might turn out to be an eastern William Jennings Bryan.

Government cannot leave business alone, Wilson told the Economic Club in early 1912. "The very thing that government cannot let alone is business, for business underlies every part of our life; the foundation of our lives, of our spiritual lives included, is economic."[2] Neither Madison nor Hamilton had put it better. But to many in that audience, Governor Wilson was an unwelcome addition to the national political scene, a moralizing, academic liberal who probably knew almost nothing about the real world.

The 1913 Underwood Tariff proved their accusations about Wilson, critics said. All it did was to lower the bars so that foreign goods could undersell American products. Wilson's supporters had confidence, however, that if the Underwood Tariff did not stimulate exports, the president would try something else. Meanwhile, Wilson fulfilled another pledge by signing into law the Federal Reserve Act, which included a provision permitting American banks to establish overseas branches, such as those Great Britain and Germany had planted abroad to help exports grow.

Almost 150 branch banks were established during the next six years, although many failed to survive the rigor of overseas competition. The Wilson administration next encouraged the formation of a National Foreign Trade Council. "We have learned the lesson now," Secretary of Commerce William C. Redfield told delegates to the first convention,

> that our factories are so large that their output at full time is greater than America's market can continuously and regularly absorb. . . . And because the markets of the world are greater and steadier than the markets of any country can be, and because we are strong, we are going out, you and I, into the markets of the world to get our share.[3]

At the 1915 annual meeting of the United States Chamber of Commerce, Wilson elaborated on a similar theme. Explaining to the business leaders that he had made it a habit to read consular reports for more than twenty years, the president lamented that more had not been done in the past to support the exporter:

We ought long ago to have sent the best eyes of the Government out into the world to see where the opportunities and openings for American commerce and American genius were to be found—men who were not sent out as the commercial agents of any particular set of business men in the United States, but who were eyes for the whole business community.[4]

Along a parallel line ran the high-powered campaign for a new law to exempt foreign-trade combines from the provisions of the Sherman Antitrust Act. The first serious efforts in this direction began in the Taft years—and were promptly labeled special interest pleading. But the leaders of the 1914 National Foreign Trade Convention had an unanswerable argument: if the United States was to become a low-tariff country, then it must first equip its businessmen to compete successfully in foreign markets. "England permits combinations which our Sherman Law prohibits," began one speaker, "France encourages them, and Germany not only encourages but, at times, compels its citizens to enter into them."[5]

In December 1914 Wilson, interested in this logical treatment of the consequences of low-tariff policies, approved the "principle" of a bill to exempt foreign trade organizations from antitrust laws. Missouri Governor David R. Francis anticipated a bit at the 1915 National Foreign Trade Convention: "We Democrats are willing to permit all kinds of combination for foreign commerce. No Democrat, no American, will contend that any legislative body of this country, whether State or National, should legislate for the benefit of the citizens of another country."[6] But the Federal Trade Commission, at Wilson's direction, soon completed a report calling for legislation to permit cooperation for foreign trade.

A few days after his reelection, Wilson granted an interview to a reporter who wanted to discuss his plans for the next four years. The president elaborated at great length on expectations of continued prosperity: "Not only is there the part we shall be called upon to play in the reconstruction of shattered Europe, but the great markets of South America and the Orient are calling to us. . . ." Then he turned to what Congress must do to insure there would be opportunities for "legitimate trade expansion": "American firms must be given definite authorization to cooperate for foreign selling operations; in plain words to organize for foreign trade just as the 'rings' of England and the cartels of Germany are organized."[7]

The necessary legislation, the 1918 Webb-Pomerene Act and the 1919 Edge Act permitting banks to organize in similar fashion, completed a "Commercial Preparedness" program that had begun not in 1916, nor even in 1914, but in the Taft years.

TROUBLED WATERS IN *MARE NOSTRUM*

Between 1898 and 1920, United States marines or soldiers landed on some Caribbean island or country on no less than twenty occasions. Until the 1910 Mexican Revolution began to be part of the problem, American policymakers looked to Mexico City for support in these "neighborhood" tasks. The chief troublemaker in those years was Nicaraguan dictator José Santos Zelaya, who aspired to add Honduras to his domain. His rival was Guatemala's Manuel Estrada Cabrera, another "scoundrel," but one who, in the words of an experienced diplomat, had "the good sense to be civil to our country and its citizens and to keep his cruelties . . . for home consumption."[8]

Shortly after Taft became president, the State Department informed Zelaya that his time was up: unless he signed a protocol agreeing to satisfy the complaints lodged by American citizens, it would "have to wash its hands of the matter and refer it to Congress."[9] Zelaya ignored the ultimatum. In April 1909, he added insult to injury by negotiating a large loan in London to consolidate Nicaraguan debts and to construct an east–west railroad. This plan directly conflicted with a proposed Central American railroad. Zelaya's constant threats against his neighbors and his eagerness to do business with European bankers and capitalists set a bad example for the rest of Central America.

Washington was not unhappy, then, when, as the American consul at Bluefields predicted, a revolution broke out against Zelaya. Moreover, the leading candidate for the old dictator's job had told American diplomats: "Nicaragua is rich in natural resources and under proper administration would be a credit to the Americas and a field for American commerce, instead of a pest under your nose."[10] After the revolution, Taft offered Nicaragua the blessings of the Dominican protectorate, but the Senate balked at the 1911 Knox-Castrillo Convention. Even so, private bankers agreed to lend Nicaragua $15 million. And even without ratification of the convention, United States citizens were soon collecting Nicaraguan customs, serving on claims commissions, and sitting on the boards of the national bank and railroad.

At this point some anti-American "Zelaysitas" attempted to stage a counterrevolution. Taft was advised to be firm. If the United States did "its duty promptly, thoroughly and impressively," said State Department officials, "it would strengthen our hand and lighten our task, not only in Nicaragua itself in the future, but throughout Central America and the Caribbean and would even have some moral effect in Mexico."[11] Taft had vowed to keep the peace in Central America, even if it meant he had to "knock their heads together." At hand in this crisis were two thousand soldiers and marines in the Canal Zone. They were dispatched to Nicaragua in September 1912, and the revolutionary threat evaporated. All but one hundred were withdrawn. They stayed to guard the American legation in Managua—and to remind everyone that Uncle Sam was still listening.

Wilson's secretary of state, William Jennings Bryan, renegotiated the lapsed Knox-Castrillo Convention, making it into a treaty providing for American naval bases and an open option of a future canal route. The Bryan-Chamorro Pact also included a clause similar to the Platt Amendment that granted the right of intervention to the United States in case of internal disturbances in Nicaragua. For these privileges, the United States was to give Nicaragua a $3 million cash advance. The Senate agreed to everything except the intervention provision.

The navy bases were never occupied. Bryan's objective, however, was to preclude "foreign" control. That was accomplished by the treaty. It was not so easy to remove European economic influence from the Western Hemisphere. Bryan suggested to the president that the United States government underwrite Central American loans, in effect to lend them America's credit rating. That would make it unnecessary, he said, for those countries to borrow in Europe. Wilson found the idea too "novel and radical." The secretary of state would have to find a more traditional way to achieve that end.

DEFINING THE JUST AND THE UNJUST

Wilson had established another guideline: whenever and wherever possible, Bryan was to prevent revolutions by "those who seek to seize the power of government to advance their own personal interests or ambition."[12] This was a tall order indeed. Not only was the United States thus committed to preventing revolutions without just cause, but apparently the president expected his Department of State to be able to tell the difference. Undaunted, Bryan promptly informed the American minister in the Dominican Republic, once again in turmoil despite the customs protectorate, that the United States would use every "legitimate" means to restore order. The minister reported back that he had written both sides "that revolution would never again bring a government into power here."[13]

The proposed Dominican "solution" was based on an old idea that the United States should call the rival revolutionary leaders together, at which time they would select one of their number to serve as provisional president until "free" elections could be held. Once the election was over, the new president could count on American support. "Say to any who may feel aggrieved or who may be disposed to resort to violence," Bryan explained, "that the good offices of this Government can be counted upon at all times to assist in the establishment of justice, in the remedying of abuses, and in the promotion of the welfare of the people."[14]

Who needed a revolution when Bryan and Wilson were thus prepared to give everyone in the hemisphere the benefit of the American Revolution? Bryan came very close to saying just that, and to denying the legitimacy of any other point of view. "Some time soon," Roosevelt had once declared, "I shall have to spank some

65

22 William Jennings Bryan.

little brigand of a South American republic." Wilson put it differently: "I am going to teach the South American republics to elect good men!" But when the Dominicans resisted, Bryan began to lose patience. "No opportunity for argument should be given to any person or faction," he cabled the American minister. "It is desired that you present plan and see that it is complied with."[15]

That proved difficult. Bryan's messages to the legation became more strident. "This government meant what it said when it declared that it would tolerate no more insurrections," he wrote on April 19, 1915, "and it will furnish whatever force may be necessary to put down insurrections and to punish those guilty of exciting or supporting insurrections."[16] In May 1916, an eight-year military occupation began. The American force remained until a new Dominican government was well established.

Haiti and the Dominican Republic shared the same island; if anything, Haiti's revolutionary troubles were worse. For more than two years Bryan tried to find some way to keep a Haitian government in power long enough to impose an American protectorate.

At one point a Haitian leader offered to give American capitalists preference in any concessions that were to be handed out, but no customs control. Bryan was shocked. Advising the president that "I think it is well for us to let them distinctly understand that this Government is not disposed to make a bargain of that kind," he drafted a reply that probably came as close as any single statement could to defining American policy and his faith in its soundness:

> While we desire to encourage in every proper way American investments in Haiti, we believe that this can be better done by contributing to stability and order than by favoring special concessions to Americans. American capital will gladly avail itself of business opportunities in Haiti when assured of peace and quiet necessary for profitable production.[17]

When American troops went into Haiti a few months later, it was said that European interests were planning to intervene. Some high officials apparently took seriously a rumor that France and Germany, who were doing everything they could to destroy one another in Europe, were secretly planning a joint intervention. The 1916 purchase of the Danish West Indies completed the conversion of the Caribbean into an American lake.

There was no longer any danger that the kaiser (or anybody else) would seize a stronghold on the coast of Central America. A military buffer zone around the nearly completed Panama Canal insured that America's strategic interests would not be put in jeopardy. Referring to the canal, Wilson told a *Saturday Evening Post* reporter early in 1914 to draw a line from New York directly south. It will end, he explained, on the west coast of Latin America. "Thus, with the Panama Canal running practically north and south, this brings those countries which have been so remote into close touch with us, and the commerce of this Western Hemisphere will travel over Central America."[18]

MEXICO HAS NO GOVERNMENT

Wilson's interview with the *Post* reporter mostly concerned Mexico. The demands that the United States restore order in

Mexico, said the president, came from those who wanted to reestablish the old-time regime of Porfirio Díaz. That old order was dead, and while Wilson sympathized with the desire for an orderly and righteous government in Mexico, his passion was for the submerged 85 percent of the population who yearned for something more.

Taft had been the first president to feel pressure for intervention when Díaz, who had ruled Mexico from 1876 to 1911, finally gave way to Francisco I. Madero. Madero's ability to control the more radical elements in his revolutionary entourage and then inaugurate a reform government was in doubt from the beginning. The American ambassador, Henry Lane Wilson, scoffed at Madero's efforts and belittled the man as a mystic who thought he was in direct communication with George Washington. Americans had invested $2 billion in Mexico, Taft wrote his wife. If Mexico went to pieces, intervention would become inevitable.

Although he sent warships into the Gulf of Mexico, Taft proved surprisingly reluctant to intervene even as conditions grew steadily worse. He may have sensed that what was beginning was no ordinary customshouse *coup d'état*. In any event, at the 1912 Republican National Convention, Taft counseled patience and restraint. In a conversation with the Mexican ambassador, the president began with assurances that he desired Madero's experiment to succeed. But, continued the ambassador's report of this conversation,

> since the impotence of the administration was palpable, with great risk to foreign interests in Mexico, he exhorted me to convince President Madero that it was a serious international necessity that such a situation should change. Mr. Taft added that while he was President, the American government would remain deaf to the call of those who were asking for intervention; but that, on the other hand, he, as President, had to see that the interests of foreigners in general, not just as those of Americans, did not continue to suffer.[19]

Madero's downfall in February 1913 led to Secretary of State Knox's admonition on the need to keep Mexican opinion in equilibrium between exaggerated apprehension and wholesome fear. Now it was up to Woodrow Wilson.

Wilson's initial reaction was repugnance at General Victoriano Huerta's method of seizing power. This soon grew into genuine hatred for the usurper, who had turned back the clock in Mexico, and for those unscrupulous Europeans who kept him in power so that they might continue to exploit that nation's natural resources. At the first cabinet discussion of the Mexican situation, someone said that all the trouble stemmed from a fight between British and American oil companies for control of the country. Unheedful of those who warned that Huerta represented the only force capable of steering Mexico through unsettled times to stability, Wilson, the political scientist, decided to make Mexico a laboratory.

Finding someone who was untainted by "dollar diplomacy," the president sent John Lind, a former governor of Minnesota, to Huerta with an offer. Lind, a Protestant who spoke no Spanish, was to inform the Mexican leader that if he would fulfill his promise to hold elections, and himself step aside, the United States govern-

23 Victoriano Huerta: Wilson's *bête noire.*

ment would try to arrange a loan for Mexico through New York bankers. It quickly became apparent that Wilson had underestimated Huerta, who made it known to the world that he had been offered a bribe to betray his country—a more foul offer had not been made to Judas Iscariot.

Lind retreated to an American warship off Veracruz. In Washington, the president announced a policy of "watchful waiting." "The present situation," he told Congress, "is incompatible with the fulfillment of international obligations on the part of Mexico, with the civilized development of Mexico herself, and with the maintenance of tolerable political and economic conditions in Central America."[20] These arguments were designed to separate Huerta from his European backers. But Wilson also had domestic critics to satisfy. They charged that the president's refusal to countenance any dealings with the vile Huerta threatened chaos. The British knew from experience that it was no small matter to meddle in a volatile situation. Did the president realize what he was risking by stirring up feelings against foreign interests?

To find out, London sent Sir William Tyrrell to Washington. Wilson was reassuring: the United States intended "not merely to force Huerta from power, but also to exert every influence it can exert to secure Mexico a better government under which all contracts and business and concessions will be safer than they have been. . . ."[21] Every consul, added the president, had been instructed to warn authorities in Mexico City and in rebel-held territory that the private property "of all foreigners" must be protected.

A few days later Wilson drafted a statement for European foreign offices that went beyond his private assurances to Tyrrell. Usurpations like those of General Huerta could not be tolerated, it began, because they menaced the peace and development of "America" as nothing else could. They put the lives and fortunes of citizens and foreigners alike in jeopardy. They allowed a dictator to invalidate "contracts and concessions" in any way he might devise for his own profit.

Wilson had gotten himself into a very murky situation. In a series of speeches and remarks, he had denounced foreign conces-

24 A skeptical view of Wilson's Mexican policy.

sions and, at least implicitly, Huerta as their tool; now he had condemned this same Huerta to the Europeans as a threat to progress and stability—and to foreign concessions. Moreover, should his policy succeed, Wilson had pledged himself to the establishment of "a better government" for Mexico. What was a better government, one that would support "contracts and business and concessions" or one that would give first priority to the needs of the submerged 85 percent?

Whether or not he saw a way out of this apparent contradiction, Wilson told Congress, "Mexico has no Government." Thus he felt justified in advancing his position from watchful waiting to open support for the "Constitutionalists" led by Venustiano Carranza. Carranza's agent was even more ambiguous than Wilson in his statements to State Department officials. Once in power, he said, Carranza would move "to accomplish the needed—and it may be radical—reforms by constitutional and legal methods, respecting at all times the rights of property, the upholding of just and equitable concessions, the observance of contract rights, and opposing confiscation and anarchy."[22]

It seemed clear to Wilson, nonetheless, that if Mexico was to have a better government, he must aid the Constitutionalists to win power. This conviction almost led to war with Huerta's government in April 1914, when the United States used a supposed insult to the flag to occupy Veracruz and Tampico. The real reason was that Wilson had wanted to prevent an arms shipment from reaching Mexico City. Finally convinced that he could not hold out against both Wilson and his domestic opponents, General Huerta departed—appropriately, on a British battleship. After a period of revolutionary turmoil, Carranza emerged in Mexico City with the title First Chief. But Wilson's troubles had only begun.

25 Pancho Villa became the recipient of American aid almost by a fluke. When it was cut off, he retaliated by attacking border cities.

A conservative landowner, Carranza had seemed the least likely of all the revolutionary leaders to cause America trouble. If anything, he was thought too conservative. Yet he was a nationalist who could not avoid confronting the issue of foreign control of Mexican resources. Growing uncertainty about Carranza and continued unrest led Bryan's successor, Robert Lansing, to permit Pancho Villa, an agrarian radical, to receive funds surreptitiously from the sale of stolen cattle in the United States. When Wilson questioned this odd practice, Lansing answered with a rationale worthy of the best the National Security Council could devise in later years:

> The reason for furnishing Villa with an opportunity to obtain funds is this: We do not wish the Carranza faction to be the only one to deal with in Mexico. Carranza seems so impossible that an appearance, at least, of opposition to him will give us an opportunity to invite a compromise of factions.[23]

Left alone, Lansing would have continued with a plan to force Carranza's withdrawal. Wilson shied at that final step. In early 1917 Carranza promulgated a new constitution that, to the immediate consternation of many foreigners, vested subsoil mineral rights in the central government. Aliens who desired concessions to exploit these resources would have to surrender the cherished "right" to invoke the support of their governments in disputes with the Mexican government. Carranza also announced new regulatory and tax measures on pre-1917 concessions.

Those who had warned that the eruption in Mexico was not a minor affair had been proved right. Mexico's challenge questioned the established world order. Here was the first "Third World" trouble-spot, the first serious clash over control of natural resources, the beginning of a new era. When Washington's protests against the offending articles brought no satisfactory response from Mexico, the administration took counsel with the bankers. Encouraged by the State Department, an international bankers' committee was formed to offer Carranza a large loan. The hope was that he would accept these funds to pay off the debts of the revolution and leave private property alone. Moreover, Wilson had acquiesced in a policy that placed the United States on roughly the same level as European "capitalist" powers. An offer of $150 million was actually made, but Carranza turned it down because it included a requirement that the petroleum question be "settled" and all foreign properties be returned.

A major consideration in the decision to attempt a multinational approach to the Mexican problem was the concern that if other Latin American nations followed Carranza's lead, the whole pattern of foreign investment and international trade would come under question. In 1919 a special interdepartmental committee concluded that "the confiscation or destruction of petroleum properties controlled by United States interests or the existence of conditions which make impossible their operation, is an injury to the national interests and an injury which cannot be remedied by apologies or pecuniary compensation after the damage has occurred."[24]

Two decades earlier McKinley had defined American well-being and prosperity in terms of Cuban tranquillity; if it was not yet proper to say that policymakers now defined the national interest in terms of the security of the Mexican oil fields, this statement approached such a conclusion. The Mexican Revolution had also forced Washington to consider the importance of cooperation among the industrial powers in the face of a general challenge to the established world order. A similar pattern developed in the American attitude toward China.

THE CHINA CONSORTIUMS

President Taft had announced a more vigorous China policy in his inaugural address. Explaining his request for stronger military and naval forces, Taft said they were necessary if the United States was to secure respect for its demands in "the international controversies that are likely to arise in the Orient." And within a few weeks the president had reversed Root's coy approach to state-supported enterprises, openly embracing "paternalism." "Call it paternalism, if you will," Secretary of State Philander Knox said in a 1911 speech, "but it is rational to hold that a fatherland owes to its children the duty of assuring them opportunity for self-advancement." International rivalry, he concluded, was a "Darwinian struggle for existence, the condition is inexorable, and the fittest survive."[25]

Knox's Darwinism had a Germanic ring: nations had to keep fit for the struggle; the concept of laissez faire could no longer be applied to international relations. As the secretary explained to a group of bankers summoned to Washington, it was their patriotic duty to submerge the question of immediate profits to the long-range goal of preserving the China market for the products of American industry. The bankers reluctantly agreed at Knox's insistence to take a one-quarter share of the Hukuang Railway loan along with German, British, and French bankers. These shares entitled each lender to claim also a one-quarter share of the supplies to build the railroad.

Up to this point the history of the First China Consortium was relatively simple: Taft saw an opening and drove a wedge into the European monopoly on China loans. Within a few months events became so complicated that not even the participants were sure of what was happening. In essence what transpired was this: Willard Straight, in a dual capacity as Harriman's advance man and State Department representative, renegotiated the 1908 memorandum for American participation in a major railway undertaking in Manchuria. Harriman's death was the first complication, for it left Straight with the responsibility for explaining the more grandiose scheme to the already skeptical members of the American group, and it cut short Harriman's private negotiations with the Russians for the purchase of the Chinese Eastern Railway. Knox then proved unsympathetic to a formal Russian-American understanding on Manchurian loans, reasserting his special brand of Darwinism when the question was posed by the Russian embassy: "It would hardly do to agree that business developed and made possible through the energy of our own people . . . should, when developed through those means, be equally divided with those who have no hand in bringing it forward."[26]

When he said those words, Knox thought he was standing on firm ground. He had heard from Straight that the Chinese had signed a contract for the Chinchow-to-Aigun line with an Anglo-American company. The more Knox thought about the Russian request for a share of the Manchurian business, the more convinced he became that an opportunity for "neutralizing" that province, in an Open Door sense, was at last at hand. For ten years American policymakers had sought the answer to John Hay's dilemma: how to succeed in China without alliances. Now it was within Secretary of State Knox's grasp.

Or so he thought on November 9, 1909, when he sent a note to London proposing that an international syndicate lend China the money to buy back from Russia and Japan the Chinese Eastern and South Manchurian railways. The syndicate would exercise supervision over Manchurian railroads for the duration of the loan. Should the others prove recalcitrant, the United States and Britain would go ahead with the Chinchow–Aigun line. It was foolproof, except for one thing. The Chinese had never ratified the Chinchow-to-Aigun contract. Russia and Japan lost no time in warning Peking not to sign the agreement. By his premature move, Knox managed only to neutralize the efforts of Harriman and Straight to gain a foothold in Manchuria. Russia and Japan drew closer to one another, and Taft was back to square one.

A consensus developed around the idea that the way to get back in the running would be to strengthen the Chinese government so that it could resist foreign pressure. It was also decided that the best way to accomplish this minor miracle would be through an American-supervised currency reform loan. The bankers, growing still more restless about their position in this Wall Street–Washington combine, insisted that the other members of the international consortium be invited to participate. Ironically, the State Department now had to fend off the complaints of other American finance groups who insisted that they were being shut out of the market. When they raised a hue and cry about monopoly and free competition, the State Department instructed its minister in China that the "Morgan syndicate" had gone beyond "open competition and reached a step where a rival would interfere and not compete."[27]

Things were approaching the absurd. Storm-warnings were going up on all sides. In the United States, Roosevelt advised his old friend in the White House that the Open Door policy had never developed into anything substantial, and that when a powerful country chose to ignore it, as Russia and Japan had just done, it disappeared completely. American interests in China, and especially Manchuria, did not justify, and Congress would not support, a war for the Open Door policy. So why continue the farce? Taft and Knox did not agree. Japan had no more right to Manchuria than any other power, especially not more than China, who, after all, *owned* Manchuria. Moreover, who could say how American interests would develop in the future, or what steps some future administration might want to take to protect them? It would, therefore, seem an "inopportune time now to let down our standard," concluded Knox.[28]

That argument, with elaborate additions, would sustain policy-makers down through the years, first in China and finally in Southeast Asia. There never seemed an opportune time "to let down our standard." In 1911 the Manchu Dynasty fell. A Chinese republic was proclaimed; but over the next three decades a succession of weak strong men attempted, unsuccessfully, to unify the country. It was anticipated, correctly, that these would-be rulers would also attempt to gain the support of foreign powers by playing one off against the other. This was a dangerous game for everyone. The Four Power Consortium took defensive steps by inviting Japan and Russia to join in presenting the first of the post-Manchu aspirants, Yüan Shih-k'ai, with no-nonsense terms: control of all funds lent to China and a monopoly of the loan business.

It was a bold maneuver, too bold it soon became apparent. The governments concerned could not guarantee to their banking groups the full support needed to impress the Chinese with their control of the situation. This was especially true in Great Britain and the United States, where the consortium was being denounced as an unnatural alliance among nations with very different objectives in China and as an unnatural restraint on trade. All Yüan and his successors had to do was to indicate a willingness to do business with other lenders, and floods of letters poured into the Foreign Office and the Department of State demanding fair treatment for nonconsortium bankers.

In the 1912 election campaign Wilson had spoken of the new spirit in the air that had reached as far as China. It was a foregone conclusion, then, that when the bankers asked Secretary of State Bryan where he stood on the question of assuring the consortium full support, the answer would not be favorable. That was all right; they were ready to get out anyway, but the bankers resented Wilson's public disavowal of what they had been told was a patriotic duty. Nor did the president's promise to support legitimate business interests in China against rivals assuage their anger.

In Japan, however, Wilson's announcement was read to mean the United States was determined to cast aside the interests of other powers in China in order to gain a favorable place for itself when concessions were distributed. And when the new American minister to China opened an all-out campaign for contracts and concessions, Tokyo felt satisfied that its first guess had been correct. If idealism was the American president's primary motivation, the Japanese wondered, then why did he give unqualified support to the petty tyrant Yüan, whose immediate goal was to destroy any progressive movement in China? And why, for that matter, was Yüan any better than Huerta?

One answer, of course, was that Wilson simply did not know very much about events in China, or their meaning; but as far as Japan was concerned, the effect of American policy was the same, and there was *no* doubt that Wilson approved the drive for increased trade and investment. Perhaps as a subtle way of reminding the Americans that their interests could not be disregarded so lightly, perhaps simply as good business, the Japanese considered giving Huerta some economic aid. Disturbed, Wilson asked the British to intervene with their ally but failed to notice any possible connections.

Meanwhile, Paul S. Reinsch, the American representative to China, moved ahead with his most ambitious scheme in order to demonstrate that even after the failure of the American Development Company and the consortium plan, the United States could carry out a major project. With the support of the American Red Cross, Reinsch managed to negotiate a $20 million loan contract for the construction of dams in the Hwai River Valley. Even the much-disappointed and chastened Willard Straight was impressed. It might indeed, he wrote Reinsch, provide "the bridge over which we can enter once again upon Chinese business."[29] But, once again, it was not to be. The outbreak of the First World War drained off any capital still available for risk ventures. Worse was to come. As soon as the war broke out, the Japanese moved against Germany in Shantung and then, in January 1915, presented China with a list of "Twenty-One Demands." If granted, these would have given Japan unquestioned supremacy among the powers in China, making that country a virtual protectorate. At first the State Department reacted cautiously, despite Reinsch's fervid appeals for a dramatic protest. The sweeping nature of the Japanese demands perhaps had taken some by surprise, although a proposal was forthcoming from Robert Lansing suggesting that Tokyo's offensive might be met with a diplomatic counterattack: a straightforward bargain giving Manchuria to Japan as a sphere of influence in exchange for a final settlement of the immigration question.

As the extent of the demands became known, and as that knowledge became fully understood, the mood in Washington changed, especially in the White House. Although Secretary of State Bryan had earlier acquiesced in at least some of the lesser demands, Wilson ordered a note sent to both Peking and Tokyo stating that the United States would not recognize any agreement that would violate "the international policy relative to China commonly known as the open door policy." In effect, Wilson had turned the clock back to 1902, when John Hay had issued his protest against a Russo-Chinese pact concerning Manchuria.

The president was not actually risking an immediate confrontation with Japan, since Tokyo had already withdrawn the most offensive of the Twenty-One Demands. Wilson explained to Bryan, however, that he hoped his caveat would influence Japan not to press any similar demands "for a very long time indeed." 79

Throughout the crisis Reinsch had bombarded the president with letters and suggestions. He proposed, for example, that Wilson ask all the powers to reaffirm the Open Door principle, an idea that the president liked and that was considered at the Paris Peace Conference.

Reinsch's most interesting suggestion, however, evolved out of his great disappointment that the Hwai River Valley conservancy plan had failed for lack of funds. Suspecting that the bankers were still sulking over the consortium issue and were, therefore, deliberately witholding funds, Reinsch suggested that the government take the lead in forming an investment organization, perhaps of a semipublic character like the Federal Reserve System:

> The main consideration is that only through such an organization can American commerce get a secure footing in China under present conditions. Opportunities are offered for your Administration to lay the foundations of a great development of American enterprise in the Far East—a development which will soon be a life necessity to our industries and for which future ages will give their thankful recognition.[30]

The timing of this letter, coming as it did when Wilson was considering the general problem of export trade organizations exempt from antitrust legislation, no doubt reinforced his concern for the future of American interests not only in the Far East but everywhere. China was part of America's future. How big a part no one could tell in 1915, but for that very reason Japan's attempt to close the Open Door must be resisted. Meanwhile, a group of capitalists and bankers were completing plans for the very sort of organization Reinsch had envisioned. The key figure was Frank A. Vanderlip, a natural heir to E. H. Harriman's Oriental visions. He even picked Harriman's old China hand, Willard Straight, to run the diplomatic side of the American Investment Corporation.

At first Reinsch was delighted by the interest the AIC displayed in picking up the option on the Hwai River Valley conservancy plan. This soon turned to amazement and anger when it became clear that Straight and Vanderlip had in mind using this project—Reinsch's project—as an experiment in Japanese-American cooperation! Preliminary discussions with the members of the old consortium convinced State Department officials that there was little enthusiasm for slugging it out with Japan in China. Some arrangement had to be made for cooperation.

A survey of other bankers who had indicated interest in new China loans only confirmed this impression. Even those who had the inclination to go it alone could offer no practical suggestions as to procedure. Well, then, reasoned Secretary of State Lansing, there was nothing to do but try to make a virtue out of necessity. In January 1917, Lansing met with the Japanese ambassador and offered him a one-for-one arrangement: Manchuria for Shantung. The United States would stay clear of Manchuria if the Japanese would relinquish postwar claims to German rights in Shantung. Later in the year the secretary of state attempted to formalize this understanding—and to go beyond it in certain ways—in discussions with Special Ambassador Ishii Kikujiro.

Unfortunately, the Lansing-Ishii Agreement of November 2, 1917, never worked out quite right for the secretary's purpose. Of necessity it was ambiguous, recognizing Japan's "special interests" in China, especially in areas contiguous to its possessions (a euphemism for Manchuria), but still affirming the Open Door and China's independence. Lansing admitted that the term *special interests* "left ample room for suitable interpretations on both sides."[31] Consequently, the agreement did not reassure the Chinese. But Lansing had also had in mind a new initiative, using Japanese cooperation, to destroy European spheres of influence in China. To get a usable Open Door in China proper, he was willing to concede, however ambiguously, Japan's special interests in Manchuria, the graveyard of Hay's policy in Taft's day.

If he hoped to use Japan against European imperialists, the secretary had to have a plan to curb the former's ambitions as well. The best solution, he decided, was to resurrect the China Consortium. The old members were first encouraged to invite the participation of large banks in Chicago and the Far West. Then the State Department turned its attention to the reconstruction of the international consortium minus Germany. Russia had to be left out, too, because of the Bolshevik Revolution, but a place was reserved for whatever decent government succeeded the communists. Nor could Great Britain and France pay their way, but that had been anticipated. It was imperative to find some way to contain and control Japan, whose crude methods threatened to ruin everything for the other nations.

Moreover, despite the countinuing turmoil inside China, the United States still had faith in the ultimate success of democratic nationalism in that huge country. As Lansing and Wilson reckoned, the consortium would now be to China's advantage, since it would break the deadlock between Japan and the United States and allow foreign capital to flow into needed projects. Instead of exploitation, the new consortium would foster modernization.

Everything fit into place—except the Chinese, who were bitter about the Lansing-Ishii Agreement and skeptical of the plan to reconstruct the consortium. They feared that what Colonel House, Wilson's closest friend and adviser, predicted was right. The consortium, he wrote on July 12, 1918, was the beginning of what would ultimately prove to be the approved solution for China: "government under and by a commission of the big and interested powers."[32] Wilson had set out with new policies for Mexico and China. Four years later his advisers were working on ways of making the old policies adaptable to revolutionary situations.

TO MAKE THE WORLD SAFE FOR DEMOCRACY

The war made things more difficult in some ways, but at least Wilson could at last see in that struggle a definite opportunity to explain American ideas for a better world. For almost three years, from August 1914 to April 1917, the United States had wandered around in what Wilson called in a moment of frustration, the labyrinth of neutrality. The real cause of America's entry into the war was the stalemate. Had either side been able to mount an all-out offensive in the first months of the war, the dilemmas that led to the decisions for war would not have arisen.

There was no doubt where American sympathies lay. Germany's invasion of Belgium settled that question, although serious observers warned against taking Allied propaganda at face value.

26 A dissenting comment on loans and arms sales to belligerents.

Secretary of State Bryan was also definite on the limitations of sympathy: they did not include loans. "Loans by American bankers to any foreign nation which is at war is [sic] inconsistent with the true spirit of neutrality."[33]

Officially, that statement was never withdrawn, but during the next two and a half years private bankers extended credit and loans to the Allies totaling almost $2.3 billion. The loans themselves were not an important cause of the decision to go to war; what they represented, however, was. In the broadest sense, the loans represented an awareness that the United States could not live and prosper without Europe. Still a debtor nation in 1914, the United States relied on exports of agricultural surpluses to settle its yearly accounts. In addition, foreign purchases of cotton and wheat sustained the market price structure for those commodities and thus for large areas of the country.

British investment in the United States at the outset of the war

83

totaled more than $3.5 billion. Much of this was liquidated to provide capital to fight the war and to pay the mounting bill for imports of goods England and the Allies had ceased to produce. It was only a matter of time until the warring nations discovered that the only way the war could be won was by cutting off outside supplies to the other side. The imposition of the British maritime blockade and the German submarine counterblockade recreated the situation that led to the War of 1812.

This time, however, British policymakers were determined that if America went to war, it would be against the continental power. Sir Edward Grey, the British foreign minister, had advised his colleagues that his objective was to achieve the maximum degree of blockade without pushing the United States into a corner from which it would strike out to preserve its self-respect. Grey's careful manipulation of the cotton issue, first in persuading the cabinet not to place that commodity on the contraband list and then in picking the right moment to negotiate a secret agreement for purchase of American cotton to keep the price up when it was placed on the list, demonstrated his considerable talents in this direction.

The right moment came when the United States was embroiled with Germany over the sinking of the *Lusitania* in May 1915, but these episodes—the cotton purchase arrangement and the submarine warfare crisis—explain, at least in part, why Grey's task was not more difficult. To put it simply, the British had more options in dealing with the United States than did their opponents. Because of the natural sympathy, the economic connections, and the political similarities between the two countries, Grey had a range of possible choices and considerable room to maneuver.

Wilson interpreted submarine warfare as a moral issue, a means of distinguishing between the opposing alliances. When Bryan found himself unable to follow this reasoning, he was replaced by Robert Lansing, who wanted Wilson to go to war at once. An immediate confrontation was put off when Berlin, in the wake of the *Lusitania* crisis, agreed to restrict U-boat commanders to the same rules of naval warfare that governed surface vessels.

While Wilson was relieved that the crisis had not forced the issue of war or peace, he complained to Colonel House in September 1915 that he had never been sure that America should have remained neutral when Germany attacked Belgium. Was there not some way out of the labyrinth created by all this German "frightfulness"? To House, the president's words became a challenge. A few weeks later he proposed a new mission for himself; he would go to London with an offer that, if Sir Edward accepted it, would satisfy everyone. Reduced to its essence, the plan was to work out peace terms acceptable to the Allies. These would be presented to the Central Powers as an American offer. If it was accepted in those capitals, peace negotiations would begin; if not, the United States would "probably" enter the war on the side of the Allies.

Grey asked about the "probably" at once, but he also pointed out to House the complexity of Allied relations and war aims. What it came down to, said House in a letter to Wilson dated May 14, 1916, was that the Allies might want to be as dictatorial, if they won, as Germany. "I can foresee trouble with them."[34] Evidence for the Colonel's prediction was not long in coming. On June 23, 1916, Lansing informed the president of a special conference being held in Paris among Allied economic experts. Stimulated by French concern about a postwar *Mitteleuropa* bloc led by Germany, the Allies were considering plans for their own postwar economic alliance. The measures being discussed at Paris, the secretary of state wrote, might have "very far reaching" effects on world commerce. He recommended the formation of a neutral bloc.

Instead, Wilson responded with a series of speeches defining American war aims. And since the United States was not at war, the president could present himself as the disinterested champion of the rights of mankind, as he did on January 22, 1917, in calling for peace without victory. "There must be, not a balance of power, but a community of power; not organized rivalries, but an organized common peace." Wilson's faith in the future did not, however, prevent him from recommending legislation in the present designed to equip American interests with the legal authority to organize for foreign trade, "just as the 'rings' of England and the cartels of Germany are organized."*

* See above, pp. 62–63.

New York American

CHARACTER · QUALITY · ENTERPRISE · ACCURACY

EDITION FOR AN AMERICAN PAPER FOR THE AMERICAN PEOPLE GREATER NEW YORK

No. 12,315. Copyright, 1917, by Star Company. Registered in U. S. Patent Office. FRIDAY, APRIL 6, 1917—18 PAGES PRICE ONE CENT TWO CENTS

WAR WITH GERMANY

BAKER ASKS AN ARMY OF 1,200,000

Offers Bill for Selective Conscription of 500,000 from 19 to 25. Cost Is Set at $2,932,537,933

Many Exemptions, Including Men with Dependents, Provided. Year's Training Before Service

Washington, April 5.—Secretary of War Baker, with the approval of President Wilson, to-day presented to Congress the general staff bill to raise the army to a total of 1,200,000 within a year.

Simultaneously Secretary of the Treasury McAdoo sent to Congress estimates prepared by the War Department and approved by the President and Treasury, which call for an appropriation of $2,932,537,933 to recruit, train and equip this force.

GERMANS TWIST WILSON SPEECH

References to Plotting, Autocracy, Dynastic War and Financing Allies Cut Out by Censor

Copenhagen, April 5.—The German gaskie up to the present has had no opportunity to hear the full story of the reasons leading up to the entry of the United States into war.

Gibbons Prays God May Guide Nation in War

Baltimore, April 5.

"IN the present emergency it behooves every American citizen to do his duty, and to uphold the hands of the President and the Legislative Department in the solemn obligations that confront us," said Cardinal Gibbons to-night.

"The primary duty of a citizen is loyalty to country. This loyalty is manifested more by acts than by words; by solemn service rather than by empty declaration. It is exhibited by an absolute and unreserved obedience to his country's call.

"Will ever Congress may decide should be unequivocally complied with by every patriotic citizen. The members of both Houses of Congress are the instruments of God in guiding us in our civic duties.

"It behooves all of us, therefore, to pray that the Lord of smoke may inspire our military leaders in the present crisis as will redound to the glory of our country, to righteousness of conduct and to the future permanent peace of the nations of the world."

THREE BILLION AND A HALF IN WAR BUDGET

McAdoo Asks Congress for Huge Sum to Carry on War 2 Years. $3,000,000,000 for the Army

Money to Be Raised Principally by Taxation and to Be Immediately Available for Use

BULLETIN.

Washington, April 5.—Secretary of the Treasury McAdoo to-day asked Congress for a war budget of more than three and one-half billion dollars.

The huge sum, the first asked for the nation's war chest, is to be available immediately and is estimated to carry the United States through two years of war. More than three billions are to be expended in the army and in carrying out the plans of the War Department for strengthening the nation's defense.

HOW IT WILL BE SPENT.

The money is to be spent under the direction of the administrative departments of the government, apportioned as follows:

FOUR GERMAN SHIPS TOWED TO CITY PIER

Steamships ,Mala, Clara Mennig and Pretoria and Schooner Indra Moved by Government

Taken from Staten island Anchorages to South Brooklyn—Federal Agents Board Big Liner

BULLETIN.

At 3 o'clock this morning, when the war resolution was passed by the House, Collector of the Port Malone, with a force of customs employes, boarded the steamship Vaterland in Hoboken. It was reported he had orders to seize all the German vessels there immediately.

Three German steamships and a German sailing vessel were boarded yesterday as the Federal authorities and towed from their anchorages off Staten Island to internment docks at the foot of Sixty-ninth street, South Brooklyn. They are the steamships Mala, Clara Mennig and Pretoria and the schooner Indra.

The officers in charge of the seizure would make no statement while they were at work. They declined to say officially, was the first step to the United States is taking over the eighty-one German vessels now in American ports. The greater secrecy veiled the entire operation.

Americans in Belgium May Be Interned

London, April 5.

A DISPATCH from The Hague says:

"A frontier correspondent asserts he understands General Von Bissing, the German Governor General in Belgium, intends to order the internment of all Americans between the ages of seventeen and forty-five living in Belgium.

"The announcement adds that they will be sent to Western Germany, probably to Aix-la-Chapelle."

NAVY TO TOTAL 197,000 MEN

$468,394,551 Appropriation Is Asked—Vast Fleet to Be Built. Militia Call Soon.

Washington, April 5.—The navy will be immediately recruited to 150,000 men, the Marine Corps to 30,000, a vast fleet of auxiliary vessels will be sent to sea, and a general mobilization of the national resources will be pushed. Secretary Daniels announced to-night.

CARRANZA'S TROOPS MASS UPON BORDER

General Northern Movement of De Facto Soldiers Is Reported in Three Adjacent States

General Murguia's Army in Chihuahua on March—Washington Closely Watches Situation

El Paso, April 5—De facto troops in the States of Nuevo Leon, Coahuila and Chihuahua have begun a general movement toward the American border, according to highly reliable information received here to-night.

The movement in these three border States has been officially reported to Washington and is being watched closely.

In Chihuahua a movement is being made in a northwardly direction by General Murguia's troops. The reason given, by Carranza officials is that it is an offensive campaign against Villa.

Austria and Turkey Hope to Stay Neutral

Copenhagen, April 5.

THE expectation that Austria-Hungary and Turkey will remain neutral, for the present at least, in the conflict of Germany with the United States prevails in diplomatic circles here.

From unquestioned sources the information comes that this is the intention and desire of the two Governments, but that if Germany passes upon their fulfilling the full measure of their alliance, they will have to yield and formally declare war.

NO BREAK WITH AUSTRIA NOW

Initiative Is Expected to Come from Dual Monarchy, Washington Says.

Washington, April 5.—The United States will not sever relations or declare war with Austria, Bulgaria or Turkey, so long as those countries do not force such a step.

HOUSE BACKS UP WILSON 373 TO 5

Bitter Debate Marks End of Resolution Declaring War

Vote Taken After More Fifteen Hours of Speech Amendments to the Text

BULLETIN.

Washington, April 5 (Friday).—The war resolution passed House at 3 o'clock this morning. The vote was 373 to 50.

Amendments to the war forces in Europe, Asia or unless directed by Congress, voted down.

President Wilson will sign the resolution as soon as Vice-President Marshall has affixed his signature in the Senate.

La Follette and Stone Hanged in Effigy

Washington, April 5—Senator La Follette, of Wisconsin, opponent of war, was burned in effigy to-night in front of the Peace Monument.

Von Bernstorff New Minister to Sweden

New York—London, April (Friday)—Count Bernstorff, former German Ambassador to the United States, will be made Minister to Sweden, the newspaper says, will be recalled.

Before You Buy Anything

will pay you to consult the advertisements listed below:

	Page
A. Cluett & Co...	9
Bonwit Teller...	5
Gimbel Bros...	7
Macy...	10

The WEATHER

Fair Weather.

Clothing Friday, generally warmer. Saturday fair and not so cold.

Average Temp... 39 44

Continued on Page Two.

Germany's resumption of unrestricted submarine warfare as the only alternative to defeat triggered the final decision for war in the United States. Wilson promised Congress that victory over Germany and the Central Powers was only an interim goal:

> Our object now . . . is to vindicate the principles of peace and justice in the life of the world as against selfish and autocratic power and to set up amongst the really free and self-governed peoples of the world such a concert of purpose and of action as will henceforth insure the observance of those principles.

Who was to determine what peoples were "really free and self-governed" in this world?

Wilson's enthusiasm for a war to make the world safe for democracy, the only war Americans could (or should) fight, had been heightened by a revolution in Russia. The overthrow of Tsar Nicholas II in March 1917 had delighted Americans, especially those who wanted to see the Allies triumph. While England and France fretted about the disposition and capabilities of the provisional

27 Wilson declares war.

28   Nicholas II shovels snow in the park at Tsarskoe Selo, where the imperial family was imprisoned.

government, Wilson was telling Congress, "Here is a fit partner for a League of Honor." No country, not even the kaiser's Germany, had been more autocratic than Russia. Now, apparently, it was already "really free." Actually, Russia always had been "democratic at heart," said Wilson, and now it had shaken off autocracy in the form of a foreign crown "not in fact Russian in origin, character, or purpose."

The Russian Revolution, then, was just like the American Revolution: a rebellion against a foreign tyrant. One could therefore expect that new government to establish itself on similar principles. A few weeks after America entered the war, a frequent correspondent of Wilson's wrote: "We went into war to free Cuba and came out of it with a heavy responsibility in the Philippines. The present war is vastly greater and we may come out of it with vastly greater responsibilities for the future of Russia."[35]

Historians have pondered the influence of the Russian Revolution on Wilson's final decision for war. Perhaps it is best considered in connection with a contemporary event of seemingly far less importance, the "Zimmerman Note," which Berlin dispatched to Mexico City, proposing a German-Mexican alliance against the United States if war should come. It was fantastic that the German Foreign Office should believe that Carranza would consider an idea sure to bring about his destruction. But Wilson took the matter seriously. From an American point of view, the Russian Revolution decreased the power of reactionary imperialism in Europe and the outside world, while the Zimmerman message threatened to expand that power. By going to war, Wilson could insure the success of the "anti-imperial" forces in Europe and gain control of events in both Europe and America. He could make the world safe.

Notes

[1] From a copy in the Papers of Oscar Strauss, Library of Congress, Washington, D.C.

[2] *The Public Papers of Woodrow Wilson*, ed. Ray Stannard Baker and William E. Dodd, 6 vols. (New York: Harper & Bros., 1925–27), 2: 430–51.

[3] *Official Report of the National Foreign Trade Convention, 1914* (New York, 1914), p. 211.

[4] Baker and Dodd, eds., *Public Papers*, 2: 267–79.

[5] *Official Report, 1914*, pp. 161–62.

[6] *Official Report of the National Foreign Trade Convention, 1915* (New York, 1915), pp. 169–70.

[7] George Creel, "The Next Four Years: An Interview with the President," *Everybody's Magazine* 36 (February 1917): 129–39.

[8] Henry White to Knox, October 22, 1910, State Department File Number 710.11/46, National Archives, Washington, D.C.

[9] Memorandum by F. M. Huntington-Wilson, March 18, 1909, State Department File Number 6775/695, National Archives, Washington, D.C.

[10] Drew Linard to Assistant Secretary of State, July 5, 1909, State Department File Number 6369/131, National Archives, Washington, D.C.

[11] Quoted in Walter Scholes and Marie Scholes, *The Foreign Policies of the Taft Administration* (Columbia, Mo.: University of Missouri Press, 1970), pp. 65–66.

[12] U.S., Department of State, Declaration of Policy with Regard to Latin America, March 12, 1913, *Papers Relating to the Foreign Relations of the United States* (Washington, D.C.: Government Printing Office, 1920), p. 7.

[13] Ibid., p. 432.

[14] Ibid., p. 462

[15] U.S., Department of State, *Papers Relating to the Foreign Relations of the United States, 1914*, pp. 241–46.

[16] Bryan to American Legation in Santo Domingo, April 19, 1915, Wilson-Bryan Correspondence, National Archives, Washington, D.C.

[17] U.S., Department of State, *Papers, 1914*, pp. 370–71.

[18] Baker and Dodd, eds., *Public Papers*, 3: 111–12.

[19] Quoted in Peter Calvert, *The Mexican Revolution, 1910–1914: The Diplomacy of Anglo-American Conflict* (Cambridge: Cambridge University Press, 1968), p. 118.

[20] U.S., Department of State, *Papers, 1913*, p. 822.

[21] Quoted in Arthur S. Link, *Wilson: The New Freedom* (Princeton, N.J.: Princeton University Press, 1956), p. 376.

[22] Luis Cabrera to William Phillips, January 27, 1914, The Papers of William Jennings Bryan, Library of Congress, Washington, D.C.

[23] Lansing to Wilson, August 9, 1915, The Papers of Woodrow Wilson, Library of Congress, Washington, D.C.

[24] Economic Liaison Committee, *Petroleum Policy of the United States, 1919*, Frank L. Polk Papers, Yale University Library, New Haven, Conn.

[25] From a speech delivered December 11, 1911, in the Papers of William Howard Taft, Library of Congress, Washington, D.C.

[26] Knox to William Phillips, October 6, 1909, the Papers of Philander C. Knox, Library of Congress, Washington, D.C.

[27] Memorandum by Alvey A. Adee, October 12, 1910, State Department File Number 893.51/150, National Archives, Washington, D.C.

[28] Quoted in Tyler Dennett, *Roosevelt and the Russo-Japanese War* (New York, 1925), pp. 321–23.

[29] Straight to Reinsch, February 25, 1914, The Papers of Paul S. Reinsch, State Historical Society, Madison, Wis.

[30] Reinsch to Wilson, March 5, 1915, The Papers of Woodrow Wilson.

[31] Quoted in Charles E. Neu, *The Troubled Encounter: The United States and Japan* (New York: John Wiley, 1975), p. 93.

[32] Papers of Colonel Edward M. House, Yale University Library, New Haven, Conn.

[33] *New York Times*, August 16, 1914, quoted in Arthur S. Link, *Woodrow Wilson and the Progressive Era* (New York: Harper & Row, 1954), p. 151.

[34] Papers of Colonel House.

[35] Charles R. Crane to Wilson, June 21, 1917, The Papers of Woodrow Wilson.

Bibliography

Beers, Burton F. *Vain Endeavor: Robert Lansing's Attempts to End the American-Japanese Rivalry.* Durham, N.C.: Duke University Press, 1962. Self-explanatory.

Cline, Howard F. *The United States and Mexico.* New York: Atheneum, 1963. The standard survey, still excellent.

Croly, Herbert. *Willard Straight.* New York: Macmillan, 1924. Self-explanatory.

Kaufman, Burton I. *Efficiency and Expansion.* Westport, Conn.: Greenwood Press, 1974. A new pioneering book on government–business relations in the Wilson Administration, with emphasis on foreign-trade problems.

Lansing, Robert. *War Memoirs.* Indianapolis, Ind.: Bobbs-Merrill, 1935. The secretary answers his critics and tells a great deal about diplomacy during the First World War.

Levin, N. Gordon. *Woodrow Wilson and World Politics.* New York: Oxford University Press, 1968. The first attempt to combine revisionism and consensus interpretations of Wilson's foreign policy.

May, Ernest R. *The World War and American Isolation, 1914–1917.* Cambridge, Mass.: Harvard University Press, 1959. The standard account of our day.

Notter, Harley. *The Origins of the Foreign Policy of Woodrow Wilson.* Baltimore: Johns Hopkins Press, 1937. A thorough-going account of the president's beliefs and assumptions.

Schmidt, Hans. *The United States Occupation of Haiti: 1915–1934.* New Brunswick, N.J.: Rutgers University Press, 1971. A case study with broad implications.

Smith, Daniel. *The Great Departure: The United States and World War I, 1914–1920.* New York: John Wiley, 1965. A good, brief summary.

Splendid Isolation 4
American Style:
1919–1931

We are indeed at that changing point in our national economics that the British Empire faced in 1860, when no longer could Britain take full value in commodities for the commodities which she exported, and that if she would continue to expand, continue to progress, she had to invest the realization of these commodities abroad, and by doing so they not only extended the capacity and the absorption of British goods, but they lifted the standard of living of the entire world.

Herbert Hoover
December 10, 1920

Disillusioned by Allied bickering over colonies and mandates and by their inability to persuade England and France to grant Germany a reasonable peace, the American delegates returned from Versailles hardly anxious to face a hostile Congress. Several delegation members who had crossed the Atlantic with Wilson in full confidence that he would prevail over the "old men" of Europe came back determined to oppose the treaty and future involvement in another war on that troubled continent. Only Wilson persisted in defending the Treaty of Versailles; and, in private, he was willing to

29 Opposition to the League covenant united political opponents who had nothing else in common.

admit its one redeeming feature was the League of Nations. But many of his opponents felt the worst feature of the treaty was the League. Internationalists by any other definition, men like Elihu Root and William Howard Taft could not find common ground with the president on this issue.

A reexamination of the diplomacy of the 1920s suggests that many of Wilson's opponents on the League issue shared his belief in a community of interests among nations, especially among the industrial powers. They came to believe that adherence to the covenant would actually hamper efforts to realize this community. Obviously, the fact that the League had become a political issue in the United States was reason enough for abandoning that lost crusade and seeking another solution. But most remained convinced that the world needed both dollars and American direction to recover. His opponents were convinced that Wilson's mistake was to get himself politically entangled in a series of lesser issues. America had great assets to use to command attention to its demands. Why shackle itself to the League?

There was, then, an intimate and logical connection between American decisions to lend Germany funds to pay reparations obligations, to remove marines from the Caribbean, and to seek a Far Eastern understanding. Splendid isolation was in fact a reassertion of American liberalism as against the one-dimensionalism of Wilson's last years in office.

A DIFFICULT DECISION

Elihu Root confessed that he was perplexed about how to cast his vote on the Versailles Treaty. The former secretary of state, now a New York senator, opposed article 10 of the League covenant because, like many of his colleagues and close friends, he feared it could be twisted to mean the United States would have to support collective action to defend Japan's "right" to the Shantung peninsula. The treaty also seemed to confirm in perpetuity British and French claims to former territories of the Ottoman Empire and of Germany's African colonies and to fasten an unworkable status quo onto Europe for the foreseeable future. The only way to change things would be revolution or war.

Yet Root urged on one of the "irreconcilables," Senator Henry Cabot Lodge, the importance of American participation in a modified covenant. "The condition of Europe requires prompt action. Industry has not revived there. Its revival requires raw materials. To obtain these credit is necessary, and for this there must be peace. Satan is finding evil work for idle hands to do in Europe—evil work that affects the whole world, including the United States."[1]

Root's dilemma was to find a way between two perils: nonratification would hold up recovery and pose the danger of revolution now; ratification might mean war and revolution later. Secretary of State Lansing saw a third problem. No great defender of the treaty or the League, he was worried that a protracted debate would put the United States at an economic disadvantage: "Our economic interests do not wish to see the treaty come into force with Great Britain, France and Italy before it does with this country because their commercial agents would get a decided advantage in the matter of trade with Germany."[2] American economic interests demanded speedy ratification of some peace treaty, but personal animosity against Wilson had distracted usually intelligent men and produced this seeming impasse. "There is no getting away from the fact," Lansing noted in his diary, "that they [treaty opponents] are simply saturated with hatred of the man rather than the treaty. It is something like the feeling against Andrew Jackson."[3]

Wilson had served notice on the Senate that it would find the treaty and the League covenant so entwined as to be inseparable—there would be no peace without the League. In fact, however, he had made a bad error (not the first since the armistice): he had not made peace and the League inseparable, only himself and the League. Wilson had believed that, sooner or later, the American people would force the Senate to act favorably on the treaty. And he felt there could be no middle way, as some apparently hoped. "We ought either to go in or to stay out," Wilson explained to his private secretary. "To stay out would be fatal to the influence and

30   Wilson almost died trying to save the League, but his successors found other ways to create a community of interests among industrial nations.

even to the commercial prospects of the United States. . . . To go in would give her the leadership of the world."[4]

The president undertook a cross-country tour in the summer of 1919 to rally supporters of the League, but it ended disastrously with his breakdown and long illness. He continued to fight from his bedroom in the White House, but increasingly the work of reconstruction fell to others. The final congressional rejection of the League of Nations did set certain limitations on what policy-makers could do, but it also freed their hands in some situations. It was much easier, for example, for the United States to shape both its political and economic policies toward Germany without having to worry about League objections.

Actually, the process of freeing American policy from Allied "domination" had begun just after the armistice. Two days after the armistice was signed on November 11, 1918, the American Treasury representative in Europe recommended to his superiors that "a continuation of liberal loans from the United States Treasury . . . would strengthen the hands of those who stand for the policies of centralization . . . and would in fact constitute a large force in shaping both the domestic and international policies of European countries."[5] Government-to-government loans thus came to an abrupt halt.

The next step, which was taken in the Harding administration, was to design a tariff policy that would protect the United States against foreign dumping yet encourage the reconstruction of the world economy along liberal lines. Working behind the scenes, State and Commerce Department experts shaped the 1922 Fordney-McCumber Tariff to this purpose. They did not attempt to confront the high-tariff bloc in Congress head-on; had they done so, they would have lost. Congress had passed the Emergency Tariff of 1921 over Wilson's veto, and any effort to force the legislators back into a low-tariff frame of mind would have failed, thereby jeopardizing progress in other directions. It was hoped that flexible clauses could be written into the Fordney-McCumber bill that would improve American access to overseas markets and would aid in reintegrating the world economy.

97

31 American loans aided European recovery, but they were not always well regarded in the Continental press.

The major victory for business internationalists and their allies in government was Section 317, the so-called Open Door proviso, which gave the executive branch authority to negotiate commercial treaties based on the unconditional-most-favored-nation principle. Under that principle, any concession granted to a third power must automatically be given to the treaty signatory as well. The idea was to prevent bilateralism and special arrangements from clogging international trade routes. Nations that refused to negotiate with the United States on such a basis became subject to special tariff penalties.

Yet the Fordney-McCumber Tariff, even with Section 317, made access to the American marketplace more difficult than it had been during the Wilson years. Policymakers in the 1920s believed that the United States could not absorb the tremendous volume of exports Europe needed to balance war debts and to pay for all the goods Europeans would need for recovery. Any attempt to do so would disrupt the American economy and lead to even more nationalistic tariff laws. By undertaking the negotiation of unconditional-most-favored-nation treaties, the United States would enlarge the world marketplace for all nations and relieve pressure on its own economy.

More than most others, however, it was Herbert Hoover who had worked out the logic of America's new position; and it was Hoover who would have the greatest opportunity to put his theories into practice. Hoover joined the Harding cabinet as Secretary of Commerce after having been assured that he would have a "voice on all important economic policies of the administration." The nation's surplus capital, he told his colleagues, must be managed carefully. Foreign loans should perform the same function for twentieth-century America that they had for nineteenth-century Britain.

Disagreement arose in the administration over the degree of control the government should exercise. It would hardly do, especially for Republicans, to demand absolute authority over foreign lending: that would amount to state capitalism, the very policy the Wilson administration had so vigorously opposed at the end of the war. Whatever policy was adopted, therefore, would have to depend on voluntarism. The Commerce Department set guidelines—and hoped for the best. Successful loans, said Hoover, were always "re-productive." Loans made to purchase arms or build munitions factories, to balance budgets, or to undertake doubtful public works did not meet this standard. Borrowers also had to qualify politically: no loans should be made to governments not recognized by the United States or to those that had failed to meet their obligations. Mexico and Bolshevik Russia certainly did not qualify, but neither did any country that had not funded its war debt to the United States.

If applied rigorously, these standards might have lessened the dangers of default, but Hoover's ambition to re-create the largely automatic world of nineteenth-century capitalism by adjusting a screw here and a screw there was doomed to failure. Between 1922 and 1929 the United States exported capital at an average rate of $733 million, with the maximum, $1 billion, going out that last year. Once the upward spiral began, government officials all but abandoned attempts at control for fear of triggering a psychological crisis that might topple the whole structure, sending the American economy crashing downward into the chasms of depression. Hoover did make some belated gestures aimed at strengthening the weak foundations provided by the original guidelines. But he, too, became afraid of revealing the true state of affairs and thereby destroying investor confidence in the miraculous tower the bankers had built on the edge of a precipice.

In retrospect, Hoover still found little to fault in the theory. Even if one wrote off as much as $1 billion for bad debts, Hoover insisted in his *Memoirs,* "it certainly was a cheap method of unemployment and agricultural relief." The dollars had provided an important stimulus to recovery and growth, just as British sterling had done after the Napoleonic Wars. Political memoirs are seldom written in a spirit of repentance, but one is put off by Hoover's persistent argument that the world depression was caused by unsound internal policies in the European countries. More understandable was his belief that the loan policy he had formulated would help to reverse the trend toward "statism" in the United States and would deny funds to the worst example of that mistaken ideology: Soviet Russia.

THE BOLSHEVIK THREAT TO LIBERAL DEMOCRACY

Wilson had anticipated that Russia—freed from the tyranny of the tsars and from dependence on England and France—would stand shoulder to shoulder with him against the reactionary old men of Europe. But the Provisional Government lasted only seven months. The war had shattered the tsarist autocracy, and while the leaders of the Provisional Government were hunting for some usable remnants, Lenin seized power. The Bolshevik program was simple: Bread, Peace, Land.

No Russian government could have remained in the war and still survived. By denouncing all the belligerents in the same breath, Lenin simply made it easier to sue for peace. They were all equally guilty for the war; they were all enemies of the new Russia. The

Bolshevik leader's Marxist critique of war and capitalist society was a direct challenge to Wilsonian liberalism. If the president expected to give a lead to the Allies at the peace table, he could not fall behind now in dealing with Russia.

Wilson had welcomed the tsar's overthrow, calling revolutionary Russia "a fit partner for a League of Honor." The United States had been the first to recognize the new government; it bore some moral as well as material responsibility for its success. Now the question arose: What will Wilson do about Lenin? The Allies knew, or thought they knew, what should be done, but without Washington's concurrence, any intervention plan they might devise was unlikely to succeed. They proceeded with limited actions, helping anti-Bolshevik forces where and when possible, and grew impatient with Wilson's temporizing. There were genuine fears that without Russia a stalemate might result on the battlefield. American forces had not yet landed in France when Lenin agreed to the Treaty of Brest-Litovsk. Nevertheless, when they were candid about it, Allied leaders admitted their fear of a communist government in one of Europe's great states and their knowledge that the only way they could lead Russia back into the war would be to overthrow the Bolsheviks. Who might replace them was another problem.

When it became clear that Wilson was at least amenable to providing financial support to anti-Bolshevik armies in southern Russia, the Allies felt encouraged to approach him with a proposal for Japanese intervention, as trustee for all their interests, in Siberia. The proposal immediately put Wilson on his guard. He suspected that the Allies wished to draw him into a scheme for satisfying Japan's expansionist ambitions at Russia's expense. As he saw it, a Japanese "invasion" of Siberia would be fatal to the anti-Bolshevik cause; it would only prove Lenin right in saying that the Allies were hypocrites and enemies.

The harder the Allies pushed for the Japanese intervention, the more Wilson resisted. He pointed out that none of his military experts believed that an eastern front against Germany could be reestablished through Siberia. Moreover, American officials perceived in the Japanese ploy an even more sinister design to divide Russia into spheres of influence. If England and France could get approval for this Siberian adventure, how could Wilson deny them the right to do what they pleased elsewhere?

These suspicions only made the president more anti-Bolshevik, however, for had it not been Lenin who started all this trouble by signing a separate peace with Germany? And were not the Bolsheviks responsible for turning over 1 million square miles of old Russia to the most reactionary force in Europe? Such thoughts led Wilson to the conclusion that Lenin and his government were conscious or unconscious agents of Imperial Germany and that he must use the Siberian situation to create an area free of Bolshevism and German influence. To do less would be to fail the acid test he had set for the Allies and America in his "Fourteen Points" speech of January 8, 1918.

On that occasion the president had declared that the treatment accorded Russia by her sister nations "will be the acid test of their good will, of their comprehension of her needs as distinguished from their own interests, and of their intelligent and unselfish sympathy." All Wilson needed was the proper vehicle for converting an expedition based on Allied selfishness into a nobler undertaking. The occasion arose in the plight of two divisions of Czechoslovak troops entrained eastward along the Trans-Siberian Railway to Vladivostok. Reports that they were being attacked by former German and Austrian prisoners of war, incited by the perfidious Bolsheviks, who were determined to prevent the Czechs from joining the Allies on the Western front, provided the stimulus.

At last Wilson was ready to act. On July 18, 1918, the State Department released a statement explaining the decision to send American troops into Siberia alongside those of the other Allies. It concluded with the statement that their mission would be "to help the Czecho-Slovaks consolidate their forces and get into successful cooperation with their slavic kinsmen and to steady any efforts at self-government in which the Russians themselves may be willing to accept assistance. . . ." Nothing was said about getting the Czechs out or about which Russians were to be steadied.

32 Japanese troops in Vladivostok: Wilson's advance agents of a new order or a return to prewar imperialism?

"In short," observed the dean of American diplomatic historians, Samuel Flagg Bemis, "Woodrow Wilson, saying he would ne'er consent, consented to intervention."[6] By the end of 1918, seven thousand American troops (all of them anxious to come home) were in Siberia, but ten times that many Japanese soldiers were also there. Their mission was less complicated: "to bolster a pro-Japanese government in the Russian territories, gain control of the Chinese Eastern Railway and the Siberian railways east of Irkutsk, and harness the region to the Japanese economy."[7]

Congressional criticism of the continuing presence of American troops in Siberia after the armistice caused Wilson to formulate an additional explanation based on the Open Door policy:

> It is felt that this matter can be treated entirely apart from the general Russian problem, as, irrespective of what our policy may be toward Russia, and irrespective of [future] Russian developments, it is essential that we maintain the policy of the open door with reference to the Siberian and particularly the Chinese Eastern Railway.[8]

103

By incorporating his Russian policy into the framework of John Hay's China policy, the president hoped to blunt this criticism and reaffirm his determination to secure fair treatment for Russia. One could also see between the lines traces of the Manchurian railroad "neutralization" plan. At the peace conference, however, attention was focused on European Russia and the Bolshevik threat to Germany. The French, who had lost the most when Lenin's government repudiated Russian debts and who stood to lose even more if Germany welcomed the apostles of Marxism in the moment of defeat, proposed an all-out military attack on Petrograd to rid the world of this Red menace.

British Prime Minister David Lloyd George drew back from the French proposal. It would not succeed, he said, and if attempted "would make England Bolshevist, and there would be a Soviet in London." Wilson agreed; according to the minutes of the conference:

> He would not be surprised to find that the reason why British and United States troops would not be ready to enter Russia to fight the Bolsheviki was explained by the fact that the troops were not at all sure that if they put down Bolshevism they would not bring about a re-establishment of the ancient order.[9]

Lloyd George's counterproposal appealed to Wilson. He liked the prime minister's idea of summoning representatives of all "the different governments now at war within what used to be the Russian Empire, to a truce of God, . . . to give, so to speak, an account of themselves." It reminded Lloyd George of "the way that the Roman Empire summoned chiefs of outlying tributary states to render an account of their actions." The "coalition" approach to revolutionary crises had been tried before, in Mexico and the Caribbean, and would become a favorite, if usually unsuccessful, remedy.

It was decided at Paris to hold this "truce of God" on Prinkipo Island in the Black Sea, a remote spot selected so that Bolshevik propagandists would not have to cross any national boundary en route to the conference. But the victors worried for naught. When only Lenin responded to the invitation, the conference was canceled. Wilson had hoped that the hard knot of bolshevism might somehow be loosened at Prinkipo. At least the Allied proposal, even if the conference itself failed, would reduce the unnatural appeal bolshevism seemed to have for some nationalists who saw it as the only alternative to foreign domination.

The collapse of the conference proposal left Wilson without a Russian policy at just the worst moment. "From the look of things the crisis will soon be here," Colonel House wrote in his diary. "Rumblings of discontent every day. The people want peace. Bolshevism is gaining ground everywhere. Hungary has just succumbed. We are sitting upon an open powder magazine and some day a spark may ignite it."[10]

The diplomats had no answers left, but Wilson found what might prove to be a means of containing communism in suggestions Herbert Hoover offered for using food relief as a weapon against bolshevism. If the United States pursued a military policy in Hungary, argued the wartime Food Administrator, it would mean that we would "become a junior in this partnership of

33 Herbert Hoover emerged at the Paris Peace Conference as the leading exponent of the view that Bolshevism could be overcome by production, not military force.

four . . . and even committed to policies against our convictions."[11] Food relief in exchange for assurances that the Bolsheviks would cease "their subsidizing of disturbances abroad" offered a hope of stabilization and "a period of rest along the frontiers of Europe."

Under Hoover's instructions messages were sent to Hungary informing the Bolshevik leaders that neither food nor peace could be offered their country until a government "in which all parties are represented should be elected by the Hungarian people." Whether this was the deciding factor in the overthrow of Béla Kun a few days later, or whether his demise was already in the cards, the Hoover policy demonstrated that results against bolshevism could be obtained by other means than military invasion.

But other means did not work in Russia itself, at least not immediately. Many years later Hoover admitted that the food-relief program he started in midsummer 1921 in response to an appeal from Russian novelist Maxim Gorky probably enabled the Bolsheviks to weather the severe strain of civil war. He, like Wilson, still insisted that in the end the communist system must fail. In the meantime, Hoover once explained to Secretary of State Charles Evans Hughes, his colleague in the Harding Administration, "Americans are infinitely more popular in Russia and our government more deeply respected by even the Bolsheviks than any other," and "the relief measures will build a situation which, combined with the other factors, will enable the Americans to undertake the leadership in the reconstruction of Russia when the proper moment comes."[12]

Just before they left Versailles, the Big Four decided to support Admiral Aleksandr Kolchak, who, for a brief time, seemed close to victory in the Russian civil war. What might have happened had he succeeded in rallying the White forces is an intriguing question, but the admiral was caught and executed early in 1920. With his removal, no one was left to serve as a focus for Allied policy.

During the next few years the European powers came, each in its own way, to an "understanding" with the Soviet regime. Only the United States refused diplomatic recognition. Throughout the 1920s American policymakers continued to regard themselves as both ideological and political trustees for a future Russia. For three years after Versailles, the State Department funded the embassy of the defunct Provisional Government in Washington, keeping alive the notion that somewhere there existed the "real" Russian government.

Hoover's economic policy toward Soviet Russia was complicated and contradictory. At first he attempted to limit trade with the Russians as much as possible. Yet following the rationale of the relief program, he modified this stance in two ways: first, he felt the Russians must be made aware of American technical and commercial prowess if they were to call on the United States for a post-Bolshevik reconstruction program; second, the United States government had no right to deprive American business of an opportunity to compete in any market as long as diplomatic recognition was not involved.

Wilson's Russian policy had required the United States actually to withold relief supplies on occasion when humanitarian concerns clashed with his determination to preserve the territorial integrity of old Russia against the supposed designs of England, France, and, after the war, Germany. To a proposal that the United States extend credit to the Ukrainian Republic for the purchase of surplus stocks, Lansing replied that the "Ukrainian separatist movement . . . [was] largely the result of Austrian and German propaganda." Pending the establishment of a "modern democratic government" in Russia, United States policy should tend "rather to sustain the principle of essential Russian unity than to encourage separatism."[13]

Ideological consistency on this and other Russian questions demonstrated that while Wilson's League had been rejected, his views still governed many of his successors' actions. Moreover, most business leaders in the first half of the decade were still frightened by the Bolshevik threat, which, in the minds of some, extended to all labor organizations, even the staid American Federation of Labor. Nevertheless, for the few who were willing to risk the displeasure of their fellow "club members" in the NAM or the Chamber of Commerce, Russian business was good, that is, profitable. By the end of fiscal year 1924/25, Americans were exporting over $68 million to Russia—more than their rivals in any other nation.

Government remained ambivalent, not unlike the preacher who, while recognizing that procreation is a necessary function if his flock is to survive, wants everyone to know he disapproves of the sex act itself. These tensions were increased substantially when European countries began extending long-term credit to the Soviet Union in an effort to get a greater share for themselves. Washington drew the line there; it would not compete in such unseemly fashion for the favors of the Bolsheviki.

DEUTSCHLAND ÜBER ALLES

Sympathy for Germany as the victim of Versailles came naturally for Americans who were disillusioned by the outcome of the Great Crusade. Even Wilson felt that way at times. But sympathy supplemented other attitudes about the postwar world. The American view of war debts and reparations was difficult for policymakers to explain, even to themselves. In announcing the first wartime loan to the Allies by the United States government in 1917, a Treasury bulletin explained that the $3 billion was being made available to the Allies to enable them to do "the fighting which otherwise the American army would have to do at much expense, not only of men, but of money—money which would never be returned to America, and lives that never could be restored."

On the way to the peace conference, however, President Wilson assured the members of the American delegation that the United States would have its way in the writing of the peace treaty because the Allies were now in his hands economically. That proved not to be the case at Versailles, but over the longer run, Wilson was right. At war's end, European countries owed the United States more than $12 billion, but that was only one measure of America's economic supremacy. British and French foreign investments and foreign trade outlets, which had been sacrificed to defeat the Central Powers, wound up in American hands. And so on.

Both Democrats and Republicans believed that Germany was the

34 Eddie Rickenbacker, the premier flier, advocated restoring Germany to prominence.

key to restoring European productivity, but the reparations clauses had virtually stripped the country of liquid assets and demoralized its people. At the peace conference the American delegation had refused to recognize any connection between war debts owed the United States and reparations, although there were hints that if the Allies would reduce Germany's obligations, war debts might be scaled down.

Nothing came of this attempt to wield America's new economic leverage directly. Meanwhile, America's premier flying ace, Captain Eddie Rickenbacker, now an equally successful businessman, went on a special barnstorming tour to inform private groups about what America must do: "Germany is a tramp—out of a job, hungry, poorly clothed and desperate. It is for us to decide whether he will become a citizen or an I.W.W."[14] A large loan—"administered by the best brains we have"—was the only way to save Germany. If Germany did not become an ideological, political, and economic bulwark to Russia, it would surely become the second great power to succumb to communism. After that, all Europe would be in jeopardy.

Once British efforts to take the lead in the reconstruction of Russia had failed and after the French had moved into the Saar to take in kind what they could not collect in cash from the Germans and found themselves in a ridiculous (and potentially disastrous) situation, the Allies were ready to listen to almost any proposal from Washington. War debts were scaled down, but not forgiven, while agreement was reached that Germany should receive a large loan from British and American Bankers. Repayment of this so-called Dawes loan was to take precedence over reparations, but at least there was the chance that some reparations would in fact be paid. How much would be determined by an American reparations overseer who would, in effect, act as trustee for the German economy. In the seven years after the inauguration of the Dawes program, American private investors lent $1.2 billion to German municipalities and industries.

By this time the United States had lost interest in actually collecting the war debts. They were more useful where they were—hanging over the heads of Europeans. Not only did Washington force compliance with its German policy this way, it also secured a reversion to the gold standard. Economic policymakers were now juggling three things: war debts, reparations, and the Dawes loans. In 1929 a fourth was added: the Young Plan, which further scaled down reparations.

Considerable bitterness arose out of these arrangements, but the whole plan collapsed anyway with the onset of the Great Depression. On June 5, 1931, Germany appealed for a reparations moratorium, which Hoover converted into a general moratorium on all intergovernment debts. Within a few weeks, nevertheless, a run began on sterling that signaled the dawn of the long-feared day of reckoning. Hoover blamed European profligacy for the depression; European leaders, American mismanagement of the world economy.

MEXICO AND SOUTH

Hints of the impending economic disaster had come first from Latin America when falling prices for raw materials plunged those economies into crisis. During the 1920s the United States replaced Europe as the leading investor not only in the Caribbean, where American interests already predominated, but throughout South America as well. These investments were in all sorts of enterprises, including manufacturing, but the magnets that most attracted Americans were in agriculture, oil exploration, and mining—enterprises most subject to the rising tide of antiforeign nationalism.

Succeeding Republican administrations in the 1920s made a serious effort to reduce overt symbols of American domination in the Caribbean area, beginning with the removal of a marine garrison from Cuba in 1922 and culminating in the decision to withdraw from Nicaragua and Haiti. Congress, meanwhile, passed legislation permitting United States officers to serve in South American

35 The influx of American capital reached new heights in Latin America in the 1920s.

armies and navies, thereby initiating a kind of military-assistance program. In 1930 the State Department released the J. Reuben Clark memorandum, which downgraded the Roosevelt Corollary to the Monroe Doctrine. And Secretary of State Henry L. Stimson announced that the United States would no longer pass judgment on Latin American governments before extending diplomatic recognition.

When Nicaragua proved unable to hack it alone in 1926, the marines were sent in one more time. Explaining why this action had become necessary, Secretary of State Frank Kellogg pointed a finger at Mexico, the supposed source of Bolshevik influence in the Western Hemisphere.

Kellogg's "red scare" argument provoked a satirical response from liberal Senator George Norris of Nebraska:

> Once't there was a Bolshevik who wouldn't say his prayers,
> So Kellogg sent him off to bed, away upstairs;
> An' Kellogg heered him holler, and Coolidge heerd him bawl,
> But when they turn't the kivers down he wasn't there at all.
> They seeked him down in Mexico, they cussed him in the press,
> They seeked him round the Capitol, an' ever'where I guess.
> But all they ever found of him was whiskers, hair and clout;
> An' the Bolsheviks 'ill get you ef you don't watch out.[15]

As far as the United States was concerned in regard to Mexico, a Bolshevik was defined as anyone who wanted to challenge foreign ownership of the Mexican oil fields. By the mid-1920s, United States companies owned more than 50 percent of the producing wells. And Mexico remained the third largest oil producer in the Western Hemisphere. When Kellogg declared that Mexico was "now on trial before the world," he was talking about the difficulty in reaching a permanent settlement with Carranza's successors. Mexican leaders were anxious not to alienate the United States, but it was just not possible for them to repudiate the Constitution of 1917. Finally, in 1928, Ambassador Dwight R. Morrow reached an agreement with President Plutarco Calles stipulating that oil concessions that antedated the constitution would be guaranteed in perpetuity.

112

New trouble was brewing farther to the south. Eight of the ten republics of South America suffered revolutionary upheavals at the end of the decade. Reports from Chile contained warnings that the government intended to seize American property to satisfy the angry demands of insurgents. Another symptom of the Great Depression in Latin America was the outbreak of war between Peru and Colombia. Asked if he would land forces to protect American interests in Chile and Colombia, Stimson answered,

> not on your life. . . . If we landed a single soldier among those South Americans now, it would undo all the labor of three years, and it would put me absolutely wrong in China, where Japan has done all of this monstrous work under the guise of protecting her nationals with a landing force.[16]

CHINA IN PERIL

After several difficult bargaining sessions, American bankers had persuaded their Japanese counterparts in 1920 to enter the second China Consortium without placing major restrictions on its operations in Manchuria and Mongolia. A key victory for the Open Door policy had apparently been won by the bankers operating as agents for the State Department, but an equally difficult battle for political and military stability in the Far East had to be waged by Secretary of State Charles Evans Hughes.

The opening scene was the Washington Naval Conference of 1921/22; action began when Hughes strode to the podium to declare that the United States was ready to scrap a number of battleships and other ships then under construction if the other powers would agree to a ten-year holiday. The secretary of state's boldness took the delegates by surprise, making his other tasks easier.

For a long time American diplomats had sought, unsuccessfully, to get around, cut through, or otherwise overcome the Anglo-Japanese alliance. Hughes intended to accomplish that end, as well as naval disarmament, by substituting a number of multilateral treaties for the old imperial arrangements. China's role in this new order was uncertain. Still wracked by revolutionary disorders, China had not been able to secure a Japanese promise to return

36 A favorable comment on Charles Evans Hughes's diplomacy.

HARDING, *BROOKLYN EAGLE*

Shantung or to evacuate its troops from areas in Siberia near Manchuria. Sun Yat-sen, speaking on behalf of a revolutionary nationalist regime at Canton, refused Hughes's invitation to send representatives to participate in a unified delegation at the Washington conference. He further declared that his Kuomintang party would not recognize any of the results.

This response no doubt reinforced the secretary's determination to work with the other powers instead of seeking a direct accommodation with the nationalists or, at the least, retaining a free hand. Hughes's admirers pointed out that the secretary accomplished several things no other American diplomat had been able to do: he had brought a halt to the costly naval race just in time with a treaty that gave the United States and Great Britain a superior 5:5:3 ratio to Japan in large battleships; he managed to replace the Anglo-Japanese Treaty with a four-power security pact; and, something that had eluded secretaries of state since John Hay, he secured formal international status for the Open Door policy in the

37 Hughes sought to end the impasse with Japan.

Nine-Power Treaty. It was not quite international law yet, but it was close enough. For the present, American planners thought it essential that the industrial powers work in harmony lest, by their disagreement, the extreme nationalists and communists in China defeat them singly. It did not matter to Washington, for example, that no government in China could yet accept the consortium's terms or even that the consortium refused to offer China a loan on any terms. As long as the powers accepted these self-imposed restraints, China would not be able to play one off against the other.

The strain of waiting for China to work out its internal difficulties weighed heavily on American secretaries of state, but it was almost unendurable for Japan and Great Britain. Moreover, while speculative loans to Germany and central Europe were approved almost without question by the United States government, each loan to Japan was scrutinized to see that it did not conflict with the Open Door policy. In short, to Tokyo it appeared that the United 115

38 Frank Kellogg departed from Hughes's China policy, but Chinese nationalism required more than a tip of the hat.

States was simply biding its time while the other powers suffered.

Growing antiforeign violence in China in the mid-1920s further eroded the bonds of the Washington treaties. Despite their mutual pledges, the industrial powers began bidding for China's favor. In 1926 Secretary of State Frank Kellogg tried to bargain American support for tariff autonomy in exchange for a treaty guaranteeing favorable treatment for American trade. Japan was more alarmed, however, when Sun Yat-sen's successor, Chiang Kai-shek, began a drive to consolidate Kuomintang authority over the rich northeastern provinces.

Tokyo had supported Chiang at first, believing him to be a good alternative to communism and Russian influence in China proper. But it also backed one of his enemies, the warlord Chang Tso-lin, who controlled Manchuria. What took place when Chiang seized the Chinese Eastern Railway in midsummer 1929 left even experienced Asia experts blinking and stammering. Russia sent troops to retake the railroad, touching off a Sino-Russian "mini-war." Then Secretary of State Stimson invoked the recently signed Kellogg-Briand Peace Pact, although Soviet Russia was not a signatory and, as far as Washington was concerned, not even a legitimate government.

Japan, more afraid of Chinese communism than any of the powers, supported Russia in an effort to protect Chang Tso-lin. Tokyo also thought it might be worthwhile to approach the United States and Great Britain about the possibility of a united front against the excesses of Chinese nationalism. As part of that effort, the Japanese delegation to the 1930 London Naval Conference agreed to a continuation of the naval ratios established at Washington. But there was no response to its overtures for a tripartite understanding. The Sino-Russian conflict came to an end, but the Japanese railway guard in southern Manchuria, which was in fact (as everyone would soon know) an army, took note of Chiang's determination and the seemingly ridiculous posture of their own civilian leaders.

Throughout the 1920s, Japan had continued to be America's best Asian customer. For their part, the Japanese seemed to be committed to "liberalism." The last occupation forces Tokyo had sent to Siberia had been withdrawn; an understanding had been reached with China for the return of the Shantung peninsula; and, when Washington asked for it, Tokyo agreed to the cancellation of the Lansing-Ishii arrangement, which had become something of an embarrassment.

Serious damage had been done by the 1924 Immigration Act, which effectively excluded the Japanese, but overall relations were good between the two countries. Then came the depression. Faced with a 50 percent price decline in the American market for silk (and the apparent danger of a permanent loss of that outlet to cotton and synthetics), the threat of Chinese nationalism in Manchuria, and a growing communist movement at home, Japanese civilian leaders had little inclination or ability to resist the military.

On September 18, 1931, officers of the Kwantung army, which protected the South Manchurian Railway, and the more than 200,000 resident Japanese put into operation a secret plan for military conquest and conversion of Manchuria, which they renamed Manchukuo, into a protectorate. The Japanese even chose a new ruler, a young descendant of the Manchu emperors, Henry Pu-yi, who ultimately was given more useful employment in the Peoples' Republic of China as a flower-gardener.

Washington's initial reaction to news of the Mukden "incident" was annoyance. Preoccupied with domestic problems, Hoover was in no position, as he told his advisers, to go around "sticking pins in tigers." China's appeal to the League of Nations may have stiffened some backs in both Geneva and Washington, but the president remained fundamentally opposed to using sanctions to force the Japanese to back down. Secretary Stimson took a somewhat different view, especially as the Japanese forward movement continued into the late fall and winter of 1931. Then came the bombing and occupation of Shanghai.

Hoover did not want to get involved in anything like an anti-Japanese front, especially one that would only irritate both China and Japan. Stimson and several State Department aides felt the United States could not simply ignore the situation. The League's Lytton Commission made its report, a well-balanced document that recognized the legitimacy of Japanese complaints about conditions in Manchuria, but that urged a settlement on the basis of the status quo ante—as modified by a Sino-Japanese understanding.

In the meantime, however, Stimson had secured permission from Hoover to send a public note to both China and Japan reaffirming Wilson's stance at the time of the Twenty-One Demands in 1915. The "Stimson Doctrine" stated that the United States would not recognize any treaty that might impair "the treaty rights of the United States or its citizens in China, including those which relate to the sovereignty, the independence, or the territorial and administrative integrity of the Republic of China, nor to the international policy relative to China commonly known as the open door policy. . . ." And a few weeks later the secretary sent an

39 Japan defies the League in China.

open letter to Senator William Borah that added the warning that should the other signatory states ignore the Nine-Power Treaty, the United States would have to reconsider the military agreements signed at Washington.

Stimson's great interest in the Manchurian crisis was in reasserting the rule of law among nations, although behind this legalistic posture there still burned a faith in America's Asian destiny. In another sense, he was reaffirming the whole history of American foreign policy from the "freeing" of Cuba to the promulgation of the League of Nations. Stimson's handwritten note on his copy of the Lytton Commission report states it well: "Japan's ambitions in . . . China could not be said to be limited to settlement [of the] clash of interest in Manchuria—She (or a section of her bankers) has already put out definite claims for general exclusive hegemony [over] China's modernization."[17]

Hoover did not doubt that America's future would have to include China, but he believed that Japan must fail, and that to do anything to make the situation worse, by sanctions or, heaven forbid, military action, would only strengthen the forces of disorder throughout the world. Former Secretary of State Elihu Root had some words of caution, too, warning Stimson not to go too far against Japan and to remember that the American intervention in Cuba (and, he might have added, the exclusive rights enjoyed under the Platt Amendment and the Trade Treaty) could be read very differently in other capitals of the world. To such arguments, Stimson had a ready answer: one had to remember the American "foothold in the minds of the Chinese people which is pregnant with possibilities for good, provided we do not forfeit it."[18]

Beginning with Manchuria, the priorities in American foreign policy underwent a significant change. The threat in Asia was read as Japanese expansionism, not Chinese nationalism. In Europe Nazi Germany was to replace Soviet Russia as the greater danger to world order. The debate in the next decade centered on the problem of finding a way to contain the one, without, as Hoover feared, setting loose the other.

Notes

[1] Root to Lodge, June 19, 1919, The Papers of Elihu Root, Library of Congress, Washington, D.C.

[2] Lansing to Gary Jones, August 4, 1919, The Papers of Robert Lansing, Library of Congress, Washington, D.C.

[3] Robert Lansing, diary entry, July 3, 1919, The Papers of Robert Lansing, Library of Congress, Washington, D.C.

[4] Wilson to Joe Tumulty, June 23, 1919, The Papers of Woodrow Wilson, Library of Congress, Washington, D.C.

[5] Quoted in Burton I. Kaufman, *Efficiency and Expansion* (Westport, Conn.: Greenwood Press, 1974), p. 239.

[6] Samuel Flagg Bemis, *A Short History of American Foreign Policy and Diplomacy* (New York: Holt, 1959), p. 431.

[7] James W. Morley, *The Japanese Thrust into Siberia, 1918* (New York: Columbia University Press, 1957), pp. 308–09.

[8] Lansing to Acting Secretary of State, February 9, 1919, Declaration of Policy with Regard to Russia, *Papers Relating to the Foreign Relations of the United States, 1919* (Washington, D.C.: Government Printing Office), pp. 246–51.

[9] Notes on a conversation held in the office of M. Pichon at the Quai d'Orsay, January 16, 1919, Paris Peace Conference, *Papers Relating to the Foreign Relations of the United States* (Washington D.C.: Government Printing Office), 3: 588–93.

[10] Charles Seymour, ed., *The Intimate Papers of Colonel House*, 4 vols. (Boston: Houghton Mifflin, 1926–28), 4: 389.

[11] Quoted in Herbert Hoover, *The Ordeal of Woodrow Wilson* (New York: McGraw-Hill, 1958), p. 119.

[12] Quoted in E. H. Carr, *The Bolshevik Revolution, 1917–1923*, 3 vols. (New York: Macmillan, 1953), 3: 356–57.

[13] Lansing to American Commission to Negotiate Peace, October 29, 1919, Declaration of Policy with Regard to Russia, *Papers Relating to the Foreign Relations of the United States, 1919*, pp. 783–84.

[14] Rickenbacker Machine Company to Hughes, January 4, 1923, State Department File Number 862.51/1601, National Archives, Washington, D.C.

[15] Quoted by Robert F. Smith in "Republican Policy and the Pax Americana, 1921–1932," in William Appleman Williams, *From Colony to Empire* (New York: John Wiley, 1972), pp. 265–66.

[16] Quoted in Bryce Wood, *The Making of the Good Neighbor Policy* (New York: Columbia University Press, 1961), p. 45.

[17] From a copy in the Papers of Henry L. Stimson, Yale University Library, New Haven, Conn.

[18] Quoted in Christopher Thorne, *The Limits of Foreign Policy* (London: Hamish Hamilton, 1972), p. 195.

Bibliography

Borg, Dorothy. *American Policy and the Chinese Revolution, 1925–1928.* New York: Octagon Books, 1968. At once detailed and comprehensive, the work of one of our best historians.

Brandes, Joseph. *Herbert Hoover and Economic Diplomacy: Department of Commerce Policy, 1921–1928.* Pittsburgh: University of Pittsburgh Press, 1962. A sympathetic account of Hoover's battles with European cartels.

Feis, Herbert. *The Diplomacy of the Dollar.* New York: Norton, 1966. Short and to the point.

Filene, Peter G. *Americans and the Soviet Experiment, 1917–1933.* Cambridge, Mass.: Harvard University Press, 1967. A good place to start on this complicated problem.

Iriye, Akira. *After Imperialism: The Search for a New Order in the Far East, 1921–1931.* Cambridge, Mass.: Harvard University Press, 1965. A finely textured, multiarchival examination of conflict and cooperation.

Mayer, Arno. *Politics and Diplomacy of Peacemaking.* New York: Knopf, 1967. Already a classic, this study of the forces of movement and the forces of position has influenced all writing about Versailles and its aftermath.

Neumann, William L. *America Encounters Japan: From Perry to MacArthur.* New York: Harper & Row, 1965. A quiet and persuasive critique of American policy vis-à-vis Japan.

Parrini, Carl P. *Heir to Empire: United States Economic Diplomacy, 1916–1923.* Pittsburgh: University of Pittsburgh Press, 1969. An explanation of how American policymakers faced the challenge of re-creating the world order.

Smith, Robert F. *The United States and Revolutionary Nationalism in Mexico, 1916–1923.* Chicago: University of Chicago Press, 1972. Another example of the continuity in American policy.

Williams, William Appleman. *American–Russian Relations, 1781–1947.* New York: Rinehart, 1952. Especially strong on the 1920s and Hoover's complicated approach.

Wilson, Joan Hoff. *American Business and Foreign Policy, 1920–1933.* Boston: Beacon Press, 1973. The beginnings of second-generation studies of economic factors in diplomacy, and very valuable beginnings.

Capitalism in 5
Crisis: 1931–1941

Tariff walls—Chinese Walls of isolation—would be futile. Freedom to trade is
essential to our economic life. We do not eat
all the food we can produce; and we do not
burn all the oil we can pump; we do not use
all the goods we can manufacture. It would
not be an American wall to keep Nazi goods
out; it would be a Nazi wall to keep us in.

Franklin D. Roosevelt
May 27, 1941

Americans continue to relive the 1930s. Democrats still seek a
successor for Franklin Delano Roosevelt, while Republicans still
search for Roosevelt's fingerprints on the Pearl Harbor disaster.
Contemporary politics begin with the New Deal. Yet it was a decade of paradoxes and sudden reversals. The New Dealers began
with the assumption that they could cure the depression at home.
By 1937, if indeed not sooner, a majority of the nation's leaders had
concluded that economic and political blocs outside the Western
Hemisphere were largely responsible for America's continuing dif-

ficulty. Hoover took little comfort from this tardy concession on the part of his enemies. He also had reversed direction. The embittered former president now reasoned, as did many others who called themselves isolationists, that collectivism had gone too far under Roosevelt. A war against the Axis would only ensure the death of liberal democracy in America.

New Dealers and interventionist Republicans reached the opposite conclusion: if the Axis were allowed to dominate the world, and by 1939 it appeared possible that it would at least make the attempt, there would be no future for liberal democracy. Having trod the gloomy paths of self-containment, the Democrats emerged at the end of the decade determined never to walk that way again. And having regained the high road, they came to see the decade just past as an aberration, ten years outside history.

WORLDS IN COLLISION

Hoover's world ended in September 1931. That month Japan moved into Manchuria, and Great Britain abandoned the gold standard. Actually the British were driven off gold by a combination of forces that signaled the beginning of a new era of managed currencies, state intervention, and extreme nationalism. Nine months later at Lausanne, the European powers made one final attempt to end the reparations—war debts tangle. Except for a token amount, German reparations would cease; so, too, would war debts payments. For years after Versailles, Washington had urged England and France to ease the burden on democratic Germany. Having failed in that endeavor, America had promulgated the Dawes and Young plans in an effort to rationalize the irrational into a workable system.

Seen from the American capital, the Lausanne decisions seemed to threaten the very basis of Western civilization. How could one condemn Japan if every nation was to do as it pleased about solemn legal and treaty obligations? Gold, said President Hoover, was a metal "enshrined in human instincts for over 10,000 years." He would not abandon it no matter what others did. The "others" were, unfortunately, doing quite a lot to make his position untenable. The British, and then other nations, found that a managed currency could be an effective export subsidy. By varying the exchange rate of the pound, they could make British goods cheaper. Germany, too, used a managed mark to gain an advantage over rivals. And Japan was not far behind.

To counteract these countermeasures, Great Britain sought to unite the Commonwealth in an imperial-preference system. Although it did not work out quite as London had imagined, the so-called Ottawa System further frightened the already nervous men in Washington. The world was suddenly, and everywhere, changed. Columbia University's famous president, Nicholas Murray Butler, declared:

> The period through which we are passing . . . is a period like the fall of the Roman Empire, like the Renaissance, like the beginning of the political and social revolutions in England and in France in the seventeenth and eighteenth centuries. . . . It is in some ways more powerful than them all; and it holds more of the world in its grip than any of them, but it certainly resembles them in its epoch-making character.[1]

Butler, a normally conservative man, demanded national planning to meet the crisis. Horror-stricken by this incredible chain of events, Hoover grasped at a British suggestion for a world economic conference to avoid final disaster. He was not prepared, however—even to make such a conference more than a symbolic gathering—to take the lead in tariff reductions; and he still assumed the Europeans would honor their obligations to the United States.

A few weeks after the British proposal was first made, the president accepted renomination. Openly admitting the seriousness of the plight of the millions of unemployed and the devastation of low farm prices, Hoover promised he would carry forward the work of reconstruction within the limits of the American system. He would oppose all efforts to curtail liberty. "Not regimented mechanisms, but free men, is our goal," he vowed. "This is my pledge to the Nation and to Almighty God."

Since the proposed world economic conference would not meet until the summer of 1933, Hoover could fulfill his pledge only if he   125

40   The land of plenty suddenly became the land of want.

was reelected or if he could persuade the Democratic winner, Franklin D. Roosevelt, to follow his advice. The New York governor had assembled a group of experts, collectively known as the brain trust, to aid him in coming to a decision on such issues. The leader of the group, Columbia University professor Raymond Moley, had few doubts about the direction the New Deal should take. "The problem," he explained, was "starvation amid plenty." The only solution was a balanced economy. Roosevelt had "to get control of the two ends of the equation—but you can't if one end is abroad."[2] The brain trust defined the embryo New Deal as *intranationalism*, a word they coined to ward off other potential advisers by creating a bond between their program and the president.

Foreign trade, they told the president-elect, was "only one-tenth of the problem" of recovery. They disagreed privately, however, on the question of the ultimate importance of a high level of exports to American prosperity. Roosevelt's insistence that he was committed to no long-range solution or doctrinaire philosophy provided a measure of reassurance to internationalists. So, too, did a visit Secretary of State Henry L. Stimson made to Hyde Park, the president-elect's home, in January 1933. At the conclusion of the discussion, which ranged over the world geographically and wandered through the debts tangle, Roosevelt issued a public statement: "American foreign policy must uphold the sanctity of international treaties."

This anodyne remark committed Roosevelt to nothing specific, but Stimson had private assurances that in regard to Manchukuo, at least, the president-elect would not change the American policy of nonrecognition. The debts were another matter, along with the forthcoming world economic conference. The brain trusters were more than a little disturbed about what they learned of Roosevelt's views concerning the Far East. Otherwise they were pleased by his insistence on keeping a free hand. Events were still running in their favor.

In Germany the Nazis came to power—a march over "the rotten corpse of liberalism and democracy," they termed their triumph. Prospects for a successful world economic conference, from an

41 Hoover's gloom did not lift as long as Franklin Roosevelt occupied the White House.

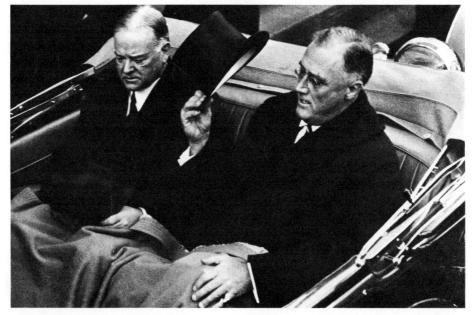

American point of view, suffered another blow with reports that the British were busy negotiating "trade agreements containing quota and preferential clauses." Apparently, an effort was being made to extend the Ottawa System to nations traditionally "friendly" with the sterling bloc.

Roosevelt's goals in the spring of 1933 did not go beyond immediate problems: farm prices, unemployment, bank failures. But the president did not discourage members of the administration from talking about the "philosophy" of the New Deal whenever they had the opportunity—in public or among themselves. Roosevelt liked it that way: the more theories the better.

Roosevelt was a skillful manipulator of other men's ideas without regard to their context, using what he needed as the occasion arose. Sometimes his closest advisers learned this the hard way. Some New Dealers had envisioned a more fundamental change from the old order, especially when, as they fully expected, the president's limited experiment in self-containment failed to produce economic recovery. Others expected an early swing back to internationalism. Only Roosevelt knew.

INSIDE INTRANATIONALISM: CORDELL HULL'S FIGHT FOR MULTILATERALISM

Roosevelt appointed his secretary of state, Cordell Hull, to head the delegation to the London Economic Conference. He staffed the remainder of the delegation with an odd assortment of experts, special interest enthusiasts, and politicians. Hull left Washington apparently convinced that he had the president's full support in seeking "an agreement between countries to lower trade barriers and stabilize the currency exchange. . . ." Why he should have felt that confidence has never become clear.

Hull's appointment as secretary of state had been considered a major victory for the internationalist wing of the Democratic party. But everything the White House had done since naming the Tennessee senator had been a rebuff to traditional low-tariff Democrats. The National Recovery Act (NRA) and the Agricultural Adjustment Act (AAA) were both premised on restricted home

42 Cordell Hull always looked worried, even after the New Deal shifted to internationalism.

production to raise prices; they were hardly compatible with an energetic effort to improve import–export levels. Roosevelt had decided, moreover, not to ask Congress for authority to negotiate tariff reductions; in fact, he had hinted that he might ask for still higher protection!

But an even greater surprise was in store for the delegates to the London Conference. Raymond Moley, Hull's archrival, suddenly appeared on the scene. He presumably brought instructions from Roosevelt to enter into a compromise stabilization agreement that would eventually end the debilitating competition between major currencies. No sooner had that maneuver been completed than the president sent his "bombshell" message repudiating all attempts to reach *any* stabilization agreement.

Persuaded by the intranationalists at home that Hoover's original plan could never succeed (the Europeans just could not give anything worthwhile in exchange for an agreement) and by his own political instincts that Americans wanted nothing more to do with Republican theories and wanting nothing so much as a dramatic break with leftover remedies, Roosevelt had acted. Moreover, he was now free to take the dollar off the gold standard.

129

Any benefits that might accrue to this last policy from increased exports were a minor consideration according to Roosevelt's point of view. The thing that had to be accomplished was a rise in farm price levels. Somehow Roosevelt had come to believe that he could force inflation at home by raising the price of gold; perhaps, feared some conservatives, that crazy streak of free silver in the Democratic heritage, which had been kept safely locked in the attic since Bryan's day, was coming out again in Roosevelt. On the evening of October 22, 1933, the president used a radio "fireside chat" to vow that he would raise prices. "If we cannot do this one way, we will do it in another. Do it we will."

A less determined man than Cordell Hull would have given up or turned the job over to a secretary of state willing to wait out this nationalistic mood in silence. But not Hull. He kept after the president on an almost daily basis, reminding him continually of the importance of getting started on a reciprocal trade treaty program. By the end of the year his efforts began to have some success. "The prospect was improving," wrote Herbert Feis,

> because by then the value of the dollar in terms of gold and other foreign currencies had so markedly declined that the competitive position of American producers was much improved. Thereby Roosevelt's monetary policy . . . was clearing the way for the step he would take in 1934 which initiated the gradual and cumulative reduction of restrictions on international trade in which, ever since, the United States has been the leader.[3]

At a meeting in the White House in late December 1933, Roosevelt told State Department advisers that if the United States was to embark on a policy to improve foreign trade, he must have greater authority to bargain with other nations than his predecessors had had. Tariff treaties in the 1920s had lagged as the Republicans depended increasingly on the extension of foreign loans to sustain the purchasing power of overseas customers. The State Department draft of new tariff legislation was the most sweeping reciprocity proposal ever presented to a jealous Congress, which had always guarded its prerogatives in foreign-trade matters despite what presidents wanted. Introduced in early 1934, the Reciprocal Trade

Agreements Act empowered the president to negotiate treaties with other nations and to generalize tariff reductions by means of a most-favored-nation clause. A pact with Brazil, for example, might thus open the market to a large number of American manufactures, since under the most-favored-nation section of the treaty every time Rio de Janeiro granted a reduction to a third country, the same lower rate would apply to American exports. The bill passed with overwhelming majorities in the House and Senate. During the debate, former Secretary of State Henry L. Stimson said in a radio address that expanded exports were the sole alternative to the "suppression of our hereditary initiative and the love of freedom."

Brooding in semiexile, Hoover had no words of praise for the "new" New Deal. But almost thirty years later he wrote to John F. Kennedy favorably comparing the proposed 1962 reciprocal trade act with his own tariff policy. Perhaps the years had dimmed his recollection or abated his fears of what a Democratic president intended to do with such power. In any event, the 1934 bill marked the end of ultranationalism. Other foreign trade measures followed. In an ironic sense, the New Deal "nationalized" the exporter, as one might say a socialist government took over a coal and steel industry. The infamous foreign loans of the Republican era were replaced by New Deal legislation creating a federal Export–Import Bank to extend credits to foreign buyers. And so on. Between 1934 and 1939 more legislation was enacted to promote foreign trade than in any other period in the nation's history. And in 1936 a tripartite stabilization agreement between England, France, and the United States completed what had been cut short at London in 1933. But none of this succeeded in lifting the seige mentality or raising the level of exports to predepression heights.

Congress demanded (and the administration willingly acquiesced) that foreign-trade laws be used in such a way as not to damage any sector of the national economy. Trade pacts were signed with fourteen countries; but while the American export balance rose from $225 million a year in 1933 to $1.4 billion in 1940, the real boom did not begin until defense spending made it possible

131

to protect the domestic economy and sell more goods at the same time. Uncle Sam substituted for the foreign buyer and did a better job—for the time being.

Although Hull constantly stressed the theoretical aspects of his trade program, saying that once it got started it should "spread like the waves of the ocean," the reality remained that all nations, including the United States, continued to discriminate against each other. On the eve of Pearl Harbor, the head of the Trade Agreements Division of the State Department reminded his colleagues that both Cuba and the Philippines discriminated against Japanese textiles at American insistence. Indeed, added Harry Hawkins, most countries that had signed trade agreements with the United States discriminated "overtly against Japan by not extending the reductions to Japanese products or covertly by thinly-disguised discriminations in the form of highly specialized tariff classifications."[4]

THE ILLUSION OF NEUTRALITY

The assumption that all other nations had to do to restore their own prosperity was to follow Washington's lead was, therefore, not one of the self-evident truths. Yet American attitudes hardened on this point as the 1930s wore on. Hull put it quite simply and forcefully in his *Memoirs:* "It is also a fact that, with very few exceptions, the countries with which we signed trade agreements joined together in resisting the Axis. The political line-up followed the economic line-up."[5]

Hull's efforts to organize the "economic line-up" to thwart the Axis powers—"This program and this policy have been constantly thrust in the face of Germany, of Japan, and other countries which seemed bent on preferences and discriminations, especially against us"[6]—suffered from Congressional restrictions on the use of trade acts but also (and more to the point in this context) from Congressional determination to devise a perfect neutrality law.

Surely it was contradictory to say that the Axis challenge would be taken up on the economic level but ignored on the political level. Yet that is what America attempted in the 1930s, ignoring

43 Students at the University of Chicago prepared for a peace march as pressure for neutrality legislation reached a high point in the mid-1930s while Europe prepared for a new war.

Woodrow Wilson's warning that the "business of neutrality" (in every sense of that phrase) was over. A majority of Congressmen wanted to believe in the illusion of neutrality and refused to recognize that to stay out of a new war would probably require a complete abandonment of cherished neutral rights. But it is only fair to admit that it is far easier to talk about inherent contradictions in the past tense. The popular myths of the day held the bankers and munitions makers responsible for American entry into the First World War. So Congress passed neutrality acts in 1935, 1936, and 1937, banning the traffic in arms and loans to belligerents. Even here it hedged in favor of the export trade by including in the 1937 law a cash-and-carry provision that permitted such sales if purchasers plunked down cash and carried the goods home in their own ships.

Roosevelt lamented that cash-and-carry worked "all right in the Atlantic," but "all wrong in the Pacific." He solved this dilemma after the 1937 invasion of North China by Japan by simply ignoring the existence of a war so that China could continue to receive arms. The episode was another instance of Congressional inability to legislate for all contingencies, its reluctance to do anything that might curtail the export trade, and the transfer of power to the White House almost by default.

The president's own policy, especially toward Europe in the 1930s, was ambivalent. He withdrew from the 1933 Geneva Disarmament Conference rather than make it seem the United States was aligned with England and France against Germany; he refused to intervene with Congress on the debt question; and he congratulated Neville Chamberlain on the outcome of the 1938 Munich Conference, which permitted German absorption of the Sudetenland. Roosevelt had played a minor role in preventing the breakdown of the talks leading to that "settlement," wiring Prime Minister Chamberlain on its conclusion the enigmatic phrase "good man."[7]

But Roosevelt also brought to an end the nonrecognition policy toward the Soviet Union at least partly because he desired a coun-

44 FDR spoke of a quarantine but admitted that he had no policy to implement the plan. Did he hope for a lead from the public?

terbalance to Germany and Japan, spent considerable sums on new ships for the navy, and in October 1937 delivered the Quarantine Speech with its famous phrase, "when an epidemic of physical disease starts to spread, the community approves and joins in the quarantine of the patient in order to protect the health of the community against the spread."

Surrounded afterward by excited journalists who wanted to know what the president planned to do, Roosevelt quickly explained that he was only describing an attitude—he was still searching for a policy. Better than any state paper, the episode of the Quarantine Speech sums up the confusions and crises of the 1930s.

WHAT MAKES GOOD NEIGHBORS?

Cuba and Mexico, quiet during the 1920s, began and ended the next decade on a revolutionary theme. In between, the struggle to negotiate what in normal times would have been a simple trade treaty with Brazil ultimately became a contest between liberal democracy and fascism in the Western Hemisphere.

Sugar prices, like those of other raw materials, collapsed at the outset of the depression. In the past, a decline in sugar prices meant a rise in Cuban revolutionary activity. This time was no exception. This time, however, Roosevelt and his advisers were concerned to avoid direct military intervention. One reason was the Pan American Conference scheduled to convene in Montevideo, at which Hull hoped to promote hemispheric acceptance of his trade-agreements program. But Cuban dictator Gerardo Machado, who, Stimson had once assured Roosevelt, could probably "hold the country safe and suppress revolutions," had fled the island at the first signs of real trouble.

After a short period of turmoil, a radical government was formed by Grau San Martín. Special Ambassador Sumner Welles, author of a lengthy memorandum to Roosevelt on the absolute necessity of renouncing the Big Stick, began pleading with Washington for just such a policy to deal with Havana's apostasy. Cuba had fallen under the control of irresponsible army men, Welles explained to

135

45   Fulgencio Batista and Grau San Martín, an old opponent, in 1944.

the State Department, and "extreme radical" students and pro-
fessors "whose theories are frankly communistic."[8]

Roosevelt and Hull held back from sending the navy, but they
accepted the special ambassador's recommendation against diplomatic recognition. If enforced long enough, nonrecognition would
topple any government in Cuba—at least in those days. In Havana,
meanwhile, Welles set about the task of organizing the opposition
to Grau San Martín, protected by the sure knowledge that the
Cuban president dared not risk an open break with the United
States by expelling him. Also, Secretary Hull told a press conference that the United States would welcome any government that

would represent the will of the people and that could maintain law and order. Grover Cleveland and William McKinley had said about the same thing four decades earlier, and Dwight Eisenhower and John Kennedy would repeat the formula in Fidel Castro's day.

Roosevelt pleaded with newsmen to "lay off this intervention stuff," but in Havana, Ambassador Welles was having some success in wooing Fulgencio Batista, Grau San Martín's chief-of-staff. In January 1934, Batista staged a coup that put Carlos Mendieta in the president's chair. But it was Batista who stood "behind the throne." Over the next quarter-century Cuban presidents came and went, but Batista stayed. Sometimes he sat in the presidential chair; sometimes he let others have a go at it. Order and stability had returned to Cuba, but liberal democracy had still not arrived. Nor would it.

Later in 1934 the United States, satisfied that Batista had a good grip on things, abrogated the Platt Amendment, reduced the tariff on Cuban sugar, and negotiated a trade agreement that provided for wide reductions on United States exports. Instead of allowing Cuba greater economic freedom, the first wave in Hull's promised tide of multilateralism, the agreement simply incorporated Cuba more fully into the American economy. It was hardly the kind of treaty to impress either the democracies or the dictatorships with America's benevolence or its tolerance for radical change.

Meanwhile, German inroads into continental Latin America had begun to disturb policymakers. It was not only the increased volume of German trade that provided cause for concern, but the broader effects of Berlin's bilateralism and barter practices. Ignoring the inconsistency of the 1934 Cuban treaty with Hull's sermons, American policymakers stoutly maintained throughout the decade that whatever volume of trade flowed into the narrow channels of bilateralism drained the pool of multilateralism. All nations thus suffered. It was also believed that a campaign against German trade methods in Latin America could have a ripple effect all the way back to Berlin and might even undermine the supposedly weak foundations of Nazism.

Brazil was a good testing ground. Depressed raw materials prices   137 made German barter offers attractive to that country in the mid-1930s. The State Department eventually designed a treaty that appealed to Rio, but even after this agreement was signed, the Brazilians found ways to negotiate barter arrangements with Germany—much to the displeasure of both American business interests and official Washington. This situation was finally remedied when the United States undertook to supply Brazil with capital to construct a steel mill complex. American private concerns had rejected the project as unprofitable; but when Brazil threatened to seek German or Japanese aid, funds were forthcoming from the United States government, foreshadowing postwar foreign-aid and development programs.

Another preview of future events came with the campaign in the late 1930s to cut off German and Italian air links with South America by lending the Latin countries funds to replace German- or Italian-owned lines with national companies. These latter, however, were usually dominated by Pan American Airways, the company once described by its president as the aerial ambassador of American business.

Cuba had posed a familiar revolutionary challenge. The situation in Brazil was more complicated. But what if *both* should come at once? Policymakers would soon find out in Mexico. In December 1934, Lázaro Cardenas assumed office, and the seemingly stalled Mexican revolution started moving again.

Cardenas nationalized the Mexican railways, greatly accelerated the pace of land expropriation, gave support to the militant trade-union movement, and established a government corporation, *Petróleos de México* (Pemex), to develop national oil reserves. Tensions began to rise when the president raised taxes on oil production, but the real threat to the foreign companies was the growing strength of the nationwide syndicate of Mexican Petroleum Workers. After advancing a series of demands that the foreign companies insisted were preposterous, the oil workers went on strike in the spring of 1937.

The companies' fear of government–labor connivance to deprive them of their property increased when the union appealed to the

46 Lázaro Cardenas inherited the oil dispute and made the most of it for Mexico.

Mexican Labor Board to resolve the dispute. The board awarded the union raises, which, declared the companies, could total 26 million *pesos* annually and would surely bankrupt them. A further appeal, this time by the companies, resulted in a Mexican Supreme Court ruling in favor of the board's decision. By this time the companies were making their position clear in another appeal—to the United States Department of State.

If Cardenas was supporting the workers, said Secretary Hull in a message to the American ambassador, then the issue ceased to be simply a question of Mexican internal affairs. Hull was righter than he knew, perhaps, but that did not make the State Department's task any simpler. When Cardenas expropriated the oil properties on March 18, 1938, Washington was faced with a set of unattractive alternatives. Choosing the best of these meant settling for much less than half a loaf, perhaps only a slice or two.

The oil companies contended, and Hull was inclined to believe they were correct, that if Cardenas was successful in challenging American properties in Mexico, others would follow suit until all

American holdings were unsafe. Yet if Hull put too much pressure on Mexico City, Cardenas might look elsewhere for support—and find it. If anything, Roosevelt was even more puzzled than his secretary of state about what to do. The recession of 1937 had brought on a new wave of labor militance in the United States, with the sitdown strike emerging as the most effective weapon in the unions' arsenal. Sometimes these strikes led to violence, but violent or not, the question of property rights versus the public welfare had once again become a heated issue.

Agriculture Secretary Henry Wallace had received a shock in midsummer 1937 at the Agricultural Labor Convention when delegates told him they were disgusted with old-line farm organizations and the administration's farm programs, which, they said, were dominated by the landlords. "They were full of enthusiasm about agricultural labor affiliating with the C.I.O. [the new industry-wide union that had sought to organize steel and automobile workers]." Wallace feared, as he wrote the president, that it "might be fatal to the future of democracy in the U.S. if labor split agriculture" this way and the two workers' groups joined in a mass movement against factory owners and landlords.[9]

There was no direct link between the oil expropriation movement in Mexico and what Henry Wallace beheld in midwestern America, but here was another instance where it was becoming more and more difficult to separate domestic and international questions. Roosevelt's public criticism of the oil companies for setting an exhorbitant price on their properties for reckoning compensation and his general uneasiness about giving the State Department free rein to deal with those "Communists" down there (Hull's phrase) were indicative of a troubled concern not only about the world, but also about the solidity of the New Deal coalition.

Washington played around with the price of silver in an effort to pressure Cardenas, but that elicited recriminations from American mineowners who still controlled a large share of the Mexican industry. Great Britain broke off diplomatic relations with Mexico City, with no appreciable effect save to provide a further stimulus to defiant celebrations of "Expropriation Day" the following year.

The oil companies declared a boycott of all Mexican petroleum products, expecting that without tankers and buyers Cardenas would drown in oil. Whoever succeeded him would be easier to deal with. It might have worked except for an enterprising American entrepreneur, William Rhoades Davis, who in the best traditions of laissez-faire capitalism offered his fleet of seventeen tankers to dispose of the oil in German and Italian markets.

When demands were made that Davis be prosecuted under the 1917 Trading with the Enemy Act, Hull confessed he was puzzled about what to do. How could the government prosecute dealers in expropriated products around the world? "This seems like a very large order."[10]

Within a few months, Davis's operation had almost made the boycott look ridiculous—with the aid, of course, of Axis customers. Pemex was reported to have left very little surplus oil for export. Once breeched, the boycott sprang leaks in other places. In March 1940, despite official frowns, the Sinclair Oil Corporation signed an agreement with Mexico City. Hull gave Sinclair a cool response, while Secretary of the Navy Frank Knox told Sinclair representatives that, regardless of price, the navy would have nothing to do with "stolen oil."

Time was growing short. Was it better to have the oil sold to Hitler? Besides, argued exporters, why should the oil companies have the right to determine Mexico's purchasing power? Roosevelt pressed for a general settlement. When Ávila Camacho replaced Cardenas later that year, Roosevelt sent word to the new president that he wanted closer relations with Mexico. This was followed by an offer to purchase other mineral products at high prices if the Mexicans would agree not to sell to the Axis. Even so, an oil settlement was not reached until the eve of Pearl Harbor.

By an exchange of notes, a Mexican-American commission was established to determine the true value of the oil fields and proper compensation. The Export-Import Bank announced a $30 million loan to Mexico for completion of the Mexico City-to-Guatemala section of the Pan-American Highway. Hull and Welles had scolded the Mexican ambassador about the sacredness of private property and the threat that expropriation posed to civilization. But Germany and Japan were greater dangers. During the war the State Department returned to the effort to persuade the Mexican government to invite the oil companies back with economic inducements. On one occasion, Roosevelt specifically disavowed a plan for lending Mexico money for an oil refinery in exchange for such an accommodation. But Mexican nationalism cooled as the depression ended. Moreover, Cardenas's successors seemed to feel that they had established their right to self-determination within the shadow of the "Yankee Colossus." They had struck something of a balance. Investment laws were drafted to encourage a postwar dollar inflow, but Pemex retained full control in the oil fields.

During the Cold War, Mexico was to play an interesting role, often voting independently of the United States, sometimes against, in the United Nations. But Mexican economic dependence on the United States grew all the while. There were hints of a new Mexican initiative among the nations of the Third World as the century entered its last quarter. New oil discoveries opened the way for either of two possibilities: cooperation with a raw materials' cartel like OPEC, or cooperation with the United States in reducing the power of such organizations. The choice would not be easy.

SHOWDOWN IN THE FAR EAST

Roosevelt's apparent endorsement of the Stimson doctrine of nonrecognition of Manchukuo in prepresidential talks with that secretary of state was a cause of some embarrassment and concern to the intranationalists. China was a soft spot in their defense. Somehow every administration seemingly had to be immunized against China fever. The Great China Market had never materialized, but ethereal or not, it was still a powerful magnet.

For a long time, too, Americans had regarded China as their next ideological frontier. Missionary sympathies ran high, especially as returning Christian spokesmen reported to local congregations about Japan's brutal attacks on the innocent Chinese. At early cabinet meetings, Roosevelt mentioned the possibility of war with

47 An interesting comment on the rivalry in China during the 1930s.

Japan, and although it was only that—a possibility—it was in the back of everyone's mind. "A declaration of non-recognition," noted a professional diplomat, "means that eventually one side or another will find itself in a position where it must 'eat crow.'"[11]

In retrospect, 1934 stands out as the critical year in the Japanese-American drama. It was in that year that Japan requested a new special arrangement, a new Lansing-Ishii understanding covering all of China and, being refused, announced the Amau Doctrine, by which it claimed a right to approve all foreign loans to China. It was also in 1934 that Tokyo demanded absolute naval equality with the United States and Great Britain and, again being refused, withdrew from the London Naval Conference. And it was in 1934 that Roosevelt, despite his own doubts, approved a Treasury De-

143

partment plan to manipulate the government's silver purchase program so that China would become more closely linked with the United States.

Actually, there were three characters in the drama, as Secretary of the Treasury Henry Morgenthau recognized. "This thing is awfully big," he said. "It's an international battle between Great Britain, Japan and ourselves and China is the bone in the middle."[12] Japan found some sympathy in Great Britain for its requests for a special arrangement over China and naval equality, but those in England who favored these policies, such as Chancellor of the Exchequer Neville Chamberlain, did so out of a desire to strike a bargain all round, including a division of colonial and Far Eastern markets. And this was precisely what policymakers in Washington were trying to avoid.

Morgenthau's readiness to take a strong stand, to go it alone if need be, alarmed State Department officials, who preferred a more measured approach to the problem. But there was never any question of withdrawing from the Far East, as the following memorandum makes clear:

> As our own population becomes more intense, as we feel increasingly the need of foreign markets, our definite concern for open markets will be more widely felt among our people and our desire for and insistence upon free opportunity to trade with and among the peoples of the Far East will be intensified. For in that region lie the great potential markets of the future.[13]

Reading that statement, one would never suppose that in the 1930s America's economic stake in Japan was actually far larger than anywhere else in Asia. China, for example, imported from the United States less than three-quarters as much as Japan did—despite a population more than seven times as large. Yet in October 1934, General William "Billy" Mitchell declared: "Japan is our most dangerous enemy, and our planes should be designed to attack her."[14] The air power enthusiast called for the construction of dirigibles and bomber planes with a range of more than six thousand miles that could reach Japan.

How can such seeming irrationality be explained? Several factors bear on the problem. First, it is clear that the United States always felt a special sympathy for China, but that sympathy included an assessment of future prospects by both missionary and merchant. China *was* a bigger market for American products, not immediately perhaps, but surely some time. Chiang Kai-shek's success in uniting the country under the Kuomintang was watched with great concern in both Japan and the United States. Chiang's conversion to Christianity, remarked on by the American ambassador, who noted in reports to the Department of State that the Chinese leader and his wife behaved decently, like "Protestant Anglo-Saxons," no doubt raised broader ideological considerations. Japan could not very well approve of this strong Western influence in China, nor could the United States easily accept the "loss" of such a friend.

But General Mitchell's warning held another meaning for Americans. Like Germany, Japan represented a worldwide threat. Roosevelt was, reported a State Department official, "likewise concerned over their [Japanese] seizure of markets throughout the world by underselling, particularly in textiles, and their oil policy."[15] If the Japanese managed to organize Manchukuo and North China, not only would the United States be deprived of access to those areas, but Japan's ability to compete around the world would increase proportionately.

By 1937 it appeared to many American observers that Japan had failed. Morgenthau was convinced that he had "saved" China, and his colleagues in the Commerce Department were in a self-congratulatory mood: "We had built up in China organizations capable of those measures of expansion which are characteristic of American enterprise where very favorable trade conditions permit."[16] The celebrations were a bit premature. On July 7, 1937, Japan launched a military attack on China proper.

If the Japanese succeeded in China, Secretary of Commerce Dan Roper advised the president, American cotton exports to Japan would be endangered—a loss of $100 million annually. He added:

> This possibility and other factors would thus combine to reduce our raw cotton exports in the next five years to probably as low as four million bales. In the absence of new domestic outlets, our domestic

145

48 Japan defied the "civilized" world in China, July 1937.

consumption would not likely exceed eight million bales. This would
call for drastic readjustments on the part of our cotton growers, in
fact, a recharting of the economy of the South and definite Federal production control procedure.[17]

In opposing Japan's forward movement, therefore, American
policymakers were not just dreaming about the Great China Market, but struggling to hold onto institutions they thought endangered at home. Moreover, it was difficult to try to draw lines between
ideological and political-economic considerations as they kept melt-
ing into one another. Immediate economic considerations, for example, dictated that America should continue to sell cotton and oil
and scrap iron to Japan, but long-range concerns had to be taken
into account as well.

Hull's advisers in the State Department recommended increasing
pressure on the presumably vulnerable Japanese economy, but in

such a fashion as to permit Tokyo every opportunity to reconsider its policies. What policy planners could not estimate, however, was the ability of the Japanese to extricate themselves from China without unacceptable consequences. Even had the American thesis, that outside pressure would discredit the warmakers, been correct, nothing in Washington's approach would enable the two nations to undertake a serious dialogue about the future. Clearly, their approaches to tomorrow and next year divided them as much as the specifics of the China problem. Hull, for example, would never consider offering diplomatic recognition of Manchukuo for accommodation and withdrawal in China.

Adopted to prevent the Japanese forward movement from succeeding, the Stimson doctrine now hindered a settlement of the "China incident" on better terms than America had any reason to expect. Having taken a stand, the United States could not back down without seeming to repudiate the foundations of its Open Door policy. On November 20, 1938, Hull stated in instructions to the American ambassador in Tokyo, "In our opinion an endeavor by any country in any part of the world to establish in favor of itself a preferred position in another country is incompatible with the maintenance of our own and the establishment of world prosperity."[18] Presumably such a blanket statement covered Manchuria, and Hull's comment must be taken not as an accountant's conclusion but as a theory of political-economy.

American policy, wrote Herbert Feis in *The Road to Pearl Harbor*, offered Japan no rewards, no advantages for returning to the "company of peaceful and orderly states and accepting a place below the salt." Viewed from Tokyo that meant something else: a continuation of economic dependence on and moral approval from Western nations. Japan's super-nationalists argued that nothing more could be expected as long as the West dominated China and Asia.

On July 26, 1939, Hull announced that the United States had served notice on Japan that the 1911 Commercial Treaty between the nations would be abrogated in six months, the warning period stipulated when it was signed. After that, the United States would

49 Japan's Saturo Kurusu sealed the Axis Tripartite Pact with Galeazzo Ciano and Adolf Hitler.

be free to impose whatever restrictions it liked on Japanese-American trade. Intended to bring Japanese leaders to their senses, the decision only provided Tokyo with another argument for closer relations with Germany and Italy. Seen from Tokyo, Hull's decision made it all the more urgent that Japan seek a treaty that would permit it to resist the United States while exploiting the opportunity presented by the outbreak of war in Europe to make itself independent in raw materials. Japanese negotiators thought they achieved this goal in September 1940 with the signing of the Axis Tripartite Pact.

The Axis pact assured, in the end, the defeat of Japan's project for an Asian "Co-Prosperity Sphere." By ranging itself so definitely on the side of Germany and Italy, Japan, however little choice it had, settled any doubts about its intentions. And in Hull's mind the complicated and confusing issues of the 1930s now came down to one simple truth: the world could not continue half-slave and half-free.

Negotiations to avoid war were undertaken in the spring of 1941, but Admiral Nomura, the special ambassador charged with this mission, found Secretary Hull not much interested in specific issues: "It became evident that he is thinking about readjusting the economic situation of the world after the conclusion of this war and that he has only a passing interest in the various problems of China." Whenever Nomura tried to bring the discussion back to specifics, Hull hardly seemed to be listening. The secretary constantly mused about the future:

> I rather think that in postwar economic reconstruction, probably the principle of non-discrimination will be an all-encompassing one. . . . Now all along I've fought against the preferential system of the British Empire resulting from the Ottawa Conference, and now we

50 Hull's expression tells all: neither side had much to say to the other.

are talking it over with England. I don't want you to tell anybody about this, but don't you know, only lately Great Britain is coming around to my point of view.[19]

One result of the war, if Hull had his say, would be a German and British return to the gold standard and an "all-encompassing" multilateralism.

DR. WIN-THE-WAR

When Roosevelt wrote his required neutrality proclamation on the outbreak of war in Europe, he concluded with these sentences: "I hope the United States will keep out of this war. I believe that it will. And I give you assurance and reassurance that every effort of your Government will be directed toward that end." The president's defenders argue that these were his honest thoughts as the war began; his accusers are equally insistent that a policy of calculated deception was already under way in the White House.

The president also promised in his declaration of neutrality that the government would not withhold information from the public. Whatever Roosevelt did to aid the Allies—and it was to be quite a lot during the next twelve months—he exempted from this pledge. A journalist at presidential press conferences would have had little difficulty, however, in picking up hints that America's official neutrality was not in fact neutral, even as Roosevelt reassured the nation that every step he took was designed to keep the United States out of war.

Was neutrality a ruse, then, and if so, who was to be fooled? Roosevelt was playing, had to play, a delicate game. He could not allow the Axis powers to assume that there were no conditions under which the United States would go to war; that would only make them bolder. He most certainly was not trying to fool the Axis. The case is sometimes made that he was attempting to deceive the public, but here, too, one must be careful.

With Roosevelt's enthusiastic support, Secretary of the Treasury Morgenthau sought to direct Allied purchases to the aircraft industry, because, he reasoned, America would soon need the expanded capacity. In January 1940, the president told Morgenthau that "he would like to see our industry on such a basis that on short notice we could produce 30,000 planes a year."[20] Between 1938 and 1940 Allied war orders totaled almost $1.5 billion, but unemployment did not fall to really low levels until 1943, a powerful reminder of the persistence of the Great Depression into an era in which the economy seemed to be running in high gear.

Roosevelt may have thought that by selling, or even "lending," airplanes and ships to Allies, he could avoid actual participation in the war. The surprisingly easy German defeat of France in June 1940 no doubt caused him to reassess that possibility. Congress gave him more than he asked for in arms, but it was far more reluctant to pass a peacetime draft. One could gather from that performance that the representatives of the people in Congress would approve (or look the other way) if Roosevelt bent the neutrality laws, just as long as American boys were not being shot in some "foreign war."

The war was one year old when Roosevelt announced the destroyer-bases deal with England, the famous trade of fifty overage destroyers for ninety-nine-year leases on base facilities in the Caribbean and on Newfoundland. "This is the most important action in the reinforcement of our national defense that has been taken since the Louisiana Purchase," asserted the president. It was an intriguing choice of parallels.

Great Britain's inability to pay cash for military supplies after 1940 led to the introduction of the lend-lease bill in Congress. Roosevelt was still assuring the nation that passage of this bill was not a step toward war when, in order to guarantee delivery of the $6 billion in supplies authorized by Congress, he secretly extended the American security line in the Atlantic to twenty-six degrees west longitude. Within this area, United States navy patrol units would "seek out any ships or planes of aggressor nations. . . ." He had decided not to announce the new policy, Roosevelt informed British Prime Minister Winston Churchill, but to "let time bring out the existence of the new patrol area."[21]

Press reports soon forced the president to comment on the patrols, but he had the advantage of denying the more extreme accusations of convoying and could thus make it appear that the navy was doing nothing more than providing advance information on aggressor ships "coming to the Western Hemisphere." While some "isolationists" raised protests about the president's policy and his way of dealing with issues relating to the war by press conference repartee, the majority of Congress and the people apparently preferred to remain uninformed. "What you don't know can't hurt you." It would also seem that a majority feared and hated the Axis powers and wanted the president to do what he could to insure their defeat. "What you don't want to know can hurt the other guy—and so much the better."

Some of Roosevelt's closest advisers, including Henry L. Stimson, who had returned as Secretary of War in 1940, worried about these games the president was playing with the political system. It was not, however, a game of solitaire. In the last analysis, Franklin Roosevelt's position at the end of the depression decade left him few options, as he and others saw it, to preserve the liberal democratic state. Yet it remained for Roosevelt's successors to consider how far the executive could go in seeking to preserve that system by methods Jefferson employed in purchasing Louisiana, Lincoln adopted to fight the Civil War, and Roosevelt used to maneuver the Japanese into firing the first big shot of the war.

AND THE WAR CAME

In December 1939, Roosevelt informed Ambassador Joseph Grew in Tokyo that the United States would not negotiate a new commerical treaty with Japan as long as that nation continued its current policies. This was almost a year before Japan signed the Axis Tripartite Pact. In the intervening months Washington had tried to decide whether it should impose an oil embargo on Japan. At the outset of the final negotiations with Ambassador Nomura, Hull laid down four principles. There could be no substantive discussions until Tokyo accepted all of them: "(1) Respect for the territorial integrity and sovereignty of each and all nations [the Open Door extended to the world]; (2) support of the principle of noninterference in the internal affairs of other countries; (3) support of the principle of equality, including equality of commercial oppor-

51 and 52   Pearl Harbor: (*above*) a Japanese pilot's view of the end of the depression decade; (*below*) ground level.

tunity; (4) non-disturbance of the *status quo* in the Pacific except as the *status quo* may be altered by peaceful means."

The Japanese negotiators responded with demands that the United States compel Chiang Kai-shek to make peace on favorable terms or to lose American support and that trade restrictions be removed. On July 20, 1941, Japan occupied French Indochina. A week later the United States froze all Japanese assets, thereby imposing a total economic embargo. "United States–Japanese relations had reached an impasse," writes Norman Graebner, "not because Tokyo's demands had become greater—indeed, the Japanese, under intense economic pressure, would have accepted less after September than they would have earlier—but because the Roosevelt administration had made it increasingly clear that Tokyo could anticipate no compromise."[22]

On November 25, 1941, the War Cabinet met with President Roosevelt. Secretary Hull advised Roosevelt that negotiations had come to and end. An attack was likely within the next few days. Then they took counsel together to decide how, if it did come, "we

53   Roosevelt reports on the day of infamy and asks Congress to declare war.

should maneuver them into the position of firing the first shot without allowing too much danger to ourselves."[23] No one present that day anticipated an outright attack on the fleet at Pearl Harbor. What seemed likely was an involvement of United States forces in the Philippines when the Japanese struck south against British or Dutch possessions. Despite the terrible damage done at Pearl Harbor, Stimson wrote in his diary on the evening of December 7, "When the news first came that Japan had attacked us, my first feeling was of relief that the indecision was over and that a crisis had come in a way which would unite all our people."[24]

And history could begin again.

Notes

[1] Quoted in Charles Beard and Mary Beard, *America in Midpassage* (New York: Macmillan, 1939), p. 115.

[2] Quoted in Eliot Rosen, "Roosevelt and the Brains Trust: An Historical Overview," *Political Science Quarterly* 87 (December 1972): 531–57.

[3] Herbert Feis, *1933: Characters in Crisis* (Boston: Little, Brown, 1966), p. 264.

[4] Hawkins to Ballantine, November 10, 1941, *Papers Relating to the Foreign Relations of the United States, 1941* (Washington, D.C.: Government Printing Office), 4: 516–19.

[5] Cordell Hull, *The Memoirs of Cordell Hull*, 2 vols. (New York: Dodd Mead, 1948), 1: 365.

[6] Hull to Roosevelt, December 14, 1934, quoted in Edgar B. Nixon, ed., *Franklin D. Roosevelt and Foreign Affairs, 1933–1937*, 3 vols. (Cambridge, Mass.: Harvard University Press, 1969), 1: 365.

[7] Cited in Keith Middlemas, *The Strategy of Appeasement* (Chicago: Quadrangle Books, 1972), p. 408.

[8] Quoted in David Green, *The Containment of Latin America: A History of the Myths and Realities of the Good Neighbor Policy* (Chicago: Quadrangle Books, 1971), p. 14.

[9] Handwritten note from Wallace to Roosevelt, July 28, 1937, The Papers of Franklin Delano Roosevelt, The President's Secretary's File, Franklin Delano Roosevelt Library, Hyde Park, New York.

[10] Quoted in Bryce Wood, *The Making of the Good Neighbor Policy* (New York: W. W. Norton, 1967), p. 229.

[11] Hugh R. Wilson, *Diplomat Between Wars* (New York, 1941), pp. 180–81.

[12] Henry Morgenthau, diary entry, August 14, 1935, The Papers and Diary of Henry Morgenthau, Franklin Delano Roosevelt Library, Hyde Park, New York.

[13] Hull to Roosevelt, March 16, 1935, Roosevelt Papers.

[14] Quoted in William L. Neumann, *America Encounters Japan: From Perry to MacArthur* (New York: Harper & Row, 1965), p. 208.

[15] J. Pierrepont Moffat, diary entry, October 24, 1934, The Papers of J. Pierrepont Moffat, Houghton Library, Harvard University, Cambridge, Mass.

[16] National Foreign Trade Convention, *Official Report, 1937*, pp. 258–60.

[17] Roper to Roosevelt, November 26, 1937, Roosevelt Papers.

[18] Hull to Grew, November 20, 1938, State Department File Number 693.001/399, National Archives, Washington, D.C.

[19] Nomura to Tokyo, November 18, 1941, reprinted in U.S., Congress, Joint Committee on the Investigation of the Pearl Harbor Attack, *Hearings*, 79th Cong., 1st sess., 39 parts (Washington, D.C.: Government Printing Office, 1948), 12: 148–50.

[20] John Blum, *From the Morgenthau Diaries: Years of Urgency, 1938–1941* (Boston: Houghton Mifflin, 1965), pp. 116ff.

[21] Quoted in T. R. Fehrenbach, *FDR's Undeclared War, 1939–1941* (New York: David McKay, 1967), pp. 226–27.

[22] Dorothy Borg and Shumpei Okamoto, eds., *Pearl Harbor as History: Japanese-American Relations, 1931–1941* (New York: Columbia University Press, 1973), p. 50.

[23] Henry L. Stimson, diary entry, November 25, 1941, The Papers of Henry L. Stimson, Yale University Library, New Haven, Conn.

[24] Ibid., December 7, 1941.

Bibliography

Beard, Charles. *The Open Door at Home.* New York: Macmillan, 1934. An early statement of the perils of economic expansion and the case for self-containment.

Borg, Dorothy. *The United States and the Far Eastern Crisis of 1933 to 1938.* Cambridge, Mass.: Harvard University Press, 1964. Especially good on the 1933/34 turning points.

Cole, Wayne. *America First.* Madison, Wis.: University of Wisconsin Press, 1953. A good survey of the isolationist opposition to Roosevelt's policies.

Cronin, E. David. *Josephus Daniels in Mexico.* Madison, Wis.: University of Wisconsin Press, 1960. So far the best study of the oil crisis, replete with selections from diplomatic papers.

Divine, Robert. *The Illusion of Neutrality.* Chicago: University of Chicago Press, 1962. An insightful monograph on the fallacies of the neutrality laws.

Gleason, S. Everett, and Langer, William L. *The Challenge to Isolation, 1937–1940* and *The Undeclared War, 1940–1941.* New York: Harper & Row, 1952–53. Volumes prepared to avoid a post-Second World War revisionist uprising. They failed to do that, but are full of information.

Russett, Bruce. *No Clear and Present Danger.* New York: Harper & Row, 1972. Hardly more than a long article in length, this study assumes a familiarity with literature of the Second World War, but is still useful to the less-well-read.

Schroeder, Paul W. *The Axis Alliance and Japanese-American Relations, 1941.* Ithaca, N.Y.: Cornell University Press, 1958. Using primarily the Congressional hearings on the Pearl Harbor attack, this book is a solid critique of American policy from a realist position.

Smith, Robert F. *The United States and Cuba.* New York: Bookman and Associates, 1960. Excellent on the crisis of 1933.

From Pearl Harbor to 6
Panmunjon: 1941-1951

There is one thing that Americans value
even more than peace. It is freedom. Freedom
of worship—freedom of speech—freedom of
enterprise. It must be true that the first two
of these freedoms are related to the third.
For, throughout history, freedom of worship
and freedom of speech have been most fre-
quently enjoyed in those societies that have
accorded a considerable measure of freedom
to individual enterprise. Freedom has
flourished where power has been dispersed. It
has languished where power has been too
highly centralized. So our devotion to
freedom of enterprise, in the United States,
has deeper roots than a desire to protect the
profits of ownership. It is part and parcel of
what we call American.

Harry S. Truman
March 5, 1947

On January 6, 1941, President Franklin Delano Roosevelt delivered a moving speech about the world of the four freedoms:
freedom of speech and expression, freedom to worship God,
freedom from want, and freedom from fear. "That is no vision of a
distant millennium. It is a definite basis for a kind of world attain-

54 Roosevelt's four freedoms became America's war aims: but how could they be implemented?

able in our own time and generation. . . ." It was still almost a year before the attack on Pearl Harbor and several months before passage of the Lend-Lease bill, yet the president was voicing on behalf of the United States a complete set of war aims. Taken literally, Roosevelt's vision could require not only the defeat of the Axis powers, but also the dismantling of the European colonial empires and the overthrow of the Soviet dictatorship.

How was Roosevelt's speech to be taken? Prime Minister Winston Churchill was never quite sure. Roosevelt worried him on occasion by bringing up India or French Indochina, suggesting plans for their eventual independence, and then rambling on about a postwar trusteeship system to deal with all colonial problems. The prime minister warned his military planners in February 1944—four months before the invasion of France—that they must also give consideration to a major effort in the Pacific:

> A decision to act as a subsidiary force under the Americans in the Pacific raises difficult political questions about the future of our Malayan possessions. If the Japanese should withdraw from them or

make peace as a result of the main American thrust, the United States Government would after the victory feel greatly strengthened in its view that all possessions in the East Indian Archipelago should be placed under some international body upon which the United States would exercise a decisive concern.[1]

Far off in Moscow sat the other member of the Big Three, Joseph Stalin, impatiently waiting for D-Day, but no longer afraid that Russia could lose the war or be deprived of the fruits of victory. At Roosevelt's death, the Russian and Anglo-American armies were only about 125 miles apart—with Berlin between them. But the areas of "liberated" Europe had already become the first battle-fields of the Cold War.

AMBIGUITY AND THE BIG THREE

Roosevelt and Churchill issued an eight-point declaration of war aims on August 14, 1941, known as the Atlantic Charter. Especially significant were points 3 and 4, which pledged the two leaders of the English-speaking world to the restoration of sovereign rights and self-government to those nations that had been deprived of them and to the establishment of conditions that would allow all states access to the trade and raw materials of the world.

The impetus for such a statement on the American side had its immediate origins in fears that Churchill and Stalin had decided to divide post-Hitler Europe into spheres of influence. Troubled memories of Wilson's heroic, but eventually futile, efforts to disentangle the web of "secret treaties," as well as fresh evidence of maneuverings from the time of Munich and the 1939 Nazi-Soviet Pact, reinforced long-held views of European diplomacy and its makers.

Once Churchill returned to England from his conference with Roosevelt, however, he hedged. Faced with questions in the House of Commons, the prime minister reassured the honorable members (and himself) that the charter did not apply to "the regions and peoples which owe allegiance to the British Crown." Then came Russia's turn. The Soviet ambassador signed the charter in London, but as he did so he entered a caveat about the "historic peculiarities of particular countries,"[2] presumably (inevitably) a reference to Eastern Europe.

159

If Churchill's distinction was difficult for American planners to accept before Pearl Harbor, after the Pacific war began it became outright blasphemy. Roosevelt had to issue an American commentary on the charter, which he did, appropriately enough, on Washington's Birthday 1942, reaffirming its applicability to all the world. Was America to free Burma and Indonesia only to see them returned to colonial domination? Impossible. As for Russia's claim to dominate Eastern Europe, well, that would be dealt with at the proper time.

Meanwhile, Stalin was pressing for an immediate decision on his demand for Russia's 1941 frontiers, in essence and in detail what he had gained from the Nazi-Soviet Pact. When Foreign Minister Anthony Eden invoked the Atlantic Charter in December 1941 as his reason for being unable to give a positive reply, Stalin shot back, "I thought that the Atlantic Charter was directed against those people who were trying to establish world dominion. It now looks as if the Charter was directed against the U.S.S.R."[3]

During the next several months, Churchill reconsidered his position. He could continue to ward off unpleasant Soviet territorial demands with references to American opposition, but if he played the game that way he risked surrendering control over all postwar decisions. Thus the prime minister proposed to Stalin in 1944 that they settle territorial questions concerning southeastern Europe, an area in which Russian and British interests had clashed for well over a century.

Churchill had no intention of sneaking off to Moscow behind Roosevelt's back; indeed, he had invited the president to join him and Stalin. Churchill probably knew that Roosevelt could not make such a trip, especially with a presidential election only weeks away. But he apparently hoped for Roosevelt's blessing. What he and Stalin received instead was a warning. "There is in this global war literally no question," Roosevelt cabled, "either military or political, in which the United States is not interested."[4] Whatever Russia and England might decide, he continued, could only be temporary pending a Big Three conference later.

Nevertheless, Churchill proposed again to Stalin that they decide

UNITED
we are strong

UNITED we will win

55 Big Four unity—just as long as it did not mean spheres of influence.

land questions between them, although he cautioned the Russian leader that they should not "use the phrase 'dividing into spheres,' because the Americans might be shocked." Stalin agreed to Churchill's proposal, remarking that he did not much like Roosevelt's message. "It seemed to demand too many rights for the U.S.A. leaving too little for the Soviet Union and Great Britain who after all had a treaty of common assistance."[5]

But while Churchill and Stalin passed back and forth a piece of paper on which figures were scribbled that would determine the fate of the Balkans and Greece, an intense struggle was going on inside the Roosevelt administration. One might say the struggle was inside Roosevelt's mind, because the president, despite the rhetoric of the Four Freedoms speech, the Atlantic Charter, and his other

161

wartime pronouncements was deeply ambiguous. Realism pulled him toward the Big Three, ideology toward traditional American outlooks.

At the Atlantic Charter meeting, the president had surprised Churchill by rejecting a British suggestion that their declaration include a reference to the need for some kind of postwar organization to maintain the peace. Such a statement would create nothing but suspicion and opposition, Roosevelt explained. Moreover, "he himself would not be in favor of the creation of a new Assembly of the League of Nations, at least until after a period of time had transpired and during which an international police force composed of the United States and Great Britain had had an opportunity of functioning."[6] In 1942 the president enlarged the police force to include the Soviet Union and China. To Russian Foreign Minister V. M. Molotov, Roosevelt threw out the comment that the four major nations would find their natural role "as guarantors of eventual peace."

Roosevelt's casual way of dealing with even the most important questions troubled his friends and appalled the staid men of the State Department. To them, the Atlantic Charter meant a commitment against postwar spheres of influence. So did the United Nations declaration of January 1, 1942; and so did the 1943 Declaration of Moscow. Secretary of State Cordell Hull returned from the Russian capital with this last document in his brief case, a symbol, he thought, not only of an American victory over Old World diplomacy but of his personal triumph over the last vestiges of intranationalism in the New Deal. To make sure that everyone understood the purpose of the Moscow declaration, Hull elaborated on its meaning for the public: "As the provisions of the four-nation declaration are carried into effect, there will no longer be need for spheres of influence, for alliances, for balance of power, or any other of the special arrangements through which, in the unhappy past, the nations strove to safeguard their security or to promote their interests."[7]

The war would wipe the slate clean, or if it did not, America would. Roosevelt was more cautious. After receiving a congratulatory letter on the outcome of the 1943 Moscow Conference, he wrote that he would be lucky to accomplish half of what was promised in the public communique. Convinced that peace depended on Big Three unity, Roosevelt wanted to establish strong ties with Great Britain and Russia. Hull had no quarrel with the objective, but if political realism dictated that the Big Three get along, there was still a right way and a wrong way to get along. And Roosevelt was dangerously close to slipping into error by tactical miscalculation. Whenever State Department spokesmen discussed Big Three responsibility, they placed stress on its transitional role—a sort of preamble to a new world order.

But what about the Monroe Doctrine, surely that was America's caveat to the Atlantic Charter? Not at all, Hull would reply later in his *Memoirs*. The United States had demonstrated self-restraint in the Western Hemisphere. "But such self-restraint might not be exercised by a great power in another region, and there might develop, in consequence closed trade areas or discriminatory systems. These would . . . produce serious interregional economic conflicts, with dangerous political repercussions."[8]

Throughout the war, Hull and his aides were primarily concerned with convincing Roosevelt of these truths. He, in turn, would have to make the case with Churchill and Stalin. What came out of these internal deliberations, of course, was the United Nations, with the big-power veto in the Security Council. The crucial issue involved in the establishment of the United Nations has, however, gone largely unnoticed in the Cold War era: Was the United Nations to be a peacemaking or a peacekeeping organization? If the former, it would have an obvious active role in the negotiation of a peace settlement with Germany and its satellites; if the latter, it would be expected to uphold a prior settlement arrived at by Big Three agreement.

Stalin raised this point at dinner on February 4, 1945, the first night of the Yalta Conference, albeit in different words:

Marshal Stalin said that he was prepared in concert with the United States and Great Britain to protect the rights of the small powers but

56 Yalta: the peace that never was.

that he would never agree to having any action of any of the Great Powers submitted to the judgment of the small powers.

The President said he agreed that the Great Powers bore the greater responsibility and that the peace should be written by the Three Powers represented at this table.[9]

Had all of Hull's efforts been in vain? Every issue discussed at Yalta depended on the answer to this question. To prevent Roosevelt from sliding back into Big Three thinking (as he had just done), the State Department had prepared the Declaration of Liberated Europe, incorporating the principles of the Atlantic Charter into a recommendation for an emergency high commission to supervise elections in the "liberated" countries pending the establishment of United Nations authority. Roosevelt presented the declaration to his two "comrades-in-arms," but he refused to push the issue of an election commission.

It would have been better, some later commentators observed, never to have asked Stalin to sign such a document. Stalin was sure to ignore it, leaving Roosevelt or his successor to face the wrath of angry *emigré* groups and an indignant public opinion at home. By February 1945, Roosevelt was aware of the behavior of

164

the Red Army in Eastern Europe and of the British in Greece. Moreover, continues this interpretation, Roosevelt could ascertain from discussions concerning the establishment of a Polish provisional government that the Soviet Union would never honor the declaration. Indeed, the printed record of those conversations leaves room to wonder if Stalin did not assume that the president would wink at what happened in Poland as long as everyone put a good face on the outcome of "free" elections. In any event, the Declaration of Liberated Europe virtually committed the United States to intervene in Eastern Europe, thereby assuring a major confrontation.

For many years after Yalta a different view prevailed among Roosevelt's critics. He was accused of "selling-out" Eastern Europe and China to the Russians. Recently Aleksandr Solzhenitsyn has restated that criticism in biting words:

> World War III began immediately after World War II: The seeds were planted as that war ended, and it first saw the light of day at Yalta in 1945, as the cowardly pens of Roosevelt and Churchill, anxious to celebrate their victory with a litany of concessions, signed away Estonia, Latvia, Lithuania, Moldavia, Mongolia, condemned to death or to concentration camps millions of Soviet citizens, created an ineffectual United Nations Assembly, and finally abandoned Yugoslavia, Albania, Poland, Bulgaria, Rumania, Czechoslovakia, Hungary and East Germany.

Historians have usually explained Roosevelt's ambiguity at Yalta in less emotional terms. There was the problem of his health: he was a dying man who could not concentrate on any issue for long. Some writers have noted that in the weeks following Yalta a decisive change took place in the president's attitude toward the Soviet Union. Others believe that he continued to feel that crucial issues could be resolved—as long as everyone approached matters in a spirit of compromise.

Some of the mystery may not really be very mysterious. Roosevelt was always inclined to agree with whomever was sitting across from him in the Oval Office at the moment. He played with personalities as much as he did with political theories; yet he often succeeded by establishing personal relationships that lasted, even

165

when he felt it necessary to carry out policies disliked by an aide or supporter who had just left his office. What worked on the level of national politics, however, did not usually apply in world politics.

More important, Roosevelt's gestures in the direction of spheres of influence, balance of power, Big Four regionalism, serious as they were, allowed him to postpone a confrontation as long as possible. He thought America would be in the most advantageous position when the showdown came, but it was a moment he did not relish. Too much a Wilsonian to believe in the balance of power as a permanent solution, too little of a utopian to believe everything the Wilsonians told him, Roosevelt waited for something to turn up.

Roosevelt's death on April 12, 1945, cleared the way for others to decide what his policy would have been in the crunch. There was hardly a moment to lose. The United Nations organization meeting was about to be held in San Francisco, and the Big Three had yet to agree on the composition of the Polish provisional government.

During the war an exile government in London had stated its claim to rule postwar Poland; in 1944 a rival "Lublin Committee" appeared under Moscow's aegis. At Yalta it had been agreed that "the Provisional Government which is now functioning in Poland should therefore be reorganized on a broader democratic basis with the inclusion of democratic leaders from Poland itself and from Poles abroad." The West was at a decided disadvantage here, since, as the protocol itself stated, the only government "functioning" in Poland was Lublin. Moreover, who were "democratic leaders"? Anti-Nazis? Or pro-Soviets?

To Churchill's irate fulminations about Poland, Roosevelt had responded on March 29, 1945, that the wording of the protocol reflected a compromise, "but if we attempt to evade the fact that we placed, as clearly shown in the agreement, somewhat more emphasis on the Lublin Poles than on the other two groups from which the new Government is to be drawn I feel we will expose ourselves to the charge that we are attempting to go back on the Crimean decision."[10] Stalin could not, however, also expect to determine which group of Poles should be consulted about broadening the government.

As Washington saw things, the Polish dispute threatened the success of the United Nations organization conference, and, if this sort of problem spread, the chances for lasting peace also would be endangered. Roosevelt's death, while it removed the one man whose prestige could hold the alliance together in the dangerous days ahead, offered an opportunity for his successor to make a much-needed distinction between waging war and writing peace.

Harry Truman was up to the assignment. On April 23, 1945, he met with Molotov. The last time the Russian had been in the White House, Roosevelt had talked about the possibility of enlarging Moscow's role in world affairs, possibly Stalin would like to consider a trusteeship over some colonial area, and so on. But Truman laid it on the line: If Russia expected postwar economic aid for reconstruction, Stalin would have to comply with the Anglo-American interpretation of the Yalta decision on Poland.

But at the Potsdam Conference in July 1945, the last of the wartime summits, Truman found it difficult to get in a word when Churchill and Stalin renewed other arguments, some of which went back for a century and more. Russia was building an "iron fence" around Eastern Europe, complained the prime minister. "All fairy-tales," snorted Stalin. Although he agreed with Churchill, Truman soon tired of listening to their endless arguments. In a Washington conversation with French leader Charles de Gaulle shortly after Potsdam, Truman downgraded traditional power politics, alliances, special guarantees. "The United States possessed a new weapon," he said, "the atomic bomb, which would defeat any aggressor. What the whole world needed most was economic reestablishment. At present, all the powers, including England and Russia, were asking for assistance from the United States."[11]

LEND-LEASE DIPLOMACY

Truman's receptivity to the notion that American technological and economic superiority was more important than diplomatic 167

57 Truman takes over and informs de Gaulle that all nations need American aid.

skill arose naturally from the situation at the end of the war with Europe in ruins, but a good deal of diplomatic effort had gone into economic planning for the peace. It had begun in the 1930s with Cordell Hull's determination to open the "oyster shell," as he described the Ottawa Preference System.

At various times during the negotiations for an Anglo-American trade agreement, State Department aides would pause to lecture their British counterparts on the folly of economic nationalism, whether practiced by Nazi Germany or by the British Empire. Admitting America's past transgressions (some of them very recent, of course), Hull's aides assured Foreign Office and British Treasury representatives that the days of blind protectionism were over. Some concessions were won, in large part because London wanted to encourage collaboration on any level, but the 1938 trade agreement left the basic structure of the Imperial Preference System intact.

168

When Lend-Lease became law in March 1941, the State Department saw a new opportunity to continue the education of their British colleagues. Under Lend-Lease the United States was to provide Great Britain (and then other countries) with badly needed war material and strategic goods. At the end of the war, the recipients were to return whatever items were still serviceable and meet with American negotiators to settle all accounts. Above all, said Roosevelt's representatives when the bill was pending, there was a need and a determination to avoid another war-debts tangle. Churchill once called Lend-Lease the most unsordid act in history.

In the drafts of a master lend-lease agreement with Great Britain, however, the State Department began zeroing in on the Ottawa system. As the Department's experts set about their task, John Maynard Keynes appeared in Washington. He had been sent by the British Treasury to negotiate an amicable settlement of several economic problems that had arisen in the past few months. Keynes's frequent references to the need for postwar trade controls and the other paraphernalia of economic nationalism jangled along

58 John Maynard Keynes, the British negotiator from Lend-Lease to the 1945 loan, always remained a skeptic.

the corridors of the State Department all the way into Secretary Hull's office, where they created quite a clamor.

If his views prevailed, Assistant Secretary of State Adolf Berle wrote of Keynes's visit, "the only economic effect of the war will be that we have moved a closed-economy center from Berlin to London."[12] The British Treasury representative was equally complimentary to American plans, referring to them as "the lunatic proposals of Mr. Hull."[13] The specific point around which these arguments swirled was Article VII of the American draft, which read: "The terms and conditions upon which the United Kingdom receives defense aid . . . shall provide against discrimination in either the United States or the United Kingdom against the importation of any product originating in the other country."

Keynes made good his get-away from Washington without signing the document, and while the State Department hoped to pin down Winston Churchill at the Atlantic Conference, the wily prime minister successfully eluded his pursuers there by pointing out that he could not act without full cabinet and Commonwealth approval. Churchill even managed to water down the economic clauses of the final draft of the Atlantic Charter. But the State Department knew that their quarry could not hide forever: the British had to have a signed agreement before Congress voted on lend-lease renewal in early 1942.

Any lingering British hopes that this might not be the case were dispelled by two messages Roosevelt sent to London urging signature before the agreement became an issue with Congress, and assuring Churchill that in signing he would not be giving a commitment to end imperial preference. "I told you when you were here last, I have great confidence that we can organize a different kind of world where men shall really be free economically as well as politically."[14] What disturbed Churchill's advisers, even as they agreed that there was nothing left to do but sign the lend-lease agreement, was their feeling that Washington's view of the postwar world looked backward instead of at tomorrow's likely realities.

Trade liberalism of the sort Hull preached belonged to the nineteenth century. The British knew; they had lived it to the fullest. It was as if the State Department, and perhaps even Roosevelt himself, wanted to forget about what caused the New Deal. Talk about a world "where men shall really be free economically" sounded out of place in a world where people would probably have difficulty just getting enough to eat. Certainly British plans for a welfare state did not envision the possibility of a return to laissez faire at home or in international trade relations.

British policymakers began to suspect that the State Department, which was obviously taking the leadership role in lend-lease diplomacy, felt that America would be able to avoid either a super New Deal or a postwar depression by maintaining a very high level of exports, regardless of how this policy affected the rest of the world. Hence the constant emphasis in British proposals during wartime talks for an international conference on employment. If America attempted to export its social problem, or, if it failed to take proper precautions against difficulties in restoring the world economy, Britain (and all others closely tied to the American economy) would plunge into a new depression.

These fears were exaggerated, but an exchange between Assistant Secretary of State Will Clayton and White House adviser Harry Hopkins in late 1944 indicated that both conservatives and liberals within the Roosevelt administration thought alike on the importance of foreign trade to the maintenance of freedom at home. The exchange began with Clayton's letter to Hopkins on a prominent economist's remark that strong measures by the national government could maintain domestic employment without expanded foreign trade. "Does he face with equanimity the possibility of a reconversion in our export industries from the present level of 15 billion dollars annually to the prewar level of 3 billion dollars?" Some countries had achieved full employment by government action alone but, "Do we want to adopt the Russian system?" Hopkins agreed fully: "I just cannot understand what is going through the minds of those fellows who wash up foreign trade in such cavalier manner. It seems to me they are quite unrealistic about what makes the wheels go round."[15]

Anglo-American discussions on the postwar international

59 Bretton Woods Conference, July 4, 1944.

economy culminated in the Bretton Woods Conference in 1944, at which the two countries presented plans for the International Monetary Fund (to replace the rigid gold standard of prewar years) and the International Bank for Reconstruction and Development (to supplement and, in part, replace the private loans of the 1920s). Difficult negotiations had preceded Anglo-American agreement. Keynes still had doubts about Washington's preoccupation with realizing Hull's grand vision, but he felt that Britain could live with the Bretton Woods program while remaining free to experiment with socialist solutions to the more troublesome areas of the British economy.

Keynes was disappointed, however, at subsequent conferences at which the United States used its voting power and economic leverage to the fullest to restrict the range of experimentation to traditional capitalist solutions. Harry Dexter White, Keynes's American negotiating partner throughout the war, also felt concern about the development of "power politics" within the IMF and about the relationship between that attitude and the gearing of the American economy to a "foreign market which cannot be maintained beyond the next few years if that long."[16]

Both men were a bit wide of the mark and premature in pronouncing the Bretton Woods program a failure. It lasted for a quarter of a century—until the American economy itself was put in jeopardy by the Vietnam War. Meanwhile, however, what had developed in the management of the IMF and the World Bank had been sketched out in a Treasury Department memorandum dating from the time of the Bretton Woods Conference: "We in the United States believe that the greatest possible freedom should be given to our own businessmen engaged in international trade. But we know that this freedom will be meaningless unless other countries accord an equal measure of freedom to their businessmen."[17] Those Americans who sat on the governing boards of the IMF and World Bank never forgot these guidelines.

Great Britain had been singled out by American planners as the key to the postwar economic situation. Despite an expected decline, the actual volume of world trade that would be likely to pass through the empire and Commonwealth would make or break whatever system the experts might fashion for the future. Provision had been made for socialist economies to participate, if they were willing to abide by capitalist rules in international trade. But suppose that Great Britain attempted to lead the Commonwealth area backward into Imperial Preference or forward into a socialist community of nations? Unlikely as either of these possibilities was of realization, Washington did not want to take a chance.

In the fall of 1945 the United States agreed to lend Great Britain $3.75 billion, on condition that London in turn agree to eliminate currency exchange restrictions within the so-called sterling bloc by mid-1947. Throughout the war, Great Britain had protected its precious dollar holdings and had strengthened imperial ties on the old principle that if you owe someone $10,000 that person controls you, but if you owe $1 million, you control that person. By blocking funds paid to Commonwealth members for raw materials, London prevented a sterling crisis and (complained Washington on frequent occasions) assured its own postwar markets. Pounds that India earned, for example, could not be converted into dollars and used to purchase American goods. It was not simply that Washington coveted Commonwealth markets for American exporters. No one wanted to ruin British economic recovery, only to make sure that the Commonwealth participated fully in the Bretton Woods system.

Nevertheless, and as a result of that participation, Americans did expect to find new outlets and mutually beneficial trade relations with a truly liberated Commonwealth. "Once India gets rid of Imperial Preference," a Dominion spokesman predicted to interested listeners at the National Foreign Trade Convention in 1946, "you might as well supplant Britain as our principal supplier."

LEND-LEASE AND CONTAINMENT

Given the potential for postwar rivalry indicated by statements like the above, Russian Marxist theorists who predicted new depressions and frictions within the capitalist world may have been surprised at the smoothness and effectiveness of American economic diplomacy. They were more concerned, however, with preventing Washington from using some form of lend-lease diplomacy to forestall their own developing plans for Eastern Europe. Desirous of economic aid for reconstruction, Russian leaders were not willing to pay the American price if that meant opening up the countries of Eastern Europe to Western capitalist influences.

In truth, Stalin was not much of a gambler. But he may have thought a good wager could be made on American unwillingness to force a showdown in Eastern Europe if he refrained from interfering with communist leaders in other countries. Hard evidence of Stalin's inclination to try this, or any other, tactic is still lacking. Moreover, the situation in postwar Europe was such that no policymaker was free to act on preconceived notions.

Roosevelt clearly would have liked to persuade the Russian

leader to cooperate with American plans, and to hold out economic inducements for such cooperation, but he never found a way. Neither would his successors, who (of necessity) approached the problem from a somewhat different perspective. From the time Hitler turned on his erstwhile ally, the Soviet Union, in June 1941, both London and Washington were presented with a difficult choice.

If Britain and the United States did nothing to help Russia while Germany conquered vast areas of the Soviet Union and then signed a separate peace similar to the treaty Berlin imposed on Lenin's government twenty years earlier, how could they hope to defeat the Axis? Hitler's access to the agricultural resources and raw materials of Russia would make that task vastly more difficult and costly in terms of economics and human life—if indeed not impossible. But if they decided to supply Russia with the means of resisting the German onslaught, what would the two powers do about the Kremlin's likely postwar territorial demands?

Roosevelt was never deceived about the nature of the Stalinist system. "The Soviet Union," he once told a leftist youth convention delegation, "as everybody who has the courage to face the fact knows, is run by a dictatorship as absolute as any other dictatorship in the world."[18] But it was Churchill who gave the best answer to the immediate question of whether to aid the Soviet Union: "If Hitler invaded Hell I would make at least a favourable reference to the Devil in the House of Commons."[19]

Great Britain was not able to do much more than provide meager aid from its own small stockpiles to go along with this Churchillian rhetoric. The real substance of Western support would have to come from the United States through Lend-Lease. Close advisers encouraged Roosevelt to believe that "if we came through" with economic and military aid, the long-time suspicion between Moscow and Washington "might well be eradicated." Such aid would at least prevent a separate Russo-German peace and was the best option available for dealing with postwar problems. Roosevelt apparently agreed, congratulating Churchill in January 1942 on his continued resistance to Soviet territorial demands with the supportive statement: "The Soviet Union will need our aid for reconstruction far more than we shall need theirs."[20]

That was as close as Roosevelt ever came to formulating a policy to achieve political goals with Stalin. Speculations will never end about what might have happened had the president said at some convenient moment during one of the wartime conferences, "Well, Mr. Stalin, what *would* you be willing to do in exchange for a postwar credit of say $6 to $10 billion—allow us access to Eastern Europe?"

It was not, some argue, the sort of question one broaches in quite those terms. Besides, Roosevelt could not make such an offer on his own, if only because he could not commit Congress. Yet Roosevelt had been urged by Ambassador Averell Harriman in Moscow, who wanted to bargain for specific concessions along these lines, and by Secretary of the Treasury Morgenthau, who had in mind more general considerations, that it was essential to come forward with a concrete plan. Moreover, the Russians had even asked for a multibillion dollar credit for postwar purchases. Despite the gratuitous insinuation in Molotov's pre-Yalta bid for such aid that American capitalists would need the Russian market to stave off a new depression (an impression the Russian leadership may have gotten, by the way, not only from Marxist theory but from visiting American business leaders), Ambassador Harriman advised Washington that the Soviet government placed "high importance" on obtaining a large credit.

How does one explain, finally, that Roosevelt's marvelous inventiveness apparently deserted him on this occasion? The man who had designed the destroyer-bases deal and lend-lease could not come up with a plan by the time of the Yalta Conference or in the weeks thereafter. Instead, economic diplomacy toward Russia became bogged down in details of interest rates and payment procedures. Roosevelt had both encouragement and opportunity. He lacked inspiration. Or is the answer elsewhere? Perhaps it is in the problem of defining *access*. American policymakers appear not to have decided what degree of independence they sought for Eastern Europe, nor Stalin to have decided what degree he was willing to allow at war's end.

Whatever the reason, the first attempt to use economic aid as a diplomatic weapon came when Truman, in a dramatic confrontation, warned Molotov to get in line over Poland. No policy, he instructed the Russian foreign minister on April 23, 1945, could succeed in the United States unless it enjoyed public support. Congress must approve and authorize any economic measures in the foreign field. He hoped, Truman ended their conversation, that Molotov would keep that point in mind as postwar discussions began.

It was hardly the way one talked to a close ally, especially before the war had ended, but what were the new president's choices? His problems were not Roosevelt's; his success or failure would not be judged by the achievement of V-E or V-J Day, but by the terms of peace. Roosevelt had given no lead for economic diplomacy with the Russians. There was scarcely time for Truman, even had he been suited for the role, to develop the kind of personal relationship Roosevelt had established with Churchill and Stalin. As he saw it, the best way to avoid an even more serious confrontation in the future was to define his policy now, before positions became frozen.

Molotov could not easily respond, however, on the same level without appearing to yield to unlimited demands. If Truman got what he wanted in Poland, what would he ask next? Molotov complained bitterly to Secretary of State Edward R. Stettinius that an attempt was being made to shove the Soviet Union back into the ranks of second-rate powers. Truman abruptly stopped lend-lease aid to the Soviet Union after V-E Day, then restored it on a more selective basis for the duration of the Pacific war. Relief aid continued as well while Truman and his aides sought the magic formula that Roosevelt had failed to find in three years of searching. For a time the possibility was discussed of using credits and loans to entice former German satellites into defying the Soviet Union before Peoples' Democracies were firmly established and all nations but Russia excluded. That proved to be a false hope.

No one in Washington argued that American capitalism depended on any or all of the Eastern European countries as outlets for manufactured goods and as sources of raw materials. That notion would

177

have seemed ridiculous to policymakers and business leaders alike. Hull had not argued in 1938 that American business needed Manchuria and North China; what he had said, and it still applied, was that the United States regarded an endeavor by any country "in any part of the world" to establish for itself a preferred position as "incompatible with the maintenance of our own and the establishment of world prosperity." In the case of postwar Europe, a Russian sphere of influence in the East would divide the continent into capitalist and communist blocs, with serious economic and political consequences. A tier of communist states presented the possibility, as Ambassador Harriman once put it, of a second tier, and a third tier, and so on. By withholding raw materials, the ruble bloc could influence the political behavior of Western Europe. A ruble bloc, operating on communist principles (as defined by Stalin and the Politburo), could disrupt the world marketplace, hinder recovery, and endanger the economies of states "unfriendly" to the Soviet Union. There were, in short, many reasons to prevent the Soviets from establishing themselves in Eastern Europe—but so far no way to do it. As Truman said after Potsdam, America had the atom bomb, but, however much policymakers hoped it might be useful in making the Russians "more manageable," neither he nor his successors ever unlocked the secret of atomic diplomacy. Possession of the bomb may have given Truman a badly needed boost and may have encouraged him to take more risks in pressing Stalin to allow a measure of access to Eastern Europe, but that was all it did as far as Europe was concerned.

THE TRUMAN DOCTRINES

President Truman had promised the nation after Potsdam that Rumania, Bulgaria, and Hungary were not going to become "spheres of influence of any one power." He assigned Secretary of State James F. Byrnes the task of fulfilling that pledge. All things considered, Byrnes did pretty well. After a false start at the London Foreign Ministers' Conference in the fall of 1945, the secretary made a wise tactical decision to take one step backward into Big Three diplomacy. Although Truman was not pleased with Byrnes's

60 Foreign Minister V. M. Molotov speaks out for the "rights" of small nations.

nonchalant attitude about keeping the White House informed, the secretary pinned Stalin down to a large peace conference to approve draft treaties with the former German satellites.

When the conference assembled the following summer in Paris, Foreign Minister Molotov complained at length about American insistence on equality of opportunity. Suppose, he stated, that in some "war-weakened state, you have this so-called equal opportunity for, let us say, American capital—that is, the opportunity for it to penetrate unhindered into Rumanian industry, or Yugoslav industry and so forth: what, then, will remain of Rumania's national industry, or of Yugoslavia's national industry?"[21]

Nevertheless, peace treaties assuring all members of the United Nations equal economic opportunities in the countries now under Russian domination for at least eighteen months were agreed on at a final session of the elongated peace conference. By the time an

61 Winston Churchill discusses the "iron curtain" that had fallen between Russia and the West.

agreement was reached, in November 1946, the Cold War had spread to other areas. Eastern Europe, the locale of the original conflict, was now only a sideshow in what had taken on all the aspects of a global struggle.

Churchill, defeated in the British general elections of 1945, came to the United States in early 1946 to receive an honorary degree at Westminster College in Truman's home state of Missouri. While Truman sat behind him on the stage, Churchill described the "iron *curtain*" that had descended across Europe from Stettin in the Baltic to Trieste in the Adriatic, warned of the communist fifth columns "throughout the world," which constituted a "growing challenge and peril to Christian civilization," and concluded by thanking God that the knowledge, method, and raw materials for the atom bomb "are at present largely retained in American hands."

Meanwhile, Russia's second application for a large credit, this time for $1 billion, was inexplicably lost in the State Department, apparently while the economic experts were off pressing for an international trade organization that would prohibit any member from seeking exclusive or preferential advantages "in the territory of any non-member which would result, directly or indirectly, in discrimination against the trade of any other member." Translated into plain English, this obtuse phrase meant that ITO members would be forbidden from entering into bilateral agreements with the Soviet Union that might restrict their ability to participate in the American-sponsored system.

As the year wore on, American policymakers seemed undecided about whether to try to isolate the Soviet bloc or to continue their efforts to force its early disintegration. A military move against the Red Army was out of the question. There were not enough atomic bombs available to insure a speedy defeat of Russia in what would probably become the Third World War. For a time at least, it was necessary to concede to Stalin control of an area vaster than any the tsars had claimed. Eventually discussion centered around the recommendations of a hitherto unknown Foreign Service Officer serving in Russia, George F. Kennan. According to memoranda Kennan sent to Washington in early 1946, the successful isolation

62 George F. Kennan, the author of the most famous article of the Cold War, ultimately became the victim of his own orthodoxy.

of the Soviet bloc would promote "tendencies which must eventually find their outlet in either the break-up or the gradual mellowing of Soviet power."

This was the heart of the "containment" thesis, which first appeared in print in the July 1947 issue of the prestigious journal *Foreign Affairs*. Kennan's name, however, did not appear in the table of contents as the author of the article, "The Sources of Soviet Conduct," which was listed under the mysterious pseudonym Mr. "X," a device one policymaker later explained was used to make it possible to state an official position without committing anyone to specifics. In other words, it was the first "backgrounder" of the Cold War. Later administrations would perfect the "backgrounder" into the fine art of planting a story in the press without taking responsibility for all the information or specifics of the viewpoint thus revealed. The "backgrounder" enabled succeeding administrations to lead public opinion without violating the presumed tenets of a free-press system.

Appearing when it did, the "X" article offered Americans the hope of eventual victory in the Cold War, a victory to be won without an atomic holocaust or a toe-to-toe battle with the Red Army. "The issue of Soviet-American relations," Kennan wrote, "is in essence a test of the over-all worth of the United States as a nation among nations." The thoughtful observer would find no cause for complaint in the Kremlin's fateful challenge. "He will rather experience a certain gratitude to a Providence which, by providing the American people with this implacable challenge, has made their entire security as a nation dependent on their pulling themselves together and accepting the responsibilities of moral and political leadership that history plainly intended them to bear."[22]

Woodrow Wilson had never said it better. Neither had Theodore Roosevelt. Nor would John F. Kennedy. Although in a series of lectures given three years later he was to deprecate messianic idealism in American diplomacy, Kennan's mysticism here came right out of the legends of Manifest Destiny. And although he had recommended confronting the Russians with force wherever their expansionist urges endangered Western interests, Kennan came to re-sent what was being said and done in the name of "containment." In 1947, in fact, he was already at odds with his colleagues in the State Department over a plan for military aid to Greece and Turkey.

Whatever openings the peace treaties with former German satellites had seemed to expose in the Iron Curtain had to be ignored when conditions in Western Europe worsened during the winter of 1946/47. The situation in Greece was especially perilous. Great Britain, still gasping for breath itself, had undertaken to restore a promonarchy regime in Athens, only to find itself involved in a civil war. Greek partisans, led in some instances by communists, had vowed that there would be no return to the prewar dictatorship that had thrived under the king. They were aided by Yugoslav partisans, who, under Marshal Tito, had fought and won a similar battle. Stalin's role in the Greek civil war is less clear. In 1944 he had promised Churchill to stay out of that area, a stance the prime minister had gratefully acknowledged in the House of Commons.

When accusations concerning intervention in the Balkans started flying back and forth at Yalta and Potsdam, the Soviet leader may have decided that his earlier bargain was no longer in force and that he was free to do as he pleased. The partisans always recalled that Stalin was very free indeed with promises, but failed to deliver. However that may be, the British had come to the end of their rope in Greece by early 1947. Forewarnings of this dramatic moment had reached Washington by various routes, and on February 21, 1947, the news actually arrived via a note from the British Embassy to the State Department. World leadership had passed from England to the United States, for if Greece (and the whole Mediterranean area) were to be saved, only America could do it.

At least that was the mood that prevailed in the State Department once the British note had been circulated and little groups had gathered in Under Secretary of State Dean Acheson's office to discuss what must be done before Britain pulled out at the end of March. One overriding fear was expressed: What if Congress failed to understand? Although the Second World War had made important converts to internationalism among the Republicans from

183

America's heartland, that wing of the party was still inclined to backslide. Moreover, politics-as-usual was once again the order of the day. Within the Democratic party the New Deal coalition was in serious trouble.

In sum, as Senator Arthur Vandenberg told the president after listening to Acheson's gloomy survey of the world situation, if he wanted to get Congress to act he would have to "scare hell out of the country." Truman took Vandenberg's advice to heart. But there is no reason to doubt that he believed every word he delivered in a speech to Congress on March 12, 1947, which immediately became known as the Truman Doctrine. Truman noted in his *Memoirs* that although he was perfectly aware of the Russian threat to the "raw material balance of the world" in the Middle East–Mediterranean area, he turned down the first State Department draft of his planned message because it sounded too much like an "investment prospectus." When the second draft reached his desk, he scratched out the word *should* and wrote in *must* in the key sentence, which then read, "I believe that it must be the policy of the United States to support free peoples who are resisting attempted subjugation by armed minorities or by outside pressures."[23]

"This was America's answer to the surge of expansion of Communist tyranny. It had to be clear and free of hesitation or double talk," Truman concluded in his *Memoirs*.[24] The president was pleased with the reception of his speech; the senators and representatives rose as one man to applaud. Only one, Vito Marcantonio, the American Labor party representative from New York City, remained seated. When hearings began on legislation to implement the Truman Doctrine by providing military aid to Greece and Turkey, a somewhat different attitude prevailed. Questions arose in public sessions about the Greek government's commitment to democracy and its responsiveness to the will of the people. These problems were admitted by administration spokesmen, but they stressed that the alternative would be worse.

In private discussions, the members of the Senate Foreign Relations Committee expressed concern about the open-ended nature of the Truman Doctrine. Said Walter F. George, an administration floor leader six years before in the lend-lease debate: "I do not see how we are going to escape going into Manchuria, North China, and Korea and doing things in that area of the world. . . . You go down to the end of the road. . . ."[25]

That was the trouble with containment. No limit could be put on it. Areas that were defined as nonstrategic one day turned up the next as the newest battlefield between communist tyranny and capitalist liberty: "You go down to the end of the road. . . ." As the senators pondered this matter, Vandenberg raised another problem. Truman's message was almost like a declaration of war, he said; if Congress now refused to support him, would that not tempt the Soviets to push ahead, regardless of their original intentions? "We would have lost any chance whatsoever to find a peaceful basis of settlement with the Soviet Union. . . ." It was with some uneasiness about the future, then, that the Senate Foreign Relations Committee voted for the Truman Doctrine.

Although an effort was made during the Greek-Turkish crisis to portray the Soviet Union as threatening military action should the United States back away from the challenge, neither Truman nor his close advisers believed it likely. Why should the Russians risk an armed attack when they were doing so well already? No, the argument for the Truman Doctrine was more subtle. Thus Truman wrote: "The success of Russia in such areas [Greece and Turkey] and our avowed lack of interest would lead to the growth of domestic Communist parties in such European countries as France and Italy, where they were already significant threats."[26]

Truman's memory often reordered events and themes into a consistent pattern that never existed at the time, but contemporary evidence supports him on this point. American policymakers did view the Soviet threat primarily in political terms. This is not to say that they did not believe that the United States could be put into a position where it felt war was the only answer. However, the vast military-aid programs that grew out of the Truman Doctrine were always ancillary to the primary purpose of American policy. The term *Cold War* covers the situation well, but, as historians have found, it is well-neigh undefinable.

It was a grave decision to militarize Soviet-American competition in the atomic age, but, reasoned policymakers, it would be graver still to allow events to drift to a point where there might be no alternative to unleashing the holocaust. On June 23, 1947, Secretary of the Navy James Forrestal asked Truman at a cabinet meeting to comment on the possibility of a Russian *démarche*, accompanied by simultaneous coups in France and Italy. The president replied that the answer would have to be found in history, "the struggle between the Romans and Carthage, between Athens and Sparta, between Alexander the Great and the Persians, between France and England, between England and Germany."[27]

In this context the arms race soon took on a rationale all its own. The Greek-Turkish crisis and the Truman Doctrine had the desired effect of convincing many Americans that they were engaged in a mortal struggle with an unrelenting foe who would use any means to achieve its end. Perhaps the military image was the only way to convey to the public the urgent necessity of meeting the Soviet challenge. Kennan deplored the rhetoric of the Truman Doctrine, but he himself had used similar images in the "X" article, referring at one point to the need to confront the Russians with unalterable counterforce "at every point where they show signs of encroaching upon the interests of a peaceful world."

Kennan was much happier, however, when given the assignment of working out the details of an extensive economic-aid program for Western Europe. Soon to be known as the Marshall Plan, the primary feature that Kennan and his group of State Department planners contributed was that the Europeans propose a plan for joint action, an integrated approach that would make impossible the rebirth of economic nationalism.

REPARATIONS AND THE ORIGINS OF THE COLD WAR IN EUROPE AND ASIA

Kennan's group also recommended the early reintegration of Germany into the European economy. That would not be easy: Germany had been divided into military occupation zones, and the Russians were sure to protest that any policy to incorporate the three western zones into a reorganized and "Americanized" Europe was designed to deny them war reparations and to reestablish the German "bulwark" against the Bolshevik menace—a policy that they claimed had produced Hitler and appeasement in the 1930s.

Ever since Roosevelt had rejected the "Morgenthau Plan" in 1944 for the deindustrialization of postwar Germany, long-range planning for the future Germany had been stalled. The American attitude toward reparations, for example, had never been clearly defined. No one wanted to repeat the post-First World War reparations–debts tangle. Some policymakers also feared that by extracting heavy reparations from Germany, the victors would discredit, as Weimar had been discredited, any new German government. Finally, if Europe was to function successfully in the world economy, Germany could not be ignored.

As in the case of Eastern Europe, the key issue was not American requirements for markets and raw materials, but what a successful liberal capitalist economy in the western zones would mean to the world system the United States hoped to organize—and what failure in Germany would mean to the ultimate prospects for that system. It was now clear, argued policymakers, that Russia's intentions were far from benign. Did it make any sense to help the Kremlin by forcing Germany to pay billions in reparations?

At Yalta, Stalin had asked for $10 billion as the Soviet Union's proper due for the destruction Germany had inflicted in his country. Over Churchill's strong protests, Roosevelt had agreed to take that figure as a basis for discussion. What Roosevelt planned next to resolve the contradiction between that seeming commitment and the requirements of sound economic policy has never been learned. An intriguing suggestion is that he intended to use reparations and economic aid for Russia in tandem. When it became clear to Stalin that nothing like $10 billion could be made available, the Soviet dictator would be more amenable to some combination package involving a relaxation of the Russian grip on Eastern Europe. That might explain why Roosevelt did not come forward with a specific plan for postwar aid at Yalta.

Less speculative is the connection between State Department

recommendations for Germany in 1947 and Cordell Hull's negative report to the president on a proposed bilateral trade "deal" with Nazi Germany dated December 14, 1934. Multilateralism, concluded the secretary of state, "is the corner stone of our present foreign policy and of our reciprocal trade agreement program." By entering into a bilateral arrangement with Germany, the United States would only strengthen a regime dedicated to the destruction of liberalism. In a similar fashion, the reparations question endangered Germany's present and future, and thus the world.

But Russia and reparations were not the only obstacles in Germany. Great Britain had been assigned the Ruhr area as part of its zone of occupation. But Britain was now ruled by the Labour party, whose administrators in Germany would presumably opt for socialist solutions to recovery problems. The third western zone was run by France, which seemed bent only on forcing the Germans to pay tribute. Originally, it was France also that refused to put into operation interzonal policies desired by the other occupying powers. In early 1946, General Lucius Clay, the American commander in Germany, had ordered a halt to reparations shipments to Russia. Clay did this, he said, because no all-German agreements had been reached. In fact, Clay desired an opportunity to reconsider the German "problem" as a whole.

As might be imagined, the Russians were infuriated by Clay's action, and they continued to protest that the Marshall Plan was designed to deny them any reparations. Warning France and England that they were sacrificing their interests to American ruling circles, Soviet Foreign Minister Molotov departed Paris, where the preliminary meetings were being held, in a huff. His attendance at these ground-breaking sessions of the European Recovery Program was the result of a calculated risk by American planners. Not wanting to take the onus for dividing Europe, and wishing to project a more positive image of American policy than the Truman Doctrine, they had recommended that the secretary of state invite Russia and the satellite nations to participate.

As the policymakers had predicted, Molotov said no to the notion of an integrated European economy and forced the delegates from Czechoslovakia, who had shown great interest in the American proposal, to withdraw with him from the conference table. From Moscow, Ambassador Walter Bedell Smith drew the conclusion that the Czechoslovakian humiliation, following a hasty consultation in the Kremlin, was

> nothing less than a declaration of war by the Soviet Union on the immediate issue of the control of Europe. The lines are drawn. Our response is awaited. I do not need to point out to the Dept [Department of State] the repercussions of a failure to meet the Soviet challenge, in terms not only of the control of Europe, but of the impact which such a failure would have in the Middle and Far East and throughout the colonial world.[28]

The lines were also drawn inside Western Europe. George Kennan, the head of the Policy Planning Staff, recommended that the United States "place squarely before the French the choice between a rise in German production or no European recovery financed by the U. S."[29] Rising tensions throughout Europe in the summer and fall of 1947 thus accomplished for the United States what persuasion had failed to do. Nations caught in between, such as Austria and Czechoslovakia, found "neutralism" impossible.

Early in 1948 communist members of the Czech government refused to cooperate with the government of Eduard Beneš. Backed by the power of Soviet armies camped on the borders of the country, they demanded, and received, full power. The Czech coup of February 25, 1948, completed the division of Europe—save for one outpost of Western influence behind the Iron Curtain. Berlin, like Germany, had been divided into four occupation zones. Having overcome French opposition to their plans, American policymakers were proceeding in 1948 to introduce a trizonal currency reform, which would also be instituted in the Western sectors of Berlin. Testifying before Congress in 1947, General John Hilldring had said, "If we succeed in the program we have instituted now in western Germany, it will require all our partners in Germany, including the Soviets, to carry out their agreement arrived at Potsdam."[30]

For more than two years Clay and his political advisers had been stressing the "economic magnet" thesis, which postulated that economic recovery in West Germany would draw East Germany (and perhaps the rest of Eastern Europe) out from under Soviet control. A few weeks before the United States introduced the currency-reform measures, Secretary of State Marshall recommended to President Truman that he receive several exiled leaders from Eastern European countries in order to demonstrate continuing American interest in the area and to "give the USSR cause to speculate as to future United States intentions toward such regimes. . . ."[31] It was the anniversary week of the Truman Doctrine; this year the president went before Congress with the message that the Marshall Plan was still not enough. Europe must also have "some measure of protection against internal and external aggression." Congress had its own ideas about how to run a Cold War, however, and rejected universal military training but approved 25 percent higher funds than had been requested by the administration for a seventy-group air force.

The atmosphere could hardly have been more highly charged as the day approached for the introduction of the Western currency reforms. On March 20, 1948, the Soviet representative had stalked out of an Allied Control Council meeting in Berlin, asserting that he had not been informed of Western plans. Eleven days later the Russians began obstructing traffic entering West Berlin. On June 23, the currency reform was carried out. The next day the "Berlin Blockade" began.

For more than a year the United States supplied West Berliners with the essentials of life by an airlift that demonstrated every hour America's great technological and economic resources and its humanitarian concern. Every day of the blockade also revealed Soviet intransigence and brutality. During those twelve months Trizonia (the three western zones) became the Federal Republic of Germany, the European Recovery Program began functioning, and the North Atlantic Treaty Organization came into being. In the East, the Molotov Plan answered ERP, and the Warsaw Pact, NATO. The Russians still controlled Eastern Europe, but there was no longer any serious danger of communist unheavals in the West.

63   The Berlin airlift.

If Americans felt they had a right to exchange congratulations over the way the Cold War had stabilized in Europe, they were decidedly unhappy with each other over the denouement in Asia. China had been "lost" to the communists, and the rest of Asia, ravaged by war and aflame with nationalism, seemed in danger as well. Japan lacked the capability—perhaps also the will—to reassert its leadership. And the United States, caught between old alliances with European colonial powers and a desire to encourage nationalist leaders, was clearly floundering.

China had been awarded Big Four status during the war at American insistence. No one, not even Roosevelt, assumed that Chiang Kai-shek's government was the equal of the great powers, yet it was hoped that China would replace Japan as the principal stabilizing power in Asia. For his part, Chiang hoped that the United

64   The last days of the Open Door policy.

States, in the process of driving the Japanese out of China, would take care of the communist problem. Neither hope was realized.

In private conversations at Yalta, Roosevelt and Stalin struck a Far Eastern bargain that was to become an issue in American politics for nearly a generation. In exchange for Russian promises to enter the war against Japan within three months of V-E Day and to sign a treaty of friendship and alliance with Nationalist China, the president agreed to a restoration of old tsarist extraterritorial rights in Manchuria. What could not be compromised with Japan in the 1930s, complained critics when the accord was made public, Roosevelt blithely signed away. There was some substance to this complaint, but it is far from the complete story.

Above all else Roosevelt desired a solid relationship between 192   Russia and Nationalist China. He had been warned that Chiang's greatest danger would arise from a Russian-supported communist Chinese military offensive. Russia's signature on a treaty of friendship and alliance would supposedly deprive the Chinese Communist leader, Mao Tse-tung, of outside aid. That accomplished, it would presumably be possible to lead the communists into a coalition government dominated by the Kuomintang, thereby absorbing the revolutionary threat. Things did not work out the way Roosevelt planned, but, however unknowingly, Stalin also risked Russia's future relations with the Chinese communists by trying to cash in on the Yalta promises.

In the meantime, however, relations had cooled between the United States and the Soviet Union. By mid-summer 1945 Washington hoped to end the Pacific war before Russia came barging in across Manchuria. The atomic bombs dropped on Hiroshima and Nagasaki on August 6 and 9, 1945, brought the war to an end—but not quite fast enough. Russian forces occupied Manchuria, turned over some captured weapons to Mao's forces, then rushed on to claim Port Arthur and Dairen, as stipulated in the Yalta agreement. When Mao went to Moscow, Stalin advised him to return home and pursue the revolution through political means. The United States was by now busy ferrying between four and five hundred thousand Chinese Nationalist troops into new positions in North China and Manchuria, transporting thousands of others to Formosa, and establishing the Military Advisers' Group to advise Chiang after the war. Lend-lease continued well into 1948, totaling about $750 million. And more than fifty thousand marines remained in China after Japan's surrender, with orders to control key communications and transportation centers.

Once these preparations were completed, Truman sent a special ambassador, George C. Marshall, to "mediate" the dispute between Chiang and Mao. Disregarding American military advice, Chiang determined that he must launch a final offensive against Mao's position in Manchuria. Perhaps he expected that the American commitment was strong enough to permit him to take this risk; if things did not work out, the United States army would come to his rescue. If so, that expectation went unfulfilled.

Aside from military doubts about Nationalist strategy, political officers in the State Department had strong reservations about Chiang's capacity to unite the noncommunist forces. Total aid to Chiang, concluded the head of the Far Eastern Division, would mean "only trouble, trouble, trouble. . . ." Convinced that the Nationalists would lose a civil war, American policymakers aimed at reforming and strengthening the central government. General Marshall's integrity was a vital asset to American plans. Above all, the communists must not come to believe that his mediation was only a cover for Nationalist aggression. Marshall complained to Chiang on several occasions that his pledges of good faith were being abused for just such a nefarious purpose. Chiang's response was to invite the general who had planned the invasion of Europe to become his chief military adviser and command the Nationalist troops in their final victory. What more need be said, or could be said, of such madness?

THE AGENT THESIS AND AMERICAN COLD WAR POLICY

Ironically, as the United States lost interest in protecting Chiang from his folly, the Kuomintang leader received hints from Moscow that perhaps Russia and Nationalist China could find common cause against a revitalized Japan. Stalin's continuing underestimation of Mao's military capabilities, his seeming preoccupation with Manchurian baubles for a new Russian empire, and his exaggerated concern about Japan's likely resurgence, proved as shortsighted as any State Department notion of the Chinese communists as "agrarian reformers" easily converted to liberal democracy. The seeds of Sino-Soviet discord were planted early.

Meanwhile, however, Congress was growing increasingly unhappy with Truman's Far Eastern policy. The idea of shifting support to Japan appalled some members of the China "lobby," who had little difficulty recruiting Republicans generally on the issue that the Yalta "sell-out" and subsequent betrayals by men in high office had made Chiang's defeat inevitable. But the Democrats had managed very well to get themselves into this predicament. First there had been Roosevelt's solemn talk about the Big Four, supported by the best Office of War Information full-color shots of Chiang seated with Churchill and Roosevelt at the Cairo Conference of 1943. Even Truman was apparently taken in by this nonsense, remarking in his *Memoirs* that he had always assumed China was a unified country, only to find on assuming office that it was little more than a "geographical expression."

Second, and probably more important, the "containment" policy posited a world in which the Kremlin became responsible for everything that went wrong. Moscow's fifth column was at work around the globe, fomenting revolution in one country, stealing atomic secrets from another. A Red Scare on a level far above that that had developed after the First World War was about to become a permanent fact of life in America.

Little wonder, then, that many Americans simply assumed that "agents" had caused the "loss" of China. The presence of the Red Army in Eastern Europe, however distasteful it was to admit, could be accepted as a fortune of war. But once the "containment" formula was applied to Greece and Turkey, the distinction between areas under the control of the Red Army and areas experiencing revolutionary nationalism disappeared. The Chinese Revolution thus was regarded as part of the Kremlin's master plan for world conquest rather than something the Chinese could do on their own.

However convenient the agent thesis was (or would become) to those who regarded any disturbance of the status quo as a threat to American interests, it was difficult in those early Cold War days for ordinary citizens to understand why, if the Russians had stolen the Chinese revolution, the men in the Truman administration just shrugged their shoulders. Surely China was as important as Greece. Secretary of State Dean Acheson seemed positively and infuriatingly unmoved by the enormity of what had befallen one of America's oldest, and potentially most important, friends. At the height of this controversy, Acheson delivered a major speech on recent developments in China. He asked Americans to stop looking under the bed for answers. But in the next breath he stated that

65 Dean Acheson thought that Mao was the "spearhead of Russian imperialism."

communism was the "spearhead of Russian imperialism" and warned that those in China who were allowing themselves "to be used as puppets of Moscow" would one day face the "righteous anger, and the wrath, and the hatred of the Chinese people. . . ."[32]

Developed by Acheson and others in later speeches, this theme was consistent with the agent theory as it evolved out of the "X" article, but it had the unfortunate effect of confirming Republican criticisms of the China policy. If the Chinese communists were only puppets of Moscow, why had not someone cut the strings? Obviously a major failure had occurred, which the Democrats were trying to cover up. Thus the Democrats themselves set the stage for Senator Joseph McCarthy's dramatic entrance at Wheeling, West Virginia, waving a sheaf of papers on which, he claimed, were enscribed the names of 205 communist traitors in the State Department. The number changed from day to day, but McCarthy's message was always the same.

196   In an effort to prevent the attack of the primitives, as Acheson

liked to refer to the McCarthyite plague, from enlisting responsible Republicanism in its cause, and to infuse Far Eastern policy with some badly needed bipartisanship, Truman invited a leading Republican, John Foster Dulles, to accept responsibility for drafting a Japanese peace treaty. Since V-J Day in August 1945, General Douglas MacArthur had ruled in Tokyo with viceregal authority, ignoring the complaints of British and Russian members of the Far Eastern Commission. While this had the advantage of avoiding the difficulties with four-power control as encountered in Germany, it also meant that anything and everything that went wrong was blamed on the United States alone.

When Dulles went to Tokyo to talk with MacArthur, he found the general in a gloomy mood. Economic recovery had not followed his political reforms; the rest of the world refused to import Japanese goods. It was by no means certain that Japan would stand with the West in a confrontation with the Soviet Union and Communist China. At most, he argued, the United States had five years

66 Senator Joseph McCarthy strains to hear another "witness" to the Great Sellout.

67 General Douglas MacArthur and John Foster Dulles in Tokyo: with China gone, what would happen to Japan?

to complete its self-assumed task: the democratization and liberalization of the Japanese political economy. Dulles was impressed by what he heard. It agreed with his own beliefs. On his return to the United States, Dulles became a leading exponent of the view that the Japanese must be assured an outlet in Southeast Asia for their products.

Where else could they go? Deprived of the Chinese market, unwanted in European and American markets, the Japanese had nothing to hope for except Southeast Asia. Interestingly, this was also the conclusion of George Kennan, who told a round-table discussion group in the State Department in October 1949 that was considering what to do after China's expected fall: "Clearly we have got, if we are going to retain any hope of having healthy, stable civilization in Japan in this coming period, to achieve opening up of trade possibilities . . . on a scale far greater than anything Japan knew before." The Japanese would have to reopen some sort of empire toward the south.[33]

Japan expert Edwin O. Reischauer spoke to the same issue, with a slightly different emphasis. The Chinese communists were on a different time schedule, he began. They could afford a twenty-year industrialization program. Japan had to live immediately; it was already an industrial power. Moreover, Japan could help greatly in the revival of the whole Far Eastern economy. "I mean this whole concept of production of rice in Siam and Indo-China is premised on the supposition it can be exchanged for Japanese industrial goods."[34]

KOREA

Any idea on the Japanese side that the United States did not intend to develop that trade, Reischauer concluded, would be disastrous not only economically but ideologically as well. Dulles pondered a related ideological question: Suppose the Japanese and other Asian peoples began to feel that the United States regarded communism as the wave of the future, what then? In a memorandum written to himself after a discussion with Truman on May 18, 1950, the future secretary of state decided: "This series of disasters can probably be prevented if at some doubtful point we quickly take a dramatic and strong stand that shows our confidence and resolution. Probably this series of disasters cannot be prevented in any other way."[35]

A more doubtful point than the 38th parallel in Korea was difficult to imagine. At least three times between 1945 and 1950 the Joint Chiefs of Staff had recommended against military involvement—for any reason—on the Korean peninsula. Korea had been divided between Russia and America at war's end along the 38th parallel, and the victors could not decide what to do about a permanent government for the country. Japan had ruled Korea for forty years, although strong nationalist movements had not ceased to operate outside the country. Russia's interest in Korea—the two countries shared a few miles of border south of Vladivostok—had led to the Russo-Japanese War. After the Second World War, Stalin installed Kim Il-sung in the northern city of Pyongyang, while in the south, the old nationalist Syngham Rhee headed a rival government in Seoul. The withdrawal of most Russian and American forces was not accompanied by a political settlement. Both governments claimed to represent Korea, but Rhee held Seoul, the old capital.

Whether Stalin ordered, or stimulated, the North Korean attack on South Korea early in the morning of June 25, 1950, remains a mystery. He had reasons for doing so, including, perhaps, a belief that the United States would not support the obstreperous Rhee, who seemed determined to follow Chiang's path to disaster. Moreover, Secretary Acheson had defined Korea as outside the American "defense perimeter" earlier in the year. But Truman reacted to the attack instantaneously. He later explained that he was thinking of the failure to back Harry Stimson in Manchuria. As he thought more about the situation, additional reasons came to mind. Korea, he told advisers, was the "Greece" of the Far East, a probing action on the borders of the Free World. If not resisted there, the communists would be tempted to try the same thing in truly strategic areas—Iran, perhaps even Berlin.

It would be a mistake, however, to regard Korea as simply "Mr. Truman's War." The basic strategy of American foreign policy was a collective effort. "Containment" had recently been reexamined in light of the Russian explosion of an atomic bomb. The resulting document, National Security Council Paper Number 68 (NSC-68), dated April 14, 1950, reaffirmed Mr. "X"'s conclusions.[36] "[A]ny substantial further extension of the area under the domination of the Kremlin would raise the possibility that no coalition adequate to confront the Kremlin with greater strength could be assembled. It is in this context that this Republic and its citizens in the ascendancy of their strength stand in their deepest peril."

That still did not necessarily mean South Korea was all-important, but elsewhere in the document reference was made to the 1948 Czech coup: "The shock we sustained in the destruction of Czechoslovakia was not in the measure of Czechoslovakia's material importance to us. . . . [W]hen the integrity of Czecho-slovak institutions was destroyed, it was in the intangible scale of values that we registered a loss more damaging than the material loss we had already suffered."

Accommodation with the Soviet Union was impossible, how-ever, until a "fundamental change" took place in the "nature of the Soviet system." The first step in bringing about such a change would be the frustration of the Soviet "design" for the West's destruction. "[T]he Kremlin is inescapably militant. It is inescap-ably militant because it possesses and is possessed by a world-wide revolutionary movement, because it is the inheritor of Russian imperialism and because it is a totalitarian dictatorship. Persistent crisis, conflict and expansion are the essence of the Kremlin's militancy."

The Russian atomic bomb demonstrated another fact about the Kremlin program. With its lower standard of living, Russia could use more of its resources in special projects necessary to put it into a position to challenge the West. A full-scale effort by the United States could alter this trend. "The fact remains, however, that so long as the Soviet Union is virtually mobilized, and the United States has scarcely begun to summon up its forces, the greater capabilities of the U.S. are to that extent inoperative in the struggle for power."

That certainly seemed to be the case in the first few weeks of battle in Korea. It appeared that American aid would not be enough. Then MacArthur launched his famous Inchon offensive, a difficult amphibious operation in the rear of the North Korean army, and the complexion of the war changed. One month later he flew into Pyongyang, the first "liberated" communist capital since the Second World War. "Any celebrities here to greet me?" he de-manded. "Where's Kim Buck Too?"[37] MacArthur's forces included token regiments from United Nations members. With Russia ab-sent, the Security Council had voted to condemn North Korea's ac-tion and to send military forces to Korea. MacArthur was desig-nated United Nations Commander, but he took his orders from Washington.

The drive to the Yalu River stopped dead in its tracks when the Chinese intervened in December. Acheson later conceded that it probably had been a mistake to ignore Chinese warnings about any offensive that threatened the border with Manchuria. At the time, he dismissed them as "hot air." MacArthur refused to accept responsibility for the debacle and called for attacks on the Manchurian "sanctuary." However dubious the military strategy the general had pursued in the drive north, he was right on one point: the basic political decision to cross the 38th parallel had been made in Washington.

Beleaguered by Republican criticism of "containment" as a no-win policy, the Democrats had sought to liberate Korea—with disastrous results. Truman may well have thought, also, that in the wake of the Russian atomic explosion, the United States had to demonstrate that it had not been intimidated—and was willing to go to the Yalu to prove it. Other reasons for crossing the parallel may eventually come to light, but no reason seemed any good back in the winter of 1950/51.

Yet even during its worst moments, Korea was far from the pointless struggle over barren hillsides and muddy fields as it appeared in contemporary newsreels. It had been a stimulus to German rearmament and NATO. It permitted Truman to bolster the French position in Indochina after years of indecision and half-measures. And it gave the administration the best of reasons to demand sacrifices to fulfill the goals outlined in NSC-68.

But the war could not go on indefinitely the way it was. General MacArthur wanted to bring it to an end with an ultimatum to China: surrender or be destroyed. Aside from other considerations, no one in the Truman administration was sure it had the horses and men to stage such a John Wayne finale. How many atomic bombs would it take to destroy China's capacity to wage war in Korea, how many more to discourage Russia from attacking Western Europe? When MacArthur refused to abide by the decision to initiate peace talks, he had to be relieved of his duties. The Korean War dragged on while the soldiers waited for a decision from conference tables inside a tent compound at Panmunjon.

68 Dwight Eisenhower on hearing that MacArthur had been fired by Truman.

Notes

[1] Quoted in U.S., Department of Defense, *United States–Vietnam Relations, 1945-1967*, 12 vols. (Washington, D.C.: Government Printing Office, 1971), 1: A-15.

[2] Quotation from Walter LaFeber, ed., *The Origins of the Cold War, 1941-1947* (New York: John Wiley, 1971), pp. 34–35.

[3] Quoted in Anthony Eden, *The Reckoning* (Boston: Houghton Mifflin, 1965), pp. 334–35.

[4] Roosevelt to Stalin, October 4, 1944, in U.S., Department of State, *Foreign Relations: The Conferences at Malta and Yalta, 1945* (Washington, D.C.: Government Printing Office, 1955), p. 6.

[5] Quoted in a British memorandum of the meeting, October 9, 1944, in Premier 3, 434/7, Papers of Winston S. Churchill, Public Record Office, London.

[6] Quoted in Charles Beard, *President Roosevelt and the Coming of the War, 1941* (New Haven, Conn.: Yale University Press, 1948), p. 473.

[7] Quoted in LaFeber, *Origins of the Cold War*, p. 42.

[8] Cordell Hull, *The Memoirs of Cordell Hull*, 2 vols. (New York: Dodd Mead, 1948), 2: 1644.

[9] Bohlen minutes, tripartite dinner meeting, February 4, 1945, *Foreign Relations: Malta and Yalta*, p. 589.

[10] U.S., Department of State, *Papers Relating to the Foreign Relations of the United States, 1945* (Washington, D.C.: Government Printing Office), 5: 190–91.

[11] Note by Henri Bonnet of conversations between de Gaulle and Truman, August 22, 1945, in Charles de Gaulle, *War Memoirs: Salvation, 1944–1946, Documents* (London: Weidenfield & Nicolson, 1959), p. 286.

[12] Adolf Berle, diary entry, July 17, 1941, in *Navigating the Rapids, 1918–1971: From the Papers of Adolf Berle,* ed. Beatrice Bishop Berle and Travis Jacobs (New York: Harcourt Brace Jovanovich, 1973), p. 373.

[13] Quoted in Warren F. Kimball, "Lend-Lease and the Open Door: The Temptation of British Opulence, 1937–1942," *Political Science Quarterly* 86 (July 1971): 232–59.

[14] Roosevelt to Churchill, February 11, 1942, *Papers Relating to the Foreign Relations of the United States, 1942,* 1: 535–36.

[15] Quoted in Lloyd C. Gardner, *Economic Aspects of New Deal Diplomacy* (Madison, Wis.: University of Wisconsin Press, 1964), p. 263.

[16] From an undated speech draft, in The Papers of Harry Dexter White, Princeton University Library, Princeton, N.J.

[17] Gardner, *Economic Aspects of New Deal Diplomacy,* pp. 287–88.

[18] Quoted in Robert Sherwood, *Roosevelt and Hopkins: An Intimate History* (New York: Harper, 1948), p. 138.

[19] Winston S. Churchill, *The Grand Alliance* (Boston: Houghton Mifflin, 1951), p. 370.

[20] Quoted in Lloyd C. Gardner, *Architects of Illusion: Men and Ideas in American Foreign Relations, 1941–1949* (Chicago: Quadrangle Books, 1970), p. 33.

[21] Quoted in *Problems of Foreign Policy: Speeches and Statements, April 1945–November 1948* (Moscow: Foreign Languages Printing House, 1949), pp. 207–14.

[22] From a reprinted version of the "X" article in Thomas G. Paterson, ed., *Containment and the Cold War: American Foreign Policy Since 1945* (Reading, Mass.: Addison-Wesley, 1973), p. 33.

[23] Harry S. Truman, *Memoirs: Years of Trial and Hope* (Garden City, N.Y.: Doubleday, 1956), p. 95.

[24] Ibid., pp. 105–06.

[25] Quoted in Lloyd C. Gardner, *American Foreign Policy, Present to Past: A Narrative with Documents* (New York: Free Press, 1974), p. 320.

[26] Truman, *Years of Trial and Hope,* p. 102.

[27] Walter Millis, ed., *The Forrestal Diaries* (New York: Viking Press, 1951), p. 281.

[28] Smith to Secretary of State, July 11, 1947, *Papers Relating to the Foreign Relations of the United States, 1947,* 3: 327.

[29] Memorandum by Kennan, July 18?, 1947, Ibid., 3: 332.

[30] Quoted in Gardner, *Architects of Illusion,* p. 267.

[31] Marshall to Truman, March 11, 1948, *Papers Relating to the Foreign Relations of the United States, 1948,* 4: 407.

[32] U.S., Department of State, *American Foreign Policy, 1950–1955: Basic Documents,* 2 vols. (Washington, D.C.: Government Printing Office, 1957), 2: 2310–22.

[33] U.S., Department of State, Transcript of Round-Table Discussion on American Policy Toward China, October 6–8, 1949, p. 25.

[34] Ibid., p. 477.

[35] Memorandum by Dulles, May 18, 1950, in The Papers of John Foster Dulles, Princeton University Library, Princeton, N.J.

[36] All quotations from NSC-68, *A Report to the National Security Council by the Executive Secretary on United States Ojectives and Programs for National Security, April 14, 1950* (declassified, February 27, 1975).

[37] Quoted in David Rees, *Korea: The Limited War* (New York: St. Martin's Press, 1964), p. 123.

Bibliography

Alperovitz, Gar. *Atomic Diplomacy.* New York: Simon and Schuster, 1965. The book that really touched off the "revisionist" controversy about the origins of the Cold War.

Feis, Herbert. *The China Tangle.* Princeton, N.J.: Princeton University Press, 1953. A suitable, dispassionate survey by the most effective spokesman for the orthodox interpretation of Chiang's failings.

Freeland, Richard. *The Truman Doctrine and the Origins of McCarthyism.* New York: Knopf, 1971. A blend of domestic and foreign policy topics. Effective, if not entirely persuasive.

Gaddis, John L. *The United States and the Origins of the Cold War, 1941–1947.* New York: Columbia University Press, 1972. The premier "redemptionist" book of our times.

Gittings, John. *The World and China, 1922–1972.* New York: Harper & Row, 1974. Centered on Mao, this book opens new insights on almost every page.

Herz, Martin. *Beginnings of the Cold War.* Bloomington, Ind.: University of Indiana Press, 1966. An outstanding short account and point-by-point analysis of the division of the world into East and West.

Kolko, Gabriel. *The Politics of War.* New York: Random House, 1968. Kolko, Gabriel, and Kolko, Joyce. *The Limits of Power, 1945–1954.* New York: Harper & Row, 1972. The most massive reinterpretation of the Cold War from a revisionist point of view.

Kuklick, Bruce. *American Policy and the Division of Germany.* Ithaca, N.Y.: Cornell University Press, 1972. An excellent monograph with wide-ranging conclusions.

LaFeber, Walter. *America, Russia, and the Cold War.* New York: John Wiley, 1972. Justly famous, a breathtaking synthesis in highly readable form.

McNeill, William Hardy. *America, Britain, and Russia, 1941–1946.* London: Royal Institute of International Affairs, 1953. Still exemplary survey of the Big Three; useful for everyone.

Sherwin, Martin J. *A World Destroyed: The Atomic Bomb and the Grand Alliance.* New York: Knopf, 1975. A new look at the failure of American policymakers either to find the key to atomic diplomacy or to prevent the Cold War. Centering on the continuity of policy from Roosevelt to Truman.

The Collective Security 7
Empire: 1951–1961

The problem, of course, is where to draw the
line. This is more difficult in Asia than in
Europe. In Asia, you can draw a line and the
Communists can burrow under it with subversive activities in apparently non-
Communist areas that you can't see on the
surface. It's not difficult to marshal world
opinion against aggression, but it is quite another matter to fight against internal changes
in one country. If we take a position against
a Communist faction within a foreign
country, we have to act alone. We are confronted by an unfortunate fact—most of the
countries of the world do not share our view
that Communist control of any government
anywhere is in itself a danger and a threat.

John Foster Dulles
June 1954

General MacArthur returned from Korea to a hero's welcome.
Within hours of his dismissal, Republican leaders had met to
discuss the need for a full-scale investigation of the Truman administration's foreign and military policies. Afterward, House
Minority Leader Joseph Martin told newsmen that they had gone
so far as to discuss "the question of possible impeachments. . . ."   207

69 MacArthur's formula for victory in Korea left the legislators with some troubling thoughts.

For a time even some Democratic stalwarts felt that the administration was undone; the Republicans were determined to take everyone down with the general.

The MacArthur hearings cleared the air, much to the relief of government policymakers who feared that whatever mistakes had been made in Korea would only be made worse by Congressional efforts to find and convict those responsible for the debacle. The investigation revealed that both the general and the president had been fooled by China's decision to intervene. And MacArthur's West Point bravado stirred more fear than pride among his supporters when he declared that atomic war should be faced, if necessary, to win in Korea. Once the hearings ended, most senators and representatives were more than ready to see the old general fade away as he had rhetorically promised to do in a speech implying a readiness to be recalled for some greater task.

208   The foundations of the "containment" policy had withstood this

assault. During the Eisenhower administration it would be called "liberation," although the author of that phrase, John Foster Dulles, did have in mind some new ways of approaching old problems. The plan for building a series of collective-security pacts did not, however, originate with the Republicans. The State Department had already started laying the groundwork for Middle Eastern and Asian counterparts of NATO in the Truman years. On October 6, 1949, Congress passed the Mutual Defense Assistance Program, authorizing the supplying of United States arms, military equipment, and training assistance on a worldwide basis. NATO countries received more than three-quarters of the first appropriation, but the remainder went to nonmembers, including modest amounts for Korea and the Philippines.

And on December 30, 1949, the National Security Council met with President Truman to discuss a recent report on Asia by its staff. The report recommended, among other things, that "the

70 Acheson signs the North Atlantic Treaty, the first collective-security pact of the Cold War.

United States should act to develop and strengthen the security of the area from Communist external aggression or internal subversion. These steps should take into account any benefits to the security of Asia which may flow from the development of one or more regional groupings."[1]

In other policy documents of the era the premise for regional groupings outside Europe was given a concrete basis, as, for example, in a cable Secretary of State Acheson sent to American representatives in May 1949:

> In light Ho's [Ho Chi-minh] background, no other assumptions possible but that he outright Commie so long as (1) he fails unequivocally repudiate Moscow connections and Commie doctrine and (2) remains personally singled out for praise by internat'l Commies press and receives its support. Moreover, US not impressed by nationalist character red flag with yellow stars. Question whether Ho as much nationalist as Commie is irrelevant. All Stalinists in colonial areas are nationalists.[2]

LIBERATION

The Republicans brought back MacArthur for an encore at the 1952 Republican Convention, but the real ovation was saved for a new hero, another general, "Ike" Eisenhower. Although doctrinal purists would no doubt have preferred Ohio's Robert A. Taft as a presidential candidate, that senator's views were too "isolationist" for the liberal wing of the party, and both purists and liberals agreed that Taft lacked charisma. Eisenhower's credo—conservatism in fiscal affairs, liberalism in human affairs—seemed fine to everyone. Anything "Ike" said was fine.

Eisenhower named John Foster Dulles, the obvious choice, as his secretary of state. Dulles had spent most of his life preparing for this moment. His world view was in fact complex; it only *seemed* simple. A man of strong convictions and dour countenance, the new secretary was given to jeremiads and sermonizing in general, a habit that covered a surprisingly agile mind, misleading friend and foe alike.

210   Dulles wrote the 1952 Republican plank on foreign policy. In

71 Eisenhower for the people, Nixon for the Republicans: a perfect combination.

strident tones it condemned "containment" as a defeatist outlook that had led to the enslavement of 800 million souls in Eastern Europe and Asia, and it promised the American people a foreign policy worthy of their heritage: "liberation." Once nominated, Eisenhower cautioned Dulles against tossing such words about without qualification. Liberation was fine, Ike told him, as long as we say "by all peaceful means."

The secretary had no difficulty living with that qualification because he really had no intention of sending legions into Eastern Europe, however much he talked about the rollback of Soviet power. His view of "liberation" had as much to do with America's European allies as it did with the Soviet Union. What he apparently meant was liberation from an approach to world politics that, he believed, grew out of a Europe-oriented foreign policy dom-

211

inated by over-concern for the well-being of England and France. America should have a more independent foreign policy. He especially felt the need for such a policy toward the underdeveloped areas, as the Third World was then called.

Testifying before Congress in 1957, he remarked:

> I happened to be looking last night at the scrapbook of my wife's about my first trip out to Cairo in May 1953, nearly 4 years ago, and the whole burden of the rather unfriendly reception that I got from the press there was that we were there just in the interests of the British and the French, and there was a cartoon, for instance, of Churchill putting a mask over my face and saying, "Can't you go out there and fool the Egyptians into thinking that you are independent?" And I was presented as their stooge.[3]

Dulles was convinced that the once dynamic powers of Europe had become static. He had come away from Versailles fearing that while the status quo powers had triumphed (as a result of American aid), the world would one day pay a terrible price for their victory and the terms of peace they had imposed on the losers. The Second World War became a war against Axis aggression, but it had begun as a contest between the forces of change and the citadels of position.

The new secretary of state did not share Acheson's sympathy with the colonial powers in their self-appointed tasks of readying the "natives" for self-government. And it did matter to Dulles that Ho Chi Minh called himself a nationalist. Dulles wanted to align the United States with the newly independent nations of Asia and the Middle East. "Containment" was the wrong image in that context: it suggested reaction rather than innovation, suppression rather than liberation.

Dulles thought the coincidence of Eisenhower's inauguration and Stalin's death was of more than passing interest. It was an omen: "As Stalin dies, General Eisenhower, the man who liberated Western Europe, has become President of our great Republic, with a prestige unmatched in history." The opportunity for converting that prestige into something lasting was Dulles's—as well as the responsibility for failure should the United States miss its (last?)

chance. These thoughts weighed heavily on the secretary as he began his stewardship in 1953.

MORAL REARMAMENT

Dulles reluctantly accepted the fact of stalemate in Korea, although he was certainly determined not to give up the South Korean front against Red China. His concern about accepting a containment solution was eased by the signing of a mutual-security treaty with Syngman Rhee's government, and by the further realization that ending the Korean War was essential to "liberating" American policy from the past.

As soon as the truce had been signed, Dulles left for the Middle East. He found the entire area absorbed in narrow nationalistic concerns, which he counted an unhappy legacy of the colonial era. Moreover, Great Britain and France, contrary to their own best interests and those of the rest of the world, were doing nothing to counteract these factional tendencies. A proposal for an American-supported Middle East defense command based in Cairo, but largely under the control of the British, had originated in Washington near the end of 1951. When Dulles was appointed secretary of state, reconsideration of this policy was already underway, largely as a result of Egyptian opposition to granting Great Britain a continuing military presence. Even under King Farouk, the plan had been turned down in Cairo. Armed clashes between Egyptian and British forces had taken place. It was clear that Egypt wanted only one thing from London: complete withdrawal.

In the summer of 1952 King Farouk was deposed by the army, and men even less interested in allowing the British to remain assumed power. Appeals for an Anglo-American policy by Foreign Minister Anthony Eden failed to impress Eisenhower and Dulles, who were taken with the opportunity for increasing American influence in the area. Much to his dismay, Eden learned that a shipment of arms was on its way from the United States to Cairo. He was even more disappointed when the Eisenhower administration reversed its position on the so-called Baghdad Pact, Eden's

213

72　Neither King Farouk nor his successors worked out well for Dulles.

plan for bringing the northern tier of Middle Eastern states into a collective-security organization with the United States and Great Britain. After encouraging the idea, Washington decided against joining because of Egyptian opposition.

During his 1953 Middle Eastern tour Dulles had stopped in Karachi, where he explained to newsmen his ideas about future collective-security pacts. "Collective security organizations are more solid and dependable if they reflect not only strategic factors but a unity of culture and of faith."[4] Apparently Dulles wanted to leave the impression on his listeners that America shared an anti-colonial faith with underdeveloped nations, as opposed to British colonial habits of mind. At that moment the British position was in jeopardy not only in Egypt, but also in Iran, where a nationalist government under the leadership of Mohammed Mossadegh had expropriated the properties of the Anglo-Iranian Oil Company. Interestingly, Mossadegh had appealed to both Truman and Eisenhower for aid in his efforts to resist British pressures to return the fields to company management.

In answer to Mossadegh's first request for aid, Dean Acheson, Truman's secretary of state, had minced no words. The United States, he said, opposed any solution that might lessen "confidence in future commercial investments in Iran and . . . in the validity of contractual arrangements all over the world."[5] Understandably, Mossadegh was not much interested in protecting American "contractual arrangements" elsewhere in the world. Nor was he easily dissuaded even when Eisenhower turned him down. He courted Russian support.

How deeply the Central Intelligence Agency was involved in the uprising that toppled Mossadegh on August 19, 1953, remains conjecture. That it was involved has never been questioned. Mossadegh's pro-shah successors settled the dispute straight away on terms that granted the United States a major share in a previously exclusive British preserve.

For a long time the Iranian coup was cited as a CIA triumph in the James Bond tradition. Dulles found it a bit awkward, however, to reconcile such manipulation with his supposed determination to

73 Mohammed Mossadegh is ousted, and Iran remains in the Free World.

support genuine nationalists. Granted that an emergency situation existed in Iran before Eisenhower assumed office; granted also that 90 percent of the world's known oil reserves were then located in the Middle East—Dulles still had some explaining to do. In general, the secretary would satisfy himself (if not others) by pointing out that the colonial powers had so botched things that nationalists had started turning to Russia for support. The United States was ready to do business with nationalists, but it could not allow them to put their nations under Soviet bondage. Some variation of this rationale appeared often in Dulles's background press conferences. In 1954, he complained that "we have been maneuvered into a position we don't believe in." A reporter's notes of that conference continued: "Dulles takes a serious view of the future if the United States cannot in some way get the leadership of the colonial and dependent areas. . . . We could lick the Communists at their own game, but we cannot do it without seeming to desert our NATO allies."[6]

The real showdown came in Egypt. Even more than on Iranian oil, Great Britain and France depended on control of Suez and its environs to maintain their position in the Middle East and, for that matter, in Europe as well. Dulles had all but ordered the British troops out of Suez to satisfy the nationalist ambitions of the revolutionary junta now led by Colonel Gamel Abdul Nasser. The eighty-three-thousand-man garrison at Suez was the last military stronghold in the Middle East enjoyed by the once great imperial powers.

Prodded by his fellow officers, Nasser was making life difficult for the United States with his constant requests for military aid. The State Department had hoped that Egypt would eventually realize that Israel was in the Middle East to stay and that both nations would benefit by cooperating in the development of the area's natural resources. Instead, Nasser turned to the East.

Egypt's untamed behavior troubled Nasser's friends in Washington. In a speech on foreign-policy principles, Dulles noted matter-of-factly that "other peoples and nations who are free and want to stay free usually want to coordinate their policies with our own."[7]

It bothered Dulles that Nasser (and Nehru of India) did not recognize that "neutralism" was a shortsighted and amoral (if not actually immoral) policy, but once again he could rationalize those nations' behavior as a reaction to their colonial past.

After Nasser signed his first contract for the delivery of arms from Czechoslovakia, Dulles and Eisenhower decided to make one last effort in Egypt. A consortium of British, French, and German firms had agreed to consider the possibility of financing the Aswan Dam across the Nile. But if Nasser's dream was to come true, American and World Bank financing would also be needed. Washington soon took the lead in negotiating the contract, while the Europeans waited. A final contract was prepared for Nasser's signature in early 1956, but problems quickly developed on both sides.

According to the terms of the draft contract, Egypt would have to forgo future extravagances like communist arms and give first priority to paying off its obligations. Nasser refused to sign on that basis. Meanwhile, the State Department was having its own difficulties on Capitol Hill. Nasser's leadership of an Arab alliance directed against Israel, his decision to recognize Communist China, and the opposition of Southern cotton-growers, who wondered why anyone with sense would want to finance a potential competitor of that magnitude, created a new community of interest in Congress against any loan to Cairo.

Nervous European statesmen were aware of these underground rumblings but assumed (along with Eisenhower) that Dulles would not give Nasser an excuse for some outrageous act of defiance. Everyone agreed that Egypt must be handled with great care and let down softly. But when the Egyptian ambassador hinted at a Russian counter offer to build the dam, Dulles lost his temper in words to the effect: Let 'em try, we're not interested.

What ranks as the most bizarre series of events in the Eisenhower years was thus set in motion. News of the American pronouncement interrupted Nasser's "summit" meeting with Marshall Tito and Nehru, who with Nasser made up the Big Three of neutralism. A week later Nasser nationalized the canal. Dulles then rushed to London to persuade British and French leaders not

74 Nasser, Nehru, and Tito: the neutralist leaders in Yugoslavia, 1956.

to do anything rash. On his return, he told newsmen that he had warned against military action, especially anything involving Israelis against Arabs. It was very possible, Dulles mused, that the Soviet interest and the American interest in a peaceful solution "might coincide, though for different reasons."

As unlikely as it seemed, talks had actually begun in Moscow on this contingency basis. Meanwhile, Dulles was trying hard to persuade the British and French that they would not really lose anything if an international authority ran the Suez Canal. He told Senator Walter F. George that he saw no particular reason for not letting the Egyptians manage the canal. "I rather admire them," Dulles said in passing of the aggrieved Anglo-French statesmen, "for wanting to go down fighting. Western Europe would become a dependency of either Russia or the United States, they feel."[8]

Dulles was somewhat disturbed at the "fantastic" idea, "almost

Marxist in nature," that the French had got hold of, that the United States was trying to drive them out of the area for the sake of business interests. Actually, the Egyptian situation was just part of the "American dilemma," caught as we were between the inevitable passing of the colonial era and the Atlantic Alliance, which bound us to the colonial powers. He viewed his task rather philosophically—it was to cushion the change.

Determined to resist either Russian *or* American domination of the Middle East, the British and French took counsel with the Israelis. One day in mid-October 1956, Dulles was supposedly heard to remark to his staff: "It's very strange that we have heard nothing whatever from the British for ten days. We must try to find out what they and the French are up to."[9]

Two weeks later Israel invaded Egypt. An Anglo-French intervention, launched on the pretext of neutralizing the Suez Canal, was aimed at destroying Egyptian airfields. The Anglo-French-Israeli offensive proved ineffective. If they had to attack, moaned American policymakers, why did they make such a botch of it? Eisenhower's reaction was to go to the United Nations before the Russians got there.

75 Suez, 1956: the last Anglo-French intervention.

76 The Russian offer was made possible by Anglo-French-Israeli action against Egypt.

A worse moment for such an invasion could not have been imagined in Washington. Eisenhower was running for reelection; nothing but a major catastrophe could have prevented him from defeating Adlai Stevenson. But politicians always run scared. Ike was displeased with the British and French for acting at a time when he was, of necessity, preoccupied with domestic matters. Dulles was irritated because of the unfortunate coincidence of the invasion of Egypt and Russian action against the Hungarian "Freedom Fighters." Dulles could thunder all he wanted about the fate of enslaved countries inside the communist orbit, but what were his allies doing in the Middle East? Worse yet, Soviet Premier Nikita Khrushchev then claimed credit for forcing an Anglo-French-Israeli backdown with his threats to use nuclear missiles.

Out of this wreckage, the secretary professed to find at least one bright spot: he had finally liberated American policy from British and French entanglements. Presenting the Eisenhower Doctrine to Congress in early 1957, Dulles asked Congress to give the administration the authority it requested to extend economic and military aid to anticommunist governments in the Middle East, and, if it became necessary, to use military forces in the area. Great Britain and France should keep their troops in Europe, he concluded. "If I were an American boy . . . I'd rather not have a French and British soldier beside me, one on my right and one on my left."[10]

SEATO SUCCEEDS COLONIALISM

In the aftermath of the Suez war, the new British prime minister, Harold MacMillan, and his foreign secretary, Selwyn Lloyd, met with Eisenhower and Dulles in Bermuda for a series of private talks. In gentle fashion, MacMillan suggested that there was a "tendency" to move too fast in decolonizing the world and that the United States was responsible for some of this pressure. Eisenhower spoke about encouraging former colonies "to stay within the old framework on some autonomous basis," as Puerto Rico had

77 Was the pace of decolonization too fast—or too slow?

done. MacMillan turned for a moment to Hong Kong, surprising Dulles with the comment that the colony was no longer profitable and might have to be abandoned.

The very mention of China, however indirect, set Dulles off on a favorite lecture. If Great Britain's policy toward Communist China were "aligned with ours, we might be able to help to hold" Hong Kong. London should begin by withdrawing diplomatic recognition from Peking and by continuing to vote against Communist China's entrance into the United Nations. A "wholehearted" acceptance of United States policy was essential in that part of the world. Mac-Millan thought that these points might be considered; but the secretary was far from finished with the lecture.

Joint consultation, he continued, should become the rule. Look at what had already been accomplished in SEATO (the Southeast Asia Treaty Organization) along those lines in the short time since its establishment. "Whereas two years ago the UK did not want even to mention Communism, Lord Hume had said at last week's SEATO meeting, 'Communism is evil. We must meet it and beat it.'" And, added Dulles with a final gesture, he had quoted this remark to the Senate Foreign Relations Committee, "and it has had a good impact."[11]

Dulles's retelling of the SEATO story and its happy ending was of little comfort to MacMillan and Lloyd and stirred memories of other recent "misunderstandings." For nine years, from 1945 to 1954, the United States had watched glumly as the French managed to get themselves surrounded by the Vietminh in Indochina, until finally they were besieged at Dienbienphu. When France appealed to the United States in the spring of that last year, Washington replied that it could do nothing more until Paris promised to give the states of Indochina their independence. America was already funding much of the French war effort in Southeast Asia through foreign-aid programs, but had little or no voice in shaping the political policy. And now the French wanted air strikes to relieve their fortress!

For all their public insistence on the need to defeat communist aggression in Asia, Eisenhower and Dulles agreed in private that

222

78 Dulles shuddered at what Dienbienphu symbolized—America on the side of the static power beseiged by a revolution.

what was going on in Indochina was a colonial war that the Reds were exploiting for their own purposes. Speaking in New Delhi on May 22, 1953, Dulles had told journalists about the "extensive talks" he had had with the French concerning the need to bring the people of Vietnam to understand that "they were fighting for their own freedom."[12]

What the French were doing in Indochina jeopardized all of noncommunist Asia, just as their earlier stubbornness about Germany had nearly ruined postwar Europe. Dulles, it will be remembered, had become impressed with the Japanese need for Southeast Asia during his work on the peace treaty. Quite obviously, a prosperous Japan required expanding markets. Where were they to be found? Neither the United States nor Europe could absorb all of Japan's surplus production, perhaps not even much of it. China might, someday, but an economic connection with that huge apostle of Marxism-Maoism might also lead to the spread of that new secular religion to Japan as Buddhism once had progressed across East Asia.

The only alternative was Southeast Asia. Dulles had once tried

223

to persuade Philippine leaders to accept Japanese manufacturers as part of a general reparations settlement. His lack of success in Manila no doubt reinforced his concern about Southeast Asia proper. "There were large areas for overseas trade which would give Japan access to food and raw materials and markets," Dulles told the newsmen in New Delhi. These thoughts were very much on everyone's mind in Washington as policymakers in the Eisenhower administration discussed what ought to (and could) be done in response to the French requests for aid in Indochina. The president then introduced the American people to the domino principle. If Indochina went, so would . . . down to the end of the long line. Eisenhower drew a somber picture of Japan's future without those millions of customers in Southeast Asia. If you take them away, he warned, the Japanese would have only "one place in the world to go—that is, toward the Communist areas to live. So, the possible consequences of the loss are just incalculable."[13]

While the air force thought a couple of tactical atomic bombs could "clean those Commies out of there,"[14] army leaders had doubts about the struggle, which, they thought, would inevitably become a land war in Asia. Air power alone could not do the job. General Matthew Ridgway gauged the attitude of his colleagues and the probabilities in Indochina and concluded that intervention would in turn lead to a "preventive war" against Red China. Once that happened, he predicted, "our civilization would be doomed. We should have to rely on conquest for survival from then on, until our society crumbled as the empires of Alexander, and of Rome, crumbled from their own inner decay."[15]

How close did the United States come to going to war in the spring of 1954? In general, Eisenhower shared Ridgway's doubts about the desirability of putting foot soldiers into the jungles against guerilla insurgents. But he was anxious to do something. In early April, meetings were held between administration and congressional leaders. The results were inconclusive. Before giving Eisenhower the go-ahead, the legislators wanted to be sure that American military leaders were agreed on any proposed course of action and that America's allies were prepared to go along with whatever lay ahead. Dulles could not give such assurances. On

April 17, Vice President Richard Nixon raised a trial balloon, perhaps to test whether the congressional doubts really reflected popular opinion: "If to avoid further Communist expansion in Asia and Indochina, we must take the risk now by putting our boys in, I think the Executive has to take the politically unpopular decisions and do it."

If that was Nixon's ploy, it flopped. The next day the State Department, without releasing the "official" text of Nixon's speech, denied that there was any change in American policy. Meanwhile, Ike was out shopping for allies. He wanted the United States, France, Britain, Thailand, Australia, and New Zealand to begin conferring on a means of stopping the communists. His own proposal was to use French troops already in place, supplemented by troops from those European and Asian countries, and American supplies. The idea had little attraction outside Washington. Eisenhower even appealed to the old Bull Dog instincts of Prime Minister Winston Churchill: "If I may refer again to history; we failed to halt Hirohito, Mussolini, and Hitler by not acting in unity and in time. That marked the beginning of many years of stark tragedy and desperate peril. May it not be that our nations have learned something from that lesson? . . ."[16]

Eisenhower's pleading was to no avail: Churchill promised a cheering House of Commons that there would be no military action before the convening of a peace conference. Angered by this apparent unconcern for anything but "narrow" British interests—especially London's disinclination to see Japan's problems—Dulles went ahead with plans for an alliance of Asian nations based roughly on the NATO principle. There were, however, some crucial differences. For example, no plans were drawn up for a standing international army; instead, each nation was to be responsible for keeping order within its own borders, although it could call on the treaty powers to send aid in a crisis situation. In practice, this meant American air and naval support. Dulles hoped to include under this umbrella Formosa and the states of Indochina (Laos, Cambodia, and Vietnam), thereby solving several dilemmas at one signature.

While Dulles planned this new organization, the situation of the 225

French garrison at Dienbienphu became more desperate. Pierre Mendes-France became prime minister of France with a pledge to end the war within three months or resign. The British promised to support the idea of SEATO—but not until a serious peace effort had been made at Geneva. As delegates from the Soviet Union, Communist China, the United States, and France sat down to talk, word came that Dienbienphu had fallen. After that announcement, the outcome of the Geneva conference was never in doubt. Yet all things considered, the settlement was better than France could have expected. The final agreement provided for an independent Laos and Cambodia and for a "provisional" demarcation line at the 17th parallel in Vietnam and internationally supervised all-Vietnamese elections no later than 1956.

But the agreement was not enough for Dulles, who insisted on calling the area beneath the 17th parallel the "free territory" of Vietnam, and then a "country." He was gloomy about the chances of South Vietnam's survival (he estimated about one in ten), but he was going to do his damndest to save it. The first task was to find a potential George Washington for Vietnam. The choice fell on Ngo Dinh Diem, then residing at Maryknoll Seminary in Ossining, New York. Diem did have some credentials. Most important, he was anti-French. And he had once been offered a government position by the Vietminh leader, Ho Chi Minh. Over vigorous French opposition, the United States installed Diem in Saigon.

SEATO finally came into existence in early 1955. Dulles had another minor victory as well: the protocol of the treaty extended protection to the "three young nations" of Indochina. On the ground in Vietnam, American military advisers had been replacing French officers and doctrine with Yankee counterinsurgency techniques brought over from the Philippines, where they had been successful in containing a "Huk" uprising against Manila. These seemingly profitable ventures in nationbuilding stimulated Dulles to expand on "our pacific strategy" in the Philippine capital on March 2, 1955. Reporting on his conference with the heads of American missions in fifteen countries, he told journalists that the broad strategy was to maintain a potential of three fronts against the Chinese Communists "if they should commit open aggression—the one in Korea, the one in Formosa, and the one in Indochina. . . ." All three fronts were necessary.

He had spent a good deal of time, Dulles continued, considering the Japanese economic problem. "As Indochina becomes independent and has dollars directly available to it, there exists a competitive situation and there is a good chance of Japanese textile goods, for instance, moving into Indochina." The French were not too happy about that, Dulles conceded, and he could understand their concern. But they could not go on having a preferred position in that market if any one of "those three countries, particularly Vietnam, is to be an independent country and have its own sources of dollars." America had given the Philippines their independence, and now it was helping another country to become independent. "There is a certain drama about it which appeals to me, at least, and it is having an excellent effect in Vietnam. President Diem spoke to me about it there when we had lunch together in Saigon."

The French trade that was being dislocated was not enough to seriously affect the French economy, Dulles noted as he returned to his main theme, and the English now "recognized" that it was better to accept Japanese competition in Asia than at home. "It may not be pleasant for some individual concerns in France, but by and large the impact on the French economy will not be serious. . . . There is no desire on the part of the United States to try to displace French influence in that area. A certain displacement is, I think, inevitable."[17]

Dulles was being gentle. In private he and his aides were angry about reported French overtures to the Vietminh in an effort to maintain their business interests. If so, it would not be the first time the Europeans sacrificed principle to profit. But this time they were not going to be allowed to sacrifice the new father of his country, President Diem. Critics pointed out that Diem's reversal of Vietminh land reforms and his dictatorial methods were making him unpopular; American supporters called his regime One Man Democracy. We might not like it, or desire it for ourselves, but the Vietnamese did, and that was what counted. Eisenhower and

79 Diem—the George Washington of Southeast Asia—receives his award from the Valley Forge Freedom Foundation.

Dulles declared that conditions in the "north" (now a separate country in all American pronouncements) would not permit genuine all-Vietnamese elections. Elections in the south gave Diem 99 percent of the vote, better than any other Free World leader could muster—even better than some in the un-free world could get.

The Geneva Agreement, which the United States had never liked or signed, became an unmentionable in Washington. Almost $3 billion in foreign aid rained on Vietnam in the expectation that stability would grow in the countryside. In 1959 the Valley Forge Freedom Foundation, protectors of the Washington image, cited Diem for conspicuous and effective resistance to communism. He had made it; he *had* made it! Diem had become the George Washington of Southeast Asia!

Only a few clouds darkened this sunny day in Southeast Asia—nothing important really. There was a persistent trade deficit that had to be made up from the United States Treasury. And there was some restlessness in the countryside. But these were minor matters: all new nations had problems.

New nations always had had to face the threat of subversion and to employ extraordinary measures, which did not always meet the test of abstract democracy, in order to counter the threat. Critics of President Diem's methods might well harken to Gamel Nasser's response to similar charges. "What is a dictator?" Nasser asked American journalists. "After Washington became President, for eight years there was only one party in your country. One of Washington's ideas was that there might be civil war if there were two parties. This was his way of maintaining unity after the revolution. Was that dictatorship?"[18]

Nasser had gone astray, but most policymakers still regarded him as redeemable. After all, he still put communists in jail. Subversion—that is, communist subversion—was difficult to control on a worldwide basis, Dulles told a closed session of SEATO ministers, because some countries equated the Russian government with other legitimate governments. The first step in controlling subversion, therefore, was to recognize that the Soviet government was not legitimate. Russia was a dangerous disease-carrier, and the shortsightedness of some countries endangered all. "An individual who refuses innoculation against a contagious disease endangers not merely himself, but the community, and so it is with governments that fail to alert their people—they imperil not only themselves but their neighbors."[19] That was really taking Roosevelt's old quarantine analogy about as far as it could go. The implications of Dulles's rhetorical exercises scared the daylights out of some of his audiences, especially the Europeans and European-oriented.

THE OLD WORLD

The secretary's most famous phrases were uttered as threats not to the Russians but to America's NATO allies. "Liberation" was quickly disposed of when the United States failed to intervene in East Germany's bread riots during the summer of 1953. Any lingering doubts were put to rest when the Hungarian episode passed without a Soviet-American confrontation. The United States provided a home for political refugees, but no more. Dulles said at the time that the United States "could not accept the concept that each nation subject to injustice should attempt to remedy it by force, as this would set loose forces that would yield almost inevitably to World War III, particularly in view of the present predicament and power of the Soviet rulers."[20]

But when France hesitated on the question of admitting West Germany to a prominent position in the proposed European Defense Community, Dulles delivered dire warnings of an "agonizing reappraisal" by Washington of its whole postwar foreign policy. Even the famous "massive retaliation" speech scared the Allies more than it seemed to bother the Kremlin. The burden of that speech was that "containment" had proved too costly; henceforth, the United States would pick its own place and choose its own time for Cold War confrontations.

Moreover, Dulles was incessantly occupied with correcting what he thought were serious errors in the European approach to the rest of the world. Over and over again he impressed NATO leaders with the importance of supporting American policy. "If you like the kind of U.S. you see here, you should give it your confidence, as we apply the same policies in Asia, and join us if you will."[21] The broad strategy Dulles proposed in Europe did, in fact, closely parallel certain aspects of America's "pacific strategy."

It was for the Europeans' own good, Dulles's advisers in the State Department believed, that they be guided toward sounder policies in Africa and Asia. "Africa is in a sense a hinterland of Europe," Dulles told his heads of mission in Europe, "just as our great West was the hinterland of the East." If France continued the way it was going, it would surely turn North Africa over to the communists. To the NATO ministers themselves, Dulles gave a statistical demonstration of the importance of economic relations with the developing countries. Communism ruled 800 million people; 1600 million were in the West, but 1000 million were in the underdeveloped countries. If the 1000 million went over to communism, the situation would soon become intolerable for the Atlantic Community, with its "dependence upon broad markets and access to raw materials."[22]

Dulles's European policy had one overriding concern: to prevent a new Franco-German quarrel. The Russians, never quite sure if "liberation" was not all flourish to impress voters, remained concerned to gain international recognition and status for the German Democratic Republic (East Germany). In a certain sense, their concern ran parallel to Dulles's interest in Asian nationbuilding. Besides, suppose some future politician in Bonn or Washington felt it necessary to make good on "liberation"? (This very possibility arose late in the decade with Democratic criticism of the Republican era as the years of the locust and promises to get the country moving again.)

Russian diplomacy presented the West with two alternatives: a neutralized, disarmed Germany, or a permanently divided one. The United States opted for the latter, although Dulles had to keep up a "holy pretense" that America's aim was a reunited Germany free to participate in Western defense systems. He was not eager to meet with the Russians on the German question because he feared, quite rightly, that any apparent lessening of tensions would only encourage backsliding within the West. It had taken a supreme diplomatic effort to persuade the French to agree to German rearmament even with all the safeguards that were built into NATO and EDC. The slightest sign that Cold War tensions were easing could be disastrous for the cause of Franco-German unity in Europe.

A neutralized Germany was "objectionable to the United States," Dulles explained,

> because we believe that a Germany which was not tied to the western association would merely grow strong as a balance of power between the East and the West, with an enormous bargaining position. There would be no adequate restraints on German policy or German armament. We would completely destroy the concept of the growing unity between Germany and France which is one of the most important postwar results. Disunity between Germany and France has been the basic cause—originating cause—of two world wars.[23]

But the United States could not, at least not publicly, give up the goal of a reunified Germany. To do that would discredit Konrad Adenauer and the West German government in the eyes of its citizens. The problem was compounded by the influx of East German refugees into West Germany via Berlin. These bitter foes of the communist regime represented a potential tinderbox for stray sparks that might set off a general conflagration. As the decade ended, the Soviets were pressing hard for a settlement that would solidify the position of East Germany. Two summit conferences, the first in 1955 and the second scheduled for the spring of 1960, had the German question at the top of the agenda.

Dulles lamented the necessity of such meetings. What was there to say to the Russians? And how could you say anything without the rest of the world drawing the wrong conclusions? He advised Eisenhower to beware of photographers at the first summit: not to smile too broadly when they were around; not to be photographed holding a drink in such company. There was a serious purpose in these admonitions, which went beyond Dulles's fear of right-wing Republican sensibilities. Throughout the Cold War, he explained, the United States had maintained that the immorality of communist policies and principles was at the heart of the Soviet-American conflict. If the West was to be held together, it would not do to meet the Russians on friendly terms. If nations began trying to work out arrangements with Moscow on an individual basis, all the old differences and rivalries would surface and the West would be eaten or destroy itself.

More than an interesting gloss on William James's old puzzler about the unfilled need for a moral equivalent to war, Dulles's seemingly narrow strictures about photographers and summit conferences are consistent with, and help to explain, his anxiety to reintegrate Japan and Germany before any temporary lessening of Cold War tensions, or simple weariness, tempted America's allies to wander into the dangerous forests where the Russian bear watched and waited. He could not, for the sake of the same Western unity, refuse *all* meetings with the Russians and risk being accused of opposing peace. Hence his concern about the smallest matters and appearances.

While these considerations took first place in Dulles's mind, he was certainly aware of the importance of avoiding "needless provocations" to the Soviet Union. He responded to Khrushchev's ultimatum demanding a settlement of the Berlin question within six months with a surprising degree of flexibility. At a press conference Dulles suggested that the United States might accept East German "agents" instead of Russian soldiers at the various Berlin checkpoints, if it was made clear they were acting on behalf of the Soviet Union. The point at issue was the Russian demand that East Germany be recognized as an independent country, with full authority to protect its borders, and that the "temporary" postwar situation be brought to an end. The United States could not, for obvious reasons, easily approve any alteration in the status of Berlin and certainly could not recognize East Germany.

The "agent" concession was about as far as Dulles could go, although he also talked vaguely of some sort of German confederation brought about by other means than all-German elections. Newspaper sources reported that Dulles did not interpret the Khrushchev ultimatum as an aggressive act against the West. On the contrary, said the *Washington Post,* the Secretary saw the move as originating in Soviet fears of an East German uprising. Khrushchev's memoirs confirmed that impression in later years. The GDR, he said, faced serious problems stemming from the ambiguous status of West Berlin. "If things had continued like this much longer, I don't know what would have happened."[24]

But any weakening of Western resolve to stay in Berlin, or of its insistence that Berlin stay in the West ideologically, was out of the question. Eisenhower reluctantly entertained Khrushchev on a madcap tour of the United States, which took the Soviet leader to Hollywood (where he did the expected by criticizing the scanty costumes of chorus girls) and back again to Camp David in Maryland. There was a lot of talk about the "spirit" of Camp David, but following the visit, Soviet-American relations over Berlin actually grew more tense as the time for the Paris summit of May 1960 grew near. Khrushchev had asked that Berlin be made a "free city" and that peace treaties be signed with the *two* Germanies. On April 20, 1960, Undersecretary of State Douglas Dillon called the GDR "one of the outstanding myths in a vast Communist web of prodigious mythology." It could not stand for a single day "without the support of Soviet bayonets."[25]

Dillon's speech may have reflected a serious debate within the

80 Nikita Khrushchev in America: but neither in Hollywood nor in Camp David was there a solution to the German problem.

administration. Probably not. Dillon added in this speech to the AFL-CIO Conference on World Affairs that Berlin involved more than the immediate security of that city:

> It bears directly upon the future stability of Central Europe and the possibility of a lasting European peace. It represents a critical test of the integrity and dependability of the free world's collective security systems, because no nation could preserve its faith in collective security if we permitted the courageous people of West Berlin to be sold into slavery.

Three weeks later the Russians announced the downing of a U-2 spy plane. They concealed the fact that the pilot had been taken alive. This simple subterfuge led to some silly American statements about missing weather planes, which Khrushchev exposed

234

with great glee by producing Francis Gary Powers alive and well in the Kremlin. Eisenhower could now either disclaim responsibility for the CIA flight or take some other equally unpromising way out. Democrats were already harping on Ike's advancing senility, and the U-2 incident gave them one more thing to chew on. So Eisenhower talked about how no one wanted another Pearl Harbor, a neat way of turning things around to what everyone still suspected to have been a Democratic failure.

Khrushchev had his own domestic critics to contend with, and that may be the reason for the way he handled the situation. One wonders why, if the Soviets expected the Paris summit to go well, Khrushchev practiced the sort of entrapment technique used on Ei-

81 Francis Gary Powers in the prisoner's dock: what game was Khrushchev playing?

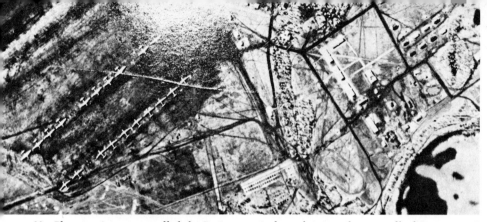

82 Photo espionage cancelled the Paris summit, but what was there to talk about anyway?

senhower. Khrushchev soon became the target of his own game: having exposed Eisenhower to the world as a liar, and an inexpert one at that, he exposed himself to Chinese and Soviet "hardliners" as something of a fool for seeking that man's trust through "peaceful coexistence."

THE INHERITANCE

The U-2 affair was only one event in a generally dismal ending for the Eisenhower era. All things considered, Vice President Richard Nixon mused, he would have preferred to be in John Kennedy's place in 1960, running against the administration. Personal loyalty to Ike still ran high. He could probably have been elected again: heart attack, ileitis, stroke, and the Twenty-Second Amendment notwithstanding. But just as certainly, the Republicans were in trouble again.

The trouble really began in 1957, when the Soviet Union launched the first satellite of the space age. Military men called for new defense expenditures to close the missile gap; educators bemoaned the American school system's apparent inability to identify future Einsteins in the primary grades and provide them with what they needed to become great scientists. Could it be that the American Century that had begun in 1941 was already over? A moderately serious recession in 1957/58 added to these woes and questionings. In San Francisco, Vice President Nixon suggested to a conference on international industrial development that the real significance of Sputnik was not military but economic:

The Kremlin has offered us a direct challenge. It proclaims to the world that a slave economy can outproduce a free economy. It promises to the developing areas of the world that the Communist system can do more for them in a shorter time than the system of private enterprise which is the economic basis of the free world. And the spectacular success of the satellite project is being held up as proof of the superiority of the Communist system.[26]

It did not matter that for the average citizen of the communist world economic conditions were just above the miserable, Nixon added. The Soviet "peaceful coexistence" offensive in the Third World, complete with a "foreign-aid" program, however short-lived and deceptive it might be, posed a real threat. If it succeeded in extending communist rule throughout Asia and Africa, the Kremlin was assured of victory "in the battle for the world." With control of those areas, the communists would hold immense resources of oil, uranium, copper, and other raw materials "essential for the economic life of the free world." America could not ignore the military danger, but the economic weapon that Sputnik represented

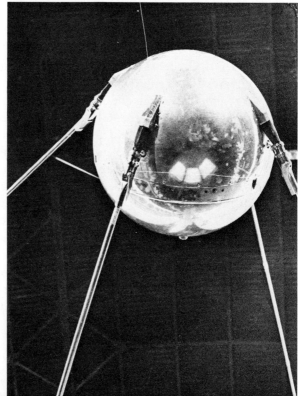

83   Sputnik.

was equally serious. "The first may never be used; the second certainly will be used."

In 1898 most Americans thought Spain's rule in Cuba was, like the Soviet regime in East Germany, completely dependent on bayonets, yet they worried about the economic threat colonialism posed to the "free world" of that time. American leaders in the 1950s still felt that issue was close to the heart of the problem. Thus Eisenhower wrote in his memoirs:

> On September 5, 1901, at the Buffalo Exposition . . . President William McKinley . . . made an eloquent plea for the expansion of international trade. The half-century intervening had, in my view, only intensified the validity of his argument. In October 1952 Joseph Stalin, in his last public political pronouncement, asserted that so much of the world had become alienated from the West that Britain, France, and the United States could make no place in international markets for the products of Germany and Japan. Stalin concluded that inevitably Britain and France would "break from the embrace of the United States," and that West Germany and Japan would "try to smash United States domination." At a crucial instant in this desperate battle for markets, Stalin predicted, would arrive the Soviet Union's "moment for the decisive blow."[27]

These thoughts guided Eisenhower's successful effort to secure congressional approval for an extension of the Reciprocal Trade Agreements Act. In addition, the focus of the World Bank's lending operations began to shift from European reconstruction to the financing of exports to less developed countries from the industrial nations. From 1952 on, more than $9.8 billion was made available for such purposes from the World Bank, of which the United States supplied only about one-third of the exports. As Nixon pointed out in his San Francisco speech, a United States program of loans and grants existed in addition to those of international agencies. From 1945 to 1957 American foreign aid already totaled $60 billion. "It laid the basis for the vast expansion of trade at a time when markets were wrenched from their traditional patterns by Communist violence," said Nixon. But there were limits to what could be done by government to export goods or ideas:

There is partly the limit imposed by budgetary problems. But above all there is the limit imposed by our conviction that free enterprise is the preferable medium for aid for the newly developing countries. In many nations the pattern of economic development is being shaped for a century ahead. If this pattern is statist, then human freedom will be the loser.[28]

The Republicans had come into power in 1953 convinced that they could put an end to all that waste in foreign aid and reverse the trend to "statist" economy at home and abroad. It was simple enough: just get rid of all those New Deal bureaucrats and leftists in the State Department. Secretary of the Treasury George Humphrey made a proposal at an early meeting of Eisenhower advisers that suggested to Dulles that his colleagues were being carried away with this kind of thinking. After reviewing the role of private capital in developing the United States in the nineteenth century, and pointing out that the rules of the financial game had changed, Dulles stated that in the second half of this century the government would have to play a larger role in the economic sector. "I said that to cut off this type of investment wholly might mean serious political consequences. South America might be lost under this policy. . . . It might be good banking to put South America through the wringer but it will come out red."[29]

Contrary to popular notions, Dulles was not the leader of the "free enterprise" purists in the Eisenhower administration. He once told an aide that he was not at all sure the United States could win the "contest" with the Soviet Union:

You know, it's like getting a bunch of people who are suffering from malnutrition, rickets, all sorts of congenital ailments—who are weak—and saying, "What you ought to do is play rugby football. Come on, get in there. Out in the field. Tackle each other. Be rough and tough." Well, you know this is madness. But after all, you say to them, "Have a free competitive system." And they say, "Good God, there must be a better way of doing things." Furthermore, you say, "The way to build up your industry is to save, become capitalists, invest—and so on." But they want a steel mill over night. They want public utilities. They want everything.[30]

239

Communist promises, Dulles mused, even if they could never be fulfilled, might be enough to tip the balance. "This is a tremendous difficulty in trying to save souls for political freedom, when the devil has so much on his side." It had been sixty years since the United States intervened militarily in Cuba. Since that time the cause of political freedom on the island had not prospered. Washington's policy had gone from "big-stick" interventionism to benign neglect (except for 1933), but the situation in Havana remained the same. During all those years the American ambassador was regarded as "the second most important man in Cuba; sometimes even more important than the President."[31]

Despite his concern that American aid policy not put Latin America through the wringer, Dulles paid little attention to affairs in the Western Hemisphere except for one episode in 1954, when the Central Intelligence Agency had to be called in to help implement an Organization of American States resolution declaring "International Communism" incompatible with the "concept" of freedom in the Americas. A provision in the resolution called on all the American states to take steps to wipe out subversion within their borders. Armed with this resolution, Dulles brought in the CIA to take on Colonel Jacobo Arbenz Guzmán, the Guatemalan leader who had expropriated United Fruit Company properties and was hoping for Czechoslovakian arms to help him resist Washington's expected reaction. He did not have to wait long.

With CIA assistance, Carlos Castillo Armas overthrew Arbenz and established a government that met all the standards of the OAS resolution. But it was not going to be so easy to deal with Cuba's Fidel Castro, who overthrew dictator Fulgencio Batista on January 1, 1959. The CIA had been involved in Cuba, too, in last-minute attempts to persuade Batista to step aside in favor of someone who would act as a safe lightning rod by absorbing the revolutionary energy building up behind Castro. Unfortunately, Batista remained stubborn—until it was too late to save anything but himself. The cigar-smoking revolutionary in American fatigues entered Havana on the crest of a wave of popular revulsion against Batista,

240

84 Fidel Castro arrives triumphantly in the outskirts of Havana, 1959: this time there were no Rough Riders on San Juan Hill.

and with the support of many in the United States. While still holed up in the mountains, Castro had become a romantic hero through a series of interviews and action photos that appeared in *Life* magazine and other mass media outlets. He continued to enjoy broad support in the American press for several months; then, beginning with the public trials and subsequent execution of Batista henchmen, liberal sympathies began to evaporate. By midsummer 1959 Cuban-American relations were strained. There was talk of cutting back on the Cuban sugar quota, a classic response and sign of displeasure. But Castro found friends in Moscow who boasted that the Monroe Doctrine was dead and said they were ready to defend Cuba with rockets.

Eisenhower's apparent inability to do anything about Castro, to prevent the "theft" of the Cuban "revolution," was, aside from all 241 other strategic and economic considerations, a terrible psychological blow to America's self-image. The Democrats may have lost John Hay's China, but now the Republicans were about to allow "free" Cuba to go by default. The clock had been turned back to 1898, only this time a "splendid little war" could mean nuclear annihilation.

Notes

[1] U.S., Department of Defense, *United States–Vietnam Relations, 1945–1967*, 12 vols. (Washington, D.C.: Government Printing Office, 1971), 1: A-57.

[2] Ibid., C-45.

[3] U.S., Congress, Senate, Committee on Foreign Relations, *Hearings: The President's Proposal on the Middle East*, 85th Cong., 1st sess. (Washington, D.C.: Government Printing Office, 1957), pp. 76–77.

[4] Press conference, May 24, 1953, copy in the Papers of John Foster Dulles, Firestone Library, Princeton University, Princeton, N.J.

[5] U.S., Department of State, *American Foreign Policy, 1950–1955*, 2 vols. (Washington, D.C.: Government Printing Office, 1957), 2: 2261–62.

[6] Quoted in Chalmers Roberts, *First Rough Draft* (New York: Praeger, 1973), p. 134.

[7] U.S., Department of State, *American Foreign Policy, 1950–1955*, 1: 110.

[8] Quoted in Roberts, *First Rough Draft*, pp. 139–40.

[9] Quoted in Robert Murphy, *Diplomat Among Warriors* (New York: Pyramid Books, 1965), pp. 424–32.

[10] Quoted in Walter LaFeber, *America, Russia, and the Cold War, 1945–1966* (New York: John Wiley, 1967), p. 197.

[11] Dinner conversation at Mid-Ocean Club, March 20, 1957, Dulles Papers.

[12] Press conference, May 22, 1953, Dulles Papers.

[13] Press conference, April 7, 1954, Public Papers of the Presidents, 1954 (Washington, D.C.: Government Printing Office, 1956), pp. 382–83.

[14] Interview with Nathan Twining, Dulles Oral History Project, Dulles Papers.

[15] Matthew B. Ridgway, *Soldier: The Memoirs of Matthew B. Ridgway* (New York: Harper, 1956), pp. 279–80.

[16] U.S., Department of Defense, *United States–Vietnam Relations, 1945–1967*, 1: B-21.

[17] Press conference, March 2, 1955, Dulles Papers.

[18] Quoted in the *New York Times*, November 5, 1959.

[19] Remarks at a closed session of SEATO ministers, March 12, 1958, Dulles Papers.

[20] Quoted in Coral Bell, *Negotiation From Strength* (New York: Knopf, 1963), p. 76.

[21] Far East Presentation, May 10, 1955, Dulles Papers.

[22] Remarks before West European Chiefs of Mission, May 9, 1958, and draft of statement, May 4, 1956, Dulles Papers.

[23] Background press conference, June 25, 1955, Dulles Papers.

²⁴ Nikita Khrushchev, *Khrushchev Remembers*, trans. Strobe Talbott (Boston: Little, Brown, 1970), p. 454.

²⁵ Quoted in Jack M. Schick, *The Berlin Crisis, 1958-1962* (Philadelphia: University of Pennsylvania Press, 1971), pp. 110–11.

²⁶ U.S., Department of State, *American Foreign Policy: Current Documents, 1957* (Washington, D.C.: Government Printing Office, 1961), p. 1435.

²⁷ Dwight D. Eisenhower, *The White House Years: Mandate for Change, 1953-1956* (Garden City, N.Y.: Doubleday, 1963), p. 208.

²⁸ U.S., Department of State, *Current Documents, 1957*, p. 1437.

²⁹ Memorandum Re NAC Meeting, September 30, 1953, October 1, 1953, Dulles Papers.

³⁰ Interview with Elliot Bell, Dulles Oral History Project, Dulles Papers.

³¹ U.S., Congress, Senate, Internal Security Subcommittee, testimony of Ambassador Earl T. Smith, *The Communist Threat to the United States Through the Caribbean: Hearings* (Washington, D.C.: Government Printing Office, 1960), p. 700.

Bibliography

Ambrose, Stephen E. *Rise to Globalism.* Baltimore: Penguin Books, 1971. Excellent interweaving of diplomatic and military history, especially good on the Eisenhower years.

Brown, Seyom. *The Faces of Power.* New York: Columbia University Press, 1968. A realist counterpart to Ambrose, also excellent on the Eisenhower and Kennedy years.

Finer, Herman. *Dulles Over Suez.* Chicago: Quadrangle Books, 1966. A bitter attack on American policy, but indispensable.

Goold-Adams, Richard. *The Time of Power: A Reappraisal of John Foster Dulles.* London: Weidenfield & Nicolson, 1962. Just what the title says, and a very interesting one.

Hammer, Ellen J. *The Struggle for Indochina, 1940-1955.* Stanford, Calif.: Stanford University Press, 1966. The most complete survey of these critical years.

Hughes, Emmet John. *The Ordeal of Power.* New York: Atheneum, 1963. The problems of striking out anew. Too much concerned with Eisenhower versus Dulles, but still a good introduction.

Kissinger, Henry. *Nuclear Weapons and Foreign Policy.* New York: Harper, 1957. One of the Dr. Strangelove books that appeared in the 1950s and was to play a role in the shaping of policy in the next decade. An exposé of "liberation" as a sham, like a movie western set.

Lukacs, John. *A New History of the Cold War.* New York: Anchor Books, 1966. A conservative view of the Cold War, centering on European questions and spheres of influence.

Randle, Robert F. *Geneva, 1954.* Princeton, N.J.: Princeton University Press, 1969. An exhaustive look at the conference that ended one war and marked the beginning of a second.

Wise, David, and Ross, Thomas B. *The Invisible Government.* New York: Random House, 1964. A compendium of "spook" tales of the 1950s.

America and the World Revolution: 1961–1976 8

Our objection with Cuba is not over the people's drive for a better life. Our objection is to their domination by foreign and domestic tyrannies. Cuban social and economic reform should be encouraged. Questions of economic and trade policy can always be negotiated. But Communist domination in this Hemisphere can never be negotiated.

John F. Kennedy
January 30, 1961

There is not an example on record of any free state even having attempted the conquest of any territory approaching the extent of Mexico without disastrous consequences. The nations conquered have in time conquered the conquerors by destroying their liberty. That will be our case. . . . This Union would become imperial and the States mere subordinate corporations. But the evil will not end there. The process will go on. The same process by which the power would be transferred from the States to the Union, will transfer the whole from this department of the Government (I speak of the Legislature) to the Executive. All the added power and added patronage which conquest will create, will pass to the Executive. In the end you put in the hands of the Executive the power of conquering you.

John C. Calhoun
January 4, 1848   245

It is usual for American presidential candidates to talk about "turning points" and "critical eras." Sometimes they even believe their own rhetoric. But no presidential candidate in the Cold War years was more convinced of—or more convincing about—America's world role than John Kennedy. On election eve 1960, Kennedy said:

> When I began my campaign for the Presidency I said that just as the issue of the campaign 100 years ago was whether the United States would continue half slave and half free, the issue of this campaign was whether the world would continue half slave and half free, or whether it would move in the direction of freedom or the direction of slavery. . . .

The New Frontiersmen were itching to get the country moving again. "Let the word go forth," the youthful president decreed in his inaugural, "from this time and place, to friend and foe alike, that the torch has been passed to a new generation of Americans. . . ." Eisenhower had entertained Kennedy for a preview briefing on world problems just a day or so before Kennedy's inauguration and, falling into the mood of the New Frontier, nodded his agreement at the latter's persistent questions about Southeast Asia: "You might have to go in there and fight it out."[1]

Eisenhower's uncharacteristic bellicosity (especially in regard to the possibility of putting foot soldiers into Asia) may have confirmed a popular Democratic myth about Eisenhower in Kennedy's mind. Searching for some way to separate Ike (and his vote-getting appeal) from the Republicans, the Democrats pictured him a "Captive Hero." Be that as it may, nothing passed between the two men that afternoon to discourage the president-elect from his chosen course. If anything, Eisenhower's solemnity may have added depth to Kennedy's already fast-moving, high-powered drive to demonstrate the reversibility of historical tides.

CUBAN COUNTDOWN

Although Kennedy had been briefed on the Cuban exile force during the campaign, he and Eisenhower apparently did not spend

85 Kennedy and Eisenhower pondered the Cold War and America's future.

time discussing the possibility of a successful military operation from Guatemala against Castro. This was curious because Cuba and the missile gap were the two principal campaign issues of 1960. Kennedy and his running mate, Senator Lyndon Baines Johnson, had belabored Republican foreign policy failures, and they blamed candidate Nixon's party both for supporting Batista all those years and then for not doing anything about Castro. New York's Republican governor, Nelson Rockefeller, himself a critic of the national administration's sluggishness, had given what he thought was the only answer: "Let's face it. The day of the big stick and the use of the marines in [maintaining?] Western Hemisphere unity is a thing of the past."[2]

247

Nixon knew better, and knew that Kennedy knew better, but he was impotent to do anything about it. The story began when Castro came to the United States in April 1959 as a guest of the American Society of Newspaper Editors. He did not make a favorable impression on Nixon, who received him in Eisenhower's absence. After their talk, the vice president wrote his impressions of the Cuban leader in a memorandum that he circulated within the administration. "At the time the State Department was evaluating Castro as one who could still be saved," Nixon told reporters some time later. "I disagreed, even though I was in a minority. My view began to gain ground slowly in the Administration, until, in March, 1960, my view prevailed. At this time, because of a decision made at the highest level, a program began and men began to be trained."[3] The memo had evaluated Castro as "a captive of the Communists—worse than a Communist because he did everything they wanted while posing as a non-Communist."

Castro had told the newspaper editors that Cuba did not want a loan, only a chance to sell sugar. He left two implications behind as he traveled on to Buenos Aires for a meeting of the Organization of American States. First, the debate within the Cuban Revolutionary Council had been resolved against accepting any aid with strings attached; second, an American economic boycott was already operating in subtle ways. At Buenos Aires he demanded that the United States make available $30 billion to Latin America over a ten-year period to be distributed as the recipients wished and through their own agencies. It was impossible, he said, to finance industrial development through foreign investment. Investors were interested only in a "favorable climate" and looked on poorer countries as an outlet for surplus capital. The governments of those countries, he added in a remark that may have revealed his position in secret economic debates within his own country, were thus placed in a very difficult situation: they must repress their own citizens or risk serious trouble with the governments of industrial nations.[4]

In Washington the speech was dismissed as utopian, although Eisenhower had already been told by close advisers that he needed to take a new look at American aid programs. This review ultimately led, in the Kennedy administration, to the Alliance for Progress, a $20 billion, ten-year program premised on the belief that private enterprise would contribute $300 million a year to a peaceful social revolution in the Western Hemisphere. An ounce of prevention against a pound of cure, but the alliance had trouble coming up with even a half ounce. Revolutions—even peaceful social ones—were risky, especially with a Fidel Castro shouting encouragement to Latin American radicals to follow the Cuban way and launching attacks against neighboring countries.

86 A comment on the Alliance for Progress.

87 This prophecy never came true: Castro found an outlet in Russia.

NOTHING LEFT BUT THE SUGAR

The Cuban way had been announced on May 17, 1959, when Castro promulgated his Agrarian Reform Law. Although few were around who remembered it, the reaction in Washington was very much like the one that had greeted the Mexican Constitution of 1917. Then, as later, the key issue in the American response had been containment and control. The usual method for discouraging Cuban obstreperousness, a cut in the sugar quota, actually made things worse. Castro simply announced that the Soviet Union had offered to exchange sugar for oil, machinery, and technicians. Military intervention, the ultimate resort in Cuban-American relations, was a hazardous business. Nevertheless, as Nixon reported in mid-1960 Eisenhower later authorized the establishment of Guatemalan training camps for Cuban exiles.

Washington had also asked its allies to stop sending arms to Cuba. On March 4, 1960, the French freighter *La Coubre* suffered an explosion on board while unloading Belgian munitions. Seventy-five persons died. "This sabotage," said Castro, "was the work of the enemies of the Revolution. . . . We have no proof, but we have the right to believe that they [American officials] are the guilty ones."[5] Then on July 9, 1960, Khrushchev stunned the world during a speech to a teachers' conference in the Kremlin: "Figuratively speaking, in case of necessity, Soviet artillerymen can support the Cuban people with their rocket fire if aggressive forces in the Pentagon dare to start an intervention in Cuba. . . . We will do everything to help Cuba in its just struggle for liberty."

Castro had shut down the Havana gambling casinos, making the American owners very unhappy. CIA agents contacted at least two of these men through a former FBI agent, Robert A. Maheu. At "that time, and nothing has happened to change my mind," Maheu stated in 1975, "I felt we were involved in a just war." The CIA wanted Maheu to convince his contacts that Castro had to be "eliminated" in connection with "the invasion of Cuba." At first the two gamblers were reluctant. Maheu added: "I personally am convinced that they agreed to join the assignment through me because they thought they were making a contribution to the national security of our country."[6]

This attempt to poison Castro was never carried out. It aborted, as did several other assassination plans, and as did the Bay of Pigs invasion in April 1961.

What began as a contingency plan for landing anti-Castro

88   The last hours of Brigade 2506.

guerillas who would join with dissidents on the island, perhaps stimulating a general uprising, might have been transformed, after Kennedy's election, into something like a conventional war force. Perhaps the Central Intelligence Agency had taken the Democratic candidate's strong words on the need to aid Cuban exiles as a private signal to proceed with an expanded version of the original plan; perhaps, instead, the agency had decided that Kennedy would have to follow through as president whatever was recommended. In either case, the CIA was mistaken. Allen Dulles, director of the agency, convinced the new president to go ahead with a landing at the Bay of Pigs with a promise and a warning. Dulles promised that the invasion would work and warned that Kennedy would have a "disposal problem" getting rid of all those exiles unless they were put ashore in Cuba.

But the president had resolved not to use American "forces" under any circumstances. Almost everything that could go wrong logistically did, but the real breakdown was in communications between Kennedy and the men who originated and planned the Bay of Pigs operation. The Cubans who waded ashore on April 17, 1961, were trained, equipped, and morally supported by the United States. Moreover, the project managers had led them to expect American intervention if things went badly. It never came. Within a matter of days, Brigade 2506 was wiped out, its members all dead, wounded, or taken prisoner.

Kennedy accepted personal responsibility for the fiasco, but he responded to a Khrushchev scolding by universalizing events at the Bay of Pigs into a world struggle between good and evil:

> I believe, Mr. Chairman, that you should recognize that free peoples in all parts of the world do not accept the claim of historical inevitability for the communist revolution. What your government believes is its own business; what it does in the world is the world's business. The great revolution in the history of man, past, present and future, is the revolution of those determined to be free.[7]

Kennedy seemed peevish as well in a speech calling on the American press to sign on for the duration of the Cold War: "We do not intend to be lectured on 'intervention' by those whose character was stamped for all time on the bloody streets of Budapest." In sum, the president's message to the American people and the world was that the only error was failure. Kennedy may not have believed that himself, but the experience of the Bay of Pigs was too shattering for the president to allow himself (or the nation) to face it honestly—not yet anyway.

THE NEW LEGIONS

Besides Cuba, the Democrats in 1960 had harped on Republican military policy, or, more specifically, lack of policy. Reliance on nuclear deterrence alone no longer sufficed in an age of guerilla subversion and counterinsurgency. Moreover, it was argued, Russia's recent technological triumphs in the space race demonstrated that the lead in missile development had passed to the other side. Eisenhower was not naive; neither was he misinformed about Russia's capabilities. The U-2 flights had provided him with what he needed to know to assess the Soviet Union's progress, but it was not information that could be used in a presidential campaign.

Disturbed by the Democrats' use of the missile gap issue to win office, Eisenhower also had trouble understanding those in his own party who had joined in this chorus of calamity. His reply to critics of all political persuasions came, fittingly enough, in a nonpolitical farewell address in which he warned against "the acquisition of unwarranted influence, whether sought or unsought, by the military-industrial complex."

That such a complex existed was hardly to be doubted. Eisenhower's implication, however, that a new conspiracy had blossomed in the very midst of happy, small-town America, misinterpreted the situation. The influence he described was not wielded by a small group of generals and government contractors but had become inherent in the structure of the corporate state. If anything, the generals had been losing influence over military policy. The outstanding business figure in the Eisenhower cabinet had been General Motors' Charles E. Wilson. In the Kennedy-Johnson

253

"COULD YOU POINT OUT THE GROUND YOU'VE TAKEN? WE'RE HERE TO SECURE AND DEVELOP IT ECONOMICALLY."

89   The American "mission" became even more complicated in the Kennedy years.

years, it was Ford's Robert McNamara. Both held the position of secretary of defense.

The argument, then, was between those who were more concerned about overheating the domestic economy than about putting out fires in the mountains and jungles of the developing nations and those who said that it must be done if the industrial nations were to survive and prosper. The first group, the pessimists, lost, largely for two reasons: first, the crises in the Third World seemed to be multiplying with each passing day. Referring to the inflexibility of America's nuclear arsenal, McNamara would shake his head and repeat: "One cannot fashion a credible deterrent out of an incredible action."[8] The proper response to trouble on the village level had to be on that level, at least in the first stages. American "defense" systems had to be better at every level, from subconflict to holocaust, for only then could one be reasonably certain that the president would not have to climb that last rung on the escalation ladder.

The second reason the "firefighters" won the internal debate over how to respond to revolutionary pressure was that they convinced enough people that the military had not been run properly since George Washington's day. A McNamara aide wrote: "President Eisenhower's farewell remarks concerning the potential dangers of the military-industrial complex marked the culmination of almost a decade of growing concern over defense management."[9] So it was all just a matter of systems analysis. Install enough computers monitored by the watchful eyes of management experts, immerse the military in sound business techniques that worked in the private sector, and just watch the results.

The Bay of Pigs experience gave an added fillip to Kennedy's determination to eradicate weakness on every echelon of military bureaucracy in the Pentagon. The missile gap nonsense quickly disappeared, as it well should have, but in its place came new shibboleths like "second-strike capability" and, for a brief, inglorious moment, "counterforce." When Kennedy assumed office the United States already had a nuclear stockpile estimated at thirty thousand megatons, or the equivalent of about ten tons of TNT for every living person. To this arsenal Kennedy added enough ICBMs (intercontinental ballistic missiles) to give the United States 750—four times what the Soviet Union possessed.

In 1967 McNamara candidly, if tardily, admitted that both sides now had too much deterrence for their own good and that the American program at the beginning of the decade, "could not possibly have left unaffected the Soviet Union's nuclear plans."[10] At the time the American buildup began, McNamara was to say, the Soviets only possessed the capability of increasing their nuclear forces. There was no hard evidence that they planned to do so, but on a worst-case basis, American construction went ahead. The counterforce strategy was a spinoff from what otherwise could be called an embarrassment of riches in the nuclear area. Cynics said it must have been adopted to satisfy some puritanical twinge: waste not, want not.

Counterforce enjoyed a brief vogue. It was introduced by the secretary of defense in a 1962 commencement speech at The University of Michigan. The point he seemed to be making was that there existed no incentive for the Soviet Union to attack anything but American cities. But by targeting our missiles on Russian military installations, we might be able to use numerical superiority to provide the other side with reason enough to avoid an attack on major urban centers.

It was never clear, unless a first strike was planned, how counterforce would work. What point could there be in striking at empty missile silos? On one occasion McNamara suggested that the world might be a safer place if both sides had second-strike capabilities, and thus, if the expanded American program did lead the Soviets to construct more missiles, maybe that was not so bad. But while McNamara talked about mutual second-strike deterrence and stability quotients, someone discovered that counterforce coupled with a defense-shelter program implied a first-strike posture. And someone else noted that the Russians could spoil things just by refusing to aim their ICBMs at Minuteman installations. Perhaps McNamara himself remembered that much of the planned missile force (existing and potential) was to consist of submarine-launched Polaris weapons, hardly compatible with a mutual counterforce scenario.

No one mourned the demise of counterforce, but other elements in the Kennedy buildup enjoyed a happier reception—none more so than the army's new Special Forces. Known at once as the Green Berets (the president's own nickname), this elite corps immediately took up the task where its European predecessor, the French Foreign Legion, had failed—in the jungles of Indochina. Alongside the Green Berets were the members of the Peace Corps, another elite group of young men and women sent out to the villages and hamlets of Asia, Africa, and Latin America. The official chronicler of the Kennedy administration, Arthur M. Schlesinger, Jr., wrote that the Peace Corps was obviously suggested by Franklin D. Roosevelt's Civilian Conservation Corps. Only the mission had changed:

> Watching the volunteers as they carried to dark slums and sullen villages examples of modesty, comradeship, hard work and optimism, one wondered whether they were not bringing some inkling of the

90 The replacement for the French Foreign Legion?

meaning of a democratic community to places hitherto inaccessible to the democratic idea, and whether future Nyereres and Sékou Tourés, even perhaps future Nkrumahs and Castros, might not catch fire from their liveliness and devotion.[11]

TWO WEEKS IN OCTOBER

Castro, always Castro. There were neither Green Berets nor Peace Corpsmen in Cuba. Access to the Cuban people, to the "dark slums and sullen villages," had long since disappeared. And the Bay of Pigs misadventure ended any hopes that the connection might be restored by some means short of the extraordinary. The American economic embargo was tightened, but since Havana now had Moscow's unqualified support, that time-honored weapon was likely to be ineffectual.

257

Meeting in January 1962 at Punta del Este, Uruguay, the members of the Organization of American States voted, fourteen to six, to expel Cuba from the inter-American organization. Tiny Haiti cast the key vote, which gave Secretary of State Dean Rusk his needed two-third's majority. Among the dissenters were the largest countries of Latin America—Brazil, Argentina, Mexico, and Chile. The American delegation had worried this might happen but went ahead anyway. On the morning of the vote, Rusk met briefly with the Haitian foreign minister, who remarked that his country desperately needed aid, and this would affect his vote. The secretary turned away but sent dictator François Duvalier's emissary a note that said that "while the United States as a matter of policy did not associate economic aid and political performance, now that Haiti itself had made the link, it had to understand that any future aid would be scrutinized in the light of its role at Punta del Este."[12]

Other votes were less costly to conscience and pocketbook. By a unanimous poll, the OAS declared "that the present Government of Cuba, which has officially identified itself as a Marxist-Leninist government, is incompatible with the principles and objectives of the inter-American system." Rusk then congratulated his fellow delegates for facing the issue. "There has been some uncertainty about whether the OAS was capable of taking hold of this crucial issue on a collective basis. I believe that uncertainty has now ended."[13]

So did Fidel Castro. Convinced that the Punta del Este meeting was the first stage in an excommunication process designed to convict him as a heretic without hope of redemption, the Cuban ruler invoked the "powers of darkness" to come to his aid. Secretary Rusk's words to the nation on Punta del Este certainly lent themselves to Castro's interpretation as much as they did to any other:

> Castro himself, in early December [1961], publicly confessed what everyone had come to know: that he is a Marxist-Leninist and would be until he dies. . . .

> No conference could, by itself, eliminate the problem of communism in this hemisphere. But the results of this conference were deeply reassuring. The hemisphere has taken a long stride forward. . . .

An empty seat at the OAS table is no cause for joy. The rest of us have no quarrel with the Cuban people—only with the regime which has fastened itself upon that country. . . .

We ourselves expelled colonialism from Cuba and provided for its independence. And that is why all delegations joined in a commom hope that we shall be able to welcome a free government of Cuba back into the family of the hemisphere.[14]

Why Khrushchev chose to respond to Cuba's appeal by placing bombers (IL-28's) and intermediate range missiles (IRBMs) on the island remains something of a mystery. Speculations range from purely military considerations to the most complicated political interpretations. Kremlinologists suspected that Khrushchev may have had in mind a package deal involving Berlin and other Cold War questions.

At a summit meeting in Vienna not long after the Bay of Pigs invasion, Kennedy and Khrushchev faced one another across the bargaining table. But there was nothing to bargain about; they were not even talking about the same things. Khrushchev was interested in Berlin and Germany; Kennedy, Cuba and the underdeveloped world. The American president told the Russian leader that his efforts to change the status quo in the Third World were fraught with disaster for them both. Khrushchev said he could not be blamed for American mistakes in supporting reactionaries and returned to a discussion of the abnormal situation in Berlin.

Both men left Vienna in a sober mood. Faced with an internal crisis in East Germany, which had become steadily worse with thousands fleeing to the West through Berlin, Khrushchev wanted American recognition of the GDR as a legitimate state. Kennedy felt, as had Eisenhower, that he could not do so without weakening the American position in Europe. Nor could he withdraw from Berlin, said his advisers, for the same reason.

Back in Washington, the president asked for $3.25 billion more from Congress for military purposes. He wanted funds for 250,000 additional soldiers and 100,000 sailors and airmen. Draft calls were doubled, and then tripled. Reservists were ordered to duty. Speaker of the House Sam Rayburn described the summer of 1961 as the most critical since 1939.

In a chilling speech on July 25, Kennedy told the nation that Berlin was a focal point—"the great testing place of Western courage and will"—where America's solemn commitment met Russian ambitions. "For the fulfillment of our pledge to that city is essential to the morale and security of Western Europe, and to the faith of the entire Free World. Soviet strategy has long been aimed, not merely at Berlin, but at dividing and neutralizing all of Europe, forcing us back on our own shores."

Over the next decade the locale would change, but never the rhetoric. It was all there: containment (and the growing fear of Soviet countercontainment), Eisenhower's domino thesis, and the supposedly discarded Dulles obsession with preventing creeping neutralism. Standing behind Kennedy in these critical weeks was former Secretary of State Acheson, who warned him against the temptation of seeking negotiations. Khrushchev's *démarche*, his threat to sign a separate peace treaty with East Germany, had nothing to do with Berlin, or Germany, or Europe. Khrushchev's hope "was that, by making us back down on a sacred commitment, he could shatter our world power and influence."[15]

Tension rose to a high point on August 14, when the West Berliners awoke to the sight and sound of East German guards putting roadblocks and barbed-wire barricades around the Russian sector. Some hardliners wanted Kennedy to knock down the "Wall," even after a permanent brick version was in place. Besides the risks that would entail, who could stop the East Germans from erecting another wall fifty to one hundred feet behind the border? Khrushchev had "solved" the East German problem in the most brutal way possible. Anyone trying to escape over the wall was shot.

Perhaps, then, the Russians hoped to force a showdown in Cuba, in the expectation that Kennedy would at last yield in Berlin. And, since the missile gap was really on the Soviet side, Khrushchev could bring Russian and American forces into a roughly equal balance by installing missiles and bombers in Cuba—a "quick fix"

91   The Berlin Wall: another Cold War monument.

until his own ICBM production caught up with American output.

According to Castro, the Punta del Este resolutions meant a second Bay of Pigs, only this time there would be no last-minute flinching. Kennedy would go all the way. What could Moscow do to protest the Cuban revolution, Castro asked? Khrushchev offered missiles and bombers. These began arriving in the summer of 1962. The cost was probably near $1 billion, although estimates vary. At any rate, the spending would be appropriate for the biggest nuclear crisis of the Cold War.

Republicans, having recovered from the presidential election, suddenly found that *they* had a Cuban issue, too. At almost every press conference Kennedy was asked to respond to charges that Russia was supplying Cuba with offensive weapons. Describing the missiles as ground-to-air types, Kennedy fended off his tormentors with a final vow that if Cuba were to become an offensive base of "significant capacity," then the United States would do whatever became necessary to protect its own security and that of its allies.

On October 14, 1962, a U-2 returned with the first undeniable   261

LAUNCH STANDS

17 MISSILE ERECTORS

92 The U-2 reports on Khrushchev's "folly."

photographic evidence of the missile installations. It now appeared that Kennedy's repeated insistence that communism in the Western Hemisphere was not negotiable was about to be put to the test. Kennedy first summoned a special committee to plan for all contingencies, then he advised British Prime Minister Harold Macmillan of the situation.

Macmillan's reaction was one of general support, but he had to remind himself "that the people of Europe and of Britain had lived in close proximity to Soviet missiles for several years." He was made uneasy by Kennedy's description of the blockade that had been recommended to him by his war council and asked for all the legal advice the American government's international lawyers could supply on what was normally an illegal operation in time of peace. Kennedy promised Macmillan that the authority for instituting such a blockade would be obtained from the OAS under the 1947 Rio Treaty. "I said that I feared that the invocation of the Rio treaty would not help us very much as I presumed that the United Kingdom had no legal obligations under its terms. Our traditional attitude with regard to the freedom of the seas would put us in an awkward position."[16]

The president passed over this reference to international law with the remark that he understood the British shipping companies still doing business with Cuba were not the most reputable. What difference that made was left for others to decide. Macmillan finally found common ground with Kennedy on the point that the Russians had steadfastly denied they were putting "offensive" weapons into Cuba. On that basis, he agreed that the Russians should be made to acknowledge their deception and to agree to an immediate removal of the missiles and bombers.

At the outset of the discussions in the special advisory group, Kennedy laid down one ground rule. Private negotiations for the removal of the missiles could not be considered. He could not, after all, negotiate such an agreement without it becoming public in some way; and then he would have to face the Republican charge that he had been caught bargaining for the removal of something he had said did not exist.

The committee divided sharply over what course to take. Advocates of an air strike to remove the weapons lost their argument because they could not assure the president an effective surgical removal of the installations. And a botched air strike might be worse than doing nothing. Other members recommended blockade, while reserving the possibility of a landing to prevent Castro and the Russian crews from completing construction on the sites. Secretary of Defense McNamara lodged an interesting dissent against both of these responses. He argued that the missiles did not really alter the balance of power, and therefore Cuba was still a political rather than a military crisis. Except for one or two others, McNamara was alone in this position.

On the night of October 22, 1962, Kennedy announced the blockade against further weapons shipments or support materials. At midweek it appeared that some of the Russian ships had stopped outside the five hundred-mile ring and were circling while waiting for instructions. Kennedy was not much encouraged by this news, and he was correct in predicting that the worst days of the crisis were yet to come. Meanwhile, photographic evidence indicated that work on the sites was proceeding. Over the weekend, October 26–27, two messages arrived from Khrushchev. One, an emotional plea for mutual restraint, offered to remove the missiles in exchange for a pledge that the United States would make no further attempt to overthrow Castro by an invasion. The other, more formal in tone, made the offer contingent on removal of American missiles from Greece and Turkey.

It was decided to answer the first as if the second had not arrived and to send Attorney General Robert Kennedy to assure the Soviet ambassador privately that the president would remove the intermediate-range missiles from Greece and Turkey within a few months. Khrushchev agreed to these terms, and the crisis was ended. Celebrated over and over again as the administration's finest hour, the Cuban missile crisis restored the president's confidence in his advisers, in flexible response, and (perhaps most of all) in himself.

On the negative side, less apparent, but ultimately more important, aspects of the crisis were these: (1) Despite Kennedy's cool outward appearance the world had very nearly gone to war over an issue that did not involve American survival. During the crisis the press was led to believe that the Russian missiles had "tipped" the nuclear balance. In a broadcast near the end of the year, Kennedy acknowledged that the weapons would only have appeared to change the balance of power. But, he said, "appearances contribute to reality."[17] (2) Despite the administration's insistence that communism in the hemisphere was not negotiable, when the moment for decision came, it was. Dean Rusk's famous comment that the two superpowers were eyeball to eyeball and the other fellow blinked was, therefore, somewhat misleading. (3) Throughout the crisis the United States had kept United Nations discussions within the Security Council because, it was apparently suspected, the American case would not have had majority support in the General Assembly. The Cuban crisis, then, might well have marked the end of American hegemony within the United Nations.

264

Another result of the crisis, which affected both Russia and the United States, was the fragmentation of the postwar bipolar security systems. Khrushchev's Chinese critics, long dissatisfied with the Russian leadership of the communist bloc, now had something more than ideology to complain about. Khrushchev was an "adventurer," one of the worst sorts in Marxist lingo, for having put the missiles into Cuba and a coward for having withdrawn them under pressure. In Western Europe, France's Charles de Gaulle used the crisis to demonstrate why his country could not rely on American definitions and decisions in the nuclear age.

SEARCH AND DESTROY

Kennedy's restored self-confidence permitted him to take the initiative over the next several months to reduce the chances of some future miscalculation during a crisis by having a Moscow to Washington "hotline" installed, to come to an agreement on a partial nuclear test ban treaty prohibiting experiments that would poison the atmosphere, and to strike out in a new direction in a famous speech at American University that reviewed the history of the Cold War with a greater degree of detachment than the public was accustomed to hearing. Were these the first soundings in preparation for something bigger?

Who can say? Those who feel that Kennedy had learned from the Cuban crisis that the United States could not impose its will on the world argue that he would not have become ensnared in the Indochina trap. "In the final analysis," Kennedy said on September 3, 1963, "it is their war. They are the ones who have to win it or lose it. We can help them, we can give them equipment, we can send our men out there as advisers, but they have to win it, the people of Vietnam." In 1961, however, 1500 American advisers were in Vietnam; at the time of Kennedy's assassination, 15,500. Neither figure proves a case. But the men who recommended the increases were men who came through the Cuban missile crisis.

McNamara, a dissenter in that crisis, was enthusiastic about winning in Southeast Asia. "Every quantitative measurement we have shows we're winning this war," he said in 1962. The commander in Saigon, General Paul Harkins, was quoted in *Stars and Stripes* on November 1, 1963: "Victory in the sense it would apply to this kind of war is just months away and the reduction of American advisors can begin any time."

As this issue of *Stars and Stripes* was being delivered to the PXs and BXs that morning, a military junta overthrew the Diem regime and took power in Saigon. Diem's inability to control dissent, his sectarian dependence on Catholic supporters, and the Vietcong insurgency in the countryside had brought him down. Official Washington knew about the impending coup; it had cut off aid to Diem on a selective basis in an unmistakable signal to the generals. Garry Wills had it right:

> If Diem was not the George Washington of South Vietnam, then we had to hope for his fall so that a true leader could take his place. Roger Hilsman, who worked in the State Department for Diem's overthrow, said we must be patient and wait for the *real* George Washington to stand up: "Like Egypt, Vietnam would find her Nasser the second time around—or the third—or the fourth."[18]

Three weeks later Kennedy was dead, and Vietnam became Lyndon Johnson's problem. Rumors of the junta's flirtation with "neutralism" were brought to Johnson the weekend of Kennedy's death by a special high-level fact-finding team his predecessor had sent to Saigon. "I am not going to lose Vietnam," Johnson promised. "I am not going to be the President who saw Southeast Asia go the way China went."[19]

The word went back to Saigon that the United States would not tolerate any more talk of surrender or neutralism. At one point Ambassador Maxwell Taylor, Kennedy's favorite military adviser, dressed down the Saigon generals as he might West Point plebes called on the carpet for some high-jinks escapade. "Do all of you understand English?" he began. "I told you all clearly at General Westmoreland's dinner we Americans are tired of coups. Apparently I wasted my words. Maybe this is because something is wrong with my French because you evidently didn't understand."[20]

The coups ceased, but this lack of understanding continued even as American troop levels rose to 500 thousand and the bombers flew more and more sorties over North Vietnam. "By December, 1967, the United States had dropped more tons of explosives—1,630,500—on North and South Vietnam than it did on all World War II targets (1,544,463 tons) and twice as many tons as were dropped during the Korean War."[21] General Nguyen Cao Ky's reply to Ambassador Taylor that day long ago began to have the haunting echo of prophecy: "We know you want stability, but you cannot have stability until you have unity. . . ." In their frustration, Americans, now engaged in a futile search-and-destroy mission throughout the South Vietnamese territory, were destroying any basis for unity outside of the Vietcong revolutionary movement itself.

It can be argued that the Cuban missile crisis, by blotting out the lessons of the Bay of Pigs, encouraged the belief that counterinsurgency was the answer to revolutionary nationalism, thus leading men who should have known better deeper into the jungles of Vietnam. Or it can be argued that sophisticated American policymakers read the outcome in Cuba to mean that revolutionary nationalists would now feel that the superpower stalemate reduced American credibility and that they could continue their subversive activities with impunity. Thus either optimism or pessimism pointed toward deeper involvement.

Yet Johnson ran as a peace candidate in 1964, assuring the electorate that he did not intend to send American boys to Indochina to do what those people should do for themselves. On August 4, he appeared on national television to inform the nation that he had ordered attacks on North Vietnamese PT-boat bases and support installations in retaliation for attacks on American warships, which had been minding their own business in the Gulf of Tonkin. Senator J. William Fulbright then shepherded the Gulf of Tonkin Resolution through the United States Senate as a preventive measure—against Republican flag-waving he thought—but with the publication of the *Pentagon Papers* in 1971, it was revealed that a draft resolution granting the president powers to wage whatever level of "limited" war he felt necessary had been prepared some time before.

Using his authority under the Gulf of Tonkin Resolution to take "all necessary measures to repel any armed attack against the forces of the United States and to prevent further aggression," Johnson initiated the bombing campaign against North Vietnam in the spring of 1965. Rumblings of dissent prompted Johnson to set the record straight, as he saw it, in a speech at Johns Hopkins University on April 7, 1965. The United States had not refused serious negotiations, but neither would it accept anything less than an independent South Vietnam:

> We will not be defeated.
>
> We will not grow tired. . . .
>
> We will use our power with restraint and with all the wisdom that we can command.
>
> But we will use it.

Should the North Vietnamese come to their senses and cease their aggression they could participate in a plan for the development of the Mekong River Valley. Johnson was prepared to ask Congress to appropriate $1 billion for this project in an effort "to replace despair with hope and terror with progress. . . ." This would be a development to "provide food and water and power on a scale to dwarf even our own TVA." America had made mistakes in the past, Johnson conceded without elaborating, but it would always oppose the effort of one nation to conquer another:

> We will do this because our own security is at stake.
>
> But there is more to it than that. For our generation has a dream. It is a very old dream. But we have the power, and now we have the opportunity to make that dream come true.
>
> For centuries nations have struggled among each other. But we dream of a world where disputes are settled by law and reason. And we will try to make it so.[22]

Johnson admitted privately that a case could be made against staying in Vietnam: "White men trying to dominate yellow, etc." But "if we pull out we might as well give up everywhere else"; besides, North Vietnam only had enough materiel and men in the south to continue fighting for another six months. Then he confided that what worried him most was the editorial policy of the *New York Times*. "I can't fight this war without the support of the NY Times."[23] Secretary McNamara was equally candid in confidential discussions, outlining two alternatives:

> Withdrawal: If the U.S. withdrew from SVN, there would be a complete shift in the world balance of power. Asia goes Red, our prestige and integrity damaged, allies everywhere shaken (even those who publicly ask us to quit bombing, etc.). At home, he foresees as a result of these calamities a bad effect on economy and a disastrous political fight that could further freeze American political debate and even affect political freedom.

> On the Other Hand: If the U.S. achieved in SVN the objectives stated by LBJ in Baltimore [the Johns Hopkins speech], there would be substantial political and economic and security gains. Way then open to combine birth control and economic expansion techniques in gigantic arc from SVN to Iran and the Middle East, bringing unimaginable developments to this region, proving worth of moderate, democratic way of growth for societies.[24]

Or, McNamara might have added, the triumph of the American Revolution.

THE DISENCHANTED

By 1968 the Vietnam War had become the dominating fact of American life. The constant assurances of light at the end of the tunnel were no longer believed, except within the president's narrowing circle of supporters, but not even critics had expected the February Tet Offensive, a massive North Vietnamese-Vietcong attack on South Vietnam's cities.

Tet jolted most of the remaining hawks off the roost, but Johnson only redoubled his vow to see the war through. Neither did Secretary of State Dean Rusk evidence any doubts. Asked by a friendly critic to explain what made domestic opposition to the war so effective, Rusk scarcely paused before saying, "The Communist apparatus is working all around the world."[25] (A few years later Nixon officials would prod investigative and intelligence agencies into illegal acts in a futile effort to prove this point.) 269

93   The American Dilemma, ca. 1965—a comment by Feiffer.

Bad news continued to come from Saigon. In the wake of the Tet "setback," during which Vietcong soldiers had even broken into the American Embassy compound, General Westmoreland had asked for two hundred thousand more troops. It did not help that Westmoreland was willing to assert that with these men he could run down the exhausted Vietcong and bring the war to a close; Johnson had heard that one before. To supply additional forces of that number, the president would have had to call up the reserves. And, what would have been equally unpopular, he would have had to ask for increased taxes. A split within the Democratic party had widened into a schism. The south supported the president, although it was thought ready to bolt in favor of a candidate who would promise a quick military victory instead of more computer body-counts. Even if he could hold the south (for how long?), Johnson had lost the "Kennedy" wing to the doves. Senator Eugene

270

94 Peace candidates in a sober mood at the funeral of Martin Luther King.

McCarthy's surprise showing in the New Hampshire primary and the threat of a Robert Kennedy candidacy left Johnson all but alone in the White House. He could not venture outside the presidential mansion without encountering protestors carrying placards denouncing him in obscene terms and touting Ho Chi Minh as the hero of the hour. The majority of Americans were puzzled and angry—puzzled that what they saw on television did not conform to official statements about the war and angry at everyone, protestors and even themselves.

In a final effort to rally support, Johnson summoned a special council of experienced Cold Warriors to the White House. The results of the discussions among the Senior Advisory Group, as it became known, convinced Johnson that he must begin to seek an end to the Vietnam War without further damage to American political and economic institutions.

Of special concern to the hard-headed realists who met with the president in the White House was the cost of the war, the balance of payments, and the gold drain. For the first time since the Second World War, America's economic supremacy was being challenged. The nation's Free World "partners" had shucked ideological restraints in a free-for-all race for markets and investments wherever they could be found. At the same time, European nations were refusing to accept the dollar in payment for American debts.

Vietnam was not the sole cause of America's predicament; Kennedy had expressed concern about the gold drain as early as 1963. A decline in exports coupled with increased imports, foreign aid spending, and foreign investments had brought about a 40 percent decline in gold reserves from post–Second World War holdings. Kennedy had given the Trade Expansion Act of 1962 top priority. "In May of 1962," he told a New Orleans audience, "we stand at a great dividing point. We must either trade or fade. We must either go backward or forward."[26] It was no longer so easy to go forward with West Germany and Japan fully recovered from the war and competing successfully in the world marketplace. Nor was it a good time to take on the added burden of a war in Vietnam. Excluding military aid, the American trade balance slipped steadily from a high point in 1964 of $6.8 billion to $.6 billion in 1968. With the war, American goods became too high priced and, sometimes, unavailable. America's share of manufactured exports in world markets fell from 28.1 percent of the total in 1955 to 20.6 percent in 1968.

These figures do not give the whole picture. For example, the return on American foreign investments had reached $5 billion a year, and other economic indicators demonstrated the continuing power of the nation's economy. But the United States was clearly living beyond its means and doing serious long-run damage to its position in the world economy. Rather than make an unpopular war more unpopular, Johnson had attempted to fight a $150 billion conflict without increased taxes or even domestic wage-and-price controls. In effect, he wanted the rest of the world to pay a large share of the costs by accepting debased dollars for goods and services. That worked for a while.

Johnson was informed by the Senior Advisory Group that he could not give Westmoreland the troops he wanted because the United States could no longer afford to fight that kind of war in Asia. A few days later the president announced he would not be a candidate for reelection. C. Douglas Dillon, a member of the Senior Advisory Group, later testified that the postwar international monetary system depended on a stable dollar. "Our continued inflation at home threatens that stability today. Without a stable dollar, world trade as we know it today would not be possible. . . . I can foresee . . . a worldwide recession or even a depression."[27]

2001: A NIXON ODYSSEY

The seriousness of the situation can perhaps be gauged by the conversion of one of the most famous of the "firefighters"—Richard M. Nixon. Nixon owed his entire political career, both its ups and downs, to the Cold War. He achieved fame as the man who ferreted out Alger Hiss early in the great postwar witch hunt. As Eisenhower's vice president, Nixon was assigned to the general's lowest staff position in charge of pinning labels on the opposition. Nixon flourished in that role, however, and seemed to take pleasure in the knowledge that liberals hated him more than anybody else in American political life except for Senator Joseph McCarthy.

Although Nixon preferred the domestic side of anticommunism, he was well known in the 1960s as a Vietnam "hawk." When he did begin to speak out, it was in the same vein as Arizona's Barry Goldwater. "Why Not Victory?" they asked. Nixon was an active lobbyist for bombing North Vietnam in 1965, citing the "immense mineral potential" of nearby Indonesia, "the region's richest hoard of natural resources," as a reason why Indochina could not be allowed to fall under communist control. The American commitment, Nixon was happy to note later, had been "a vital factor in the turnaround in Indonesia. . . . It provided a shield behind which the anti-communist forces found the courage and capacity to stage their counter-coup [of October 1965]."[28]

Even as he was writing these words, however, Nixon had become concerned about the darker side of the war. After a humiliating defeat in the 1962 California gubernatorial race, Nixon had backtracked to New York City—home base of his enemies in the Republican party. He made a "new" life for himself in a law firm specializing in international corporations and their problems. Whether he became a convert to the Establishment or simply saw an opportunity for one more go at the White House, Nixon began to address himself to a new audience. His articles had usually appeared in *Reader's Digest,* but in 1967 he tried writing for *Foreign Affairs,* an elite marketplace for high-priced intellectual products. His "Asia After Vietnam" article gained him a measure of acceptance, if not affection, with Eastern liberal Republicans. The most interesting point he made was that the People's Republic of China could not remain isolated forever.

When Robert Kennedy was assassinated, the Democrats lost the only candidate who might have succeeded in reuniting the party behind a peace platform. Nixon's nomination thus became worth something to the Republican party and to himself. During the campaign Nixon said he had a plan for ending the Vietnam War, but since the Democratic nominee, Vice President Hubert Humphrey, wanted to talk about everything except Vietnam, Nixon never had to specify details. Actually he had no plan. An offer of free advice came from Roger Hilsman, now disillusioned about finding a George Washington among the generals in Saigon. De-Americanize the war, said Hilsman; turn the responsibility back to South Vietnam. Encourage an actively reformist government that would, on its own, make contacts with the enemy. It would take a year or two for the results to become clear. "And by that time, the situation would be sufficiently fuzzed-up and the American involvement sufficiently downgraded, that Washington could go decently

95　The "new" Nixon edges out Hubert Humphrey in 1968.

to Geneva and negotiate a settlement with Hanoi and the NLF that would be a surrender in fact but not in crucial appearance."[29]

The South Vietnamese might even surprise everyone and win—but that was a long shot, and Nixon should not base policy on such an unlikely outcome. It was better to concentrate on practical matters, forgetting about falling dominos and other myths of the recent past. Variations of this scheme had been circulating for some time. Republican Senator George Aiken suggested that since America had never lost a war, we should declare a victory and come home. General James Gavin favored a "strategic enclave" posture as a prelude to a complete withdrawal at some unspecified date.

Nixon's approach combined elements from all of these plans, but it was agonizingly slow. The president reduced American forces in twenty-five thousand-man increments, just enough, it seemed, to keep Nixon one speech ahead of the antiwar movement. Vietnamization, some said, was just an attempt to gain a "decent interval" between the withdrawal of American forces and the inevitable fall of Saigon. Nixon, too, may have believed this, but if so, he never let on in public or (as far as is known) in private. On April 20, 1970, Secretary of State William Rogers told the Senate Foreign Relations Committee that Vietnamization was working well and about on schedule. There was no need to expand the war into neighboring Cambodia or Laos; indeed, if that happened it would be a confession of failure. The possibility of expansion had been discussed because of the recent North Vietnamese campaigns in Cambodia to protect their supply lines.

Rogers was not the best source of information within the Nixon administration. Ten days later the president appeared on television to inform his countrymen of an "incursion" into Cambodian territory to destroy the enemy's potential for attacking South Vietnam. All the protests during the Johnson administration were surpassed by the outburst that greeted this announcement. But a promise to remove all American troops from Cambodia within six weeks cooled things off again.

Responsibility for the "incursion" plan probably belonged to National Security Adviser Henry Kissinger. The most recent of a series of Cold War intellectuals to serve as resident-advisers in the White House, Kissinger had long felt that American policymakers missed too many opportunities to make their opponents react. The only way to create new options for yourself, he argued, was to get the other fellow reacting to your initiatives. Then the options would appear. But not in Cambodia. The domestic outcry was bad enough, but the operation proved only that the South Vietnamese still could not stand on their own.

The long shot had been tried—and it fell short. Nixon and Kissinger were reformed gamblers in the summer of 1972, when the latter indicated to the North Vietnamese negotiators in Paris that the United States would allow North Vietnamese troops to remain in South Vietnam after the cease-fire. To gain South Vietnam's acquiescence in this step, Nixon sent huge shipments of military hardware to Saigon, carried out a series of "brutalizing" air raids over North Vietnam, and assured the government of President Thieu of American support in the event that the North Vietnamese violated the truce.

96   After one last series of bombings, America gets out of Vietnam.

But no matter how the cease-fire document was presented to Thieu he knew that it meant America had given up on its self-assigned task in Southeast Asia. Senator Charles Percy visited Saigon in December 1972 while the document still lay unsigned on Thieu's desk. His message, like Kissinger's, was blunt:

> I expressed my view that continuing U.S. assistance to South Vietnam would be in jeopardy if Saigon refused to sign. I told him [Foreign Minister Tran Van Lam] that the people of the United States would not accept a continuation of the war, and that in my judgment 99 percent of the American people supported President Nixon's efforts to end the war now through a negotiated settlement.[30]

Percy's first, and most important, stop had been Japan, where he found assurances that Japan and the United States were moving toward a new era of cooperation and interdependence. "American business and agriculture have one of the greatest opportunities in history for developing an entirely new market in Japan with the potential of employing over one million American workers and   277 accounting for up to $10 billion in exports to Japan by 1976, the 200th anniversary of America's Independence."[31]

BACK TO BEGINNINGS

A post–Cold War view now predominated in the Nixon administration. Senator Percy's reactions and findings were only typical of the newly developed consensus. "It is a time when a man who knows the world will be able to forge a whole new set of alliances," Nixon told Garry Wills as he began his campaign for the presidency, "with America taking the lead in solving the big problems. We are now in a position to give the world all the good things that Britain offered in her Empire without any of the disadvantages of nineteenth-century colonialism."[32] Much to the dismay of his former right-wing supporters—who thought he had learned all the wrong things during his six-year sojourn in Rockefeller country—Nixon set about dismantling the Cold War superstructure immediately after assuming office. It had become evident that the Soviet Union, far from engaging in adventurist foreign policies, liked the world pretty much as it was, especially if it could purchase what it needed in the West. Moreover, the classic balance-of-power strategy, ignored during the many years of bipolar thinking and ideological supremacy, had a new appeal for American leaders. The Sino-Soviet split seemed to offer a marvelous opportunity to exploit the confusions and contradictions in the communist world.

As the world got closer chronologically to 1984, it moved away from George Orwell's fictional *1984*, which had depicted a future in which the bipolar structure and ideology dominated everywhere. With little fanfare, Nixon traveled to Berlin in 1969 to call for an end to Cold War tensions in the city. Two years later a four-power pact was signed. According to the agreement, guarantees of free access between West Berlin and West Germany were exchanged for assurances that West Berlin would never be incorporated into the Federal Republic. In a sense, Berlin had been "neutralized." With great fanfare, Nixon flew to Peking, walked on the Great Wall, and toasted Chairman Mao Tse-tung in the Great Banquet Hall. As a

97 Nixon in China: the Cold War becomes history.

result of that historic journey, Formosa was "neutralized." Two of the most dangerous Cold War issues thus passed into history.

A Vietnamese truce agreement was not signed until after the 1972 election, in January 1973. Once again, pledges of reconciliation and peaceful settlement were made. Kissinger had even talked about economic aid for the reconstruction of *both* Vietnams. Even had there been no new outbreak of fighting, it is very doubtful that Kissinger could have redeemed any such pledge. Turning his energies to the problems of Strategic Arms Limitation (SALT), the national security adviser, now also secretary of state, had more than enough to do in that sphere. Concomitant with the new *détente* policy was a general tightening of economic policies pursued since the end of the Second World War. In August 1971, Nixon had announced that America had been competing with one hand tied behind its back. That would have to end. And unless the industrialized nations eased restrictions on American imports, the United States would have to retaliate.

279

"THANKS A LOT."

98 A caustic comment on the end in Vietnam.

In Japan these policies became known as "Nixon Shock," but the biggest shock of all was about to explode: Watergate. Kissinger continued alone as Nixon became more and more absorbed in the desperate maneuvers that finally brought an end to his presidency. Kissinger's view of the world pictured the future in terms of another historical analogy, different from the Munich or Pearl Harbor images favored during the Cold War. As he saw it, the world now resembled the structure of the pre–First World War era, when major powers confronted one another through client states not fully under their—or anyone's—control. And the modern revolutionary, with his near-psychotic fixation on narrow questions and utopian dreams, was not unlike the Serbian patriot who had rushed forward to strike a blow for his fatherland's freedom and brought down the civilized world.

The "structure of peace" Nixon and Kissinger had been building for four years suddenly seemed dangerously weak at almost every stress point. The 1973 Yom Kippur War not only threatened big power confrontation, but the Arab oil boycott and the sudden appearance of an oil-producer's cartel (OPEC), which included countries from other parts of the world, weakened Western unity and undermined the economy of all the major industrial countries outside of the communist world.

Triggered by the oil boycott, a world recession quickly deepened into the worst slump since the prolonged Great Depression of the 1930s. Gloomy assessments and dire predictions abounded, none more frightening than Secretary Kissinger's own dark pronouncements about history repeating itself. For several years the United States had resisted efforts by the raw-materials producers to arrange among themselves, and between themselves and the industrial nations, special marketing agreements that would establish a rough parity between the prices they received and the prices paid for industrial goods. Proposals of this nature were routinely dismissed in Washington as obnoxious restraints on trade, harmful to all concerned. OPEC's success challenged that view, as well as America's presumed right to say what constituted a restraint on trade and what

99 The end of America's mission in Vietnam.

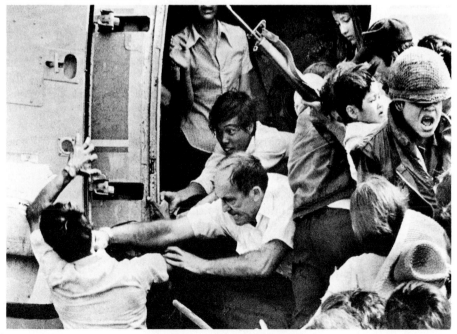

100 President Gerald Ford promises no retreats into "isolationism."

defined economic fair play. Under this pressure, Kissinger agreed to explore the possibilities of a more regulated system of international trade.

Meanwhile, however, other industrial nations complained that the United States refused to take the lead in reflating the world economy out of narrow concern for the rate of domestic inflation. But all the once-magical Keynesian words had been uttered, and the economy no longer quickened to their charm. Kissinger and Gerald Ford, Nixon's successor, discovered a new world all about them—one that they would very much have preferred not to have found at all. Everything seemed topsy-turvy in this world.

Europe's southern frontier—Turkey, Greece, Italy, and Spain—was at odds with itself and threatened by revolutionary upheavals. Portugal (like Rhode Island almost two centuries before?) was already caught in the throes of such an upheaval and was regarded as a danger to all the rest. Moreover, Angola, Lisbon's former African colony, the oldest European stronghold in that continent, had become the same sort of crisis area as the pre–First World War Balkans, complete with big-power intrigues and war alarms. The United States, using Cold War-style techniques and CIA methods, duly sent aid to "friendly" Angolan forces locked in combat with "pro-Russian" forces. Everything was confused about Angola, including a tacit Washington–Peking alliance to thwart Russian ambitions. And all this was happening at the same time that the full story of CIA involvement in assassination plots dating from Eisenhower's time finally became public.

Ike's almost casual reference to Patrice Lumumba at a National Security Council meeting had led, like Henry II's remark about Becket, to a CIA scheme for "neutralizing" the untrustworthy Congolese leader. Unlike King Henry's men, the CIA operatives moved too slowly, and when they were finally ready, Lumumba was already dead—"neutralized" by other enemies. They were not too late in Chile, however, although the plan of action against Marxist President Salvador Allende was somewhat less direct. Vast sums of money were spent over a period of years to prevent an Allende election victory, and no avenues went unexplored for making things difficult for his government once Allende assumed power in 1970. "The CIA," stated a Senate report, "was instructed by President Nixon to play a direct role in organizing a military coup d'etat in Chile to prevent Allende's accession to the presidency."

Included in these measures were ingenious manipulations of the media against Allende and even plans to kidnap the commander of the Chilean armed forces, General René Schneider. Finally, Ambassador Edward Korry delivered a blunt warning to a former president of Chile that

> not a nut or bolt will be allowed to reach Chile under Allende. Once Allende comes to power, we shall do all within our power to condemn

283

101 The last frontier?

Chile and the Chileans to utmost deprivation and poverty, a policy designed for a long time to come to accelerate the hard features of a Communist society in Chile.[33]

Chile was "saved" for the Free World by Allende's overthrow and death in 1973, but it was too late to do much about South Vietnam and Cambodia, both of which "fell" to the Communists in the spring of 1975. Laos soon followed suit, albeit in less dramatic fashion. Confronted by the complete collapse of the South Vietnamese regime, Gerald Ford did not hesitate to ask Congress for yet another appropriation to shore up the crumbling defense system around Saigon. Politics played a large part in this unnecessary postscript to America's longest war, but Ford also met the most glaring examples of "exceptional" CIA behavior and wrongdoing with little more than promises to do better in the future. He still professed to see the greatest danger in America's future in talk of a new isolationism. At Notre Dame University he said: "While we pursue a world in which there is unity and diversity, we must continue to support security against aggression and subversion. To do otherwise would invite greater violence. We are counseled to withdraw from the world and go it alone. I have heard that song before. I am here to say I am not going to dance to it."

Ford's efforts to blunt the current almost daily revelations of CIA involvement in a variety of illegal acts throughout the world and at home thus ended on a note of reaffirmation of American exceptionalism. He promised administrative changes, but added, "I wouldn't rule out necessary political activities by the United States if it involves our security." Where did security end and empire begin? The course of American history from the Louisiana Purchase to the Truman Doctrine and beyond reflected the difficulty Americans had in drawing a dividing line.

Their leaders would impose a liberal-democratic vision on the world, if only because they could not draw that line or feel secure at home until, as Wilson had put it, the world had been made safe for democracy. During the First World War Wilson promised Mexican newspaper editors that the time would come when Mexico would be able to welcome foreign capital without fear. The old empires would never dominate the world again:

> So soon as you can admit your own capital and the capital of the world to the free use of the resources of Mexico, it will be one of the most wonderfully prosperous countries in the world. And when you have the foundations of established order, and the world has come to its senses again, we shall, I hope, have the very best connections that will assure us all a permanent cordiality and friendship.

In the Cold War that vision confronted its greatest challenge, which, American leaders insisted, emanated from the Kremlin. But while billions were spent on atomic weaponry, the only fighting that took place was in Korea, the Middle East, Cuba, Indochina. So great was the evil to be overcome, said the authors of NSC-68, that extraordinary measures were warranted—indeed compelled:

> Our free society, confronted by a threat to its basic values, naturally will take such action, including the use of military force, as may be required to protect those values. The integrity of our system will not be jeopardized by any measures, covert or overt, violent or non-violent, which serve the purposes of frustrating the Kremlin design, nor does the necessity for conducting ourselves so as to affirm our values in actions as well as words forbid such measures, provided only that they are appropriately calculated to that end and are not so excessive or misdirected as to make us enemies of the people instead of the evil men who have enslaved them.[34]

Unfortunately, each new measure, whether it was the plan to assassinate Fidel Castro or the Phoenix Program for killing Vietcong political leaders, was always "appropriately calculated" and justified in the name of national security. Watergate awoke many to the danger that the "integrity of our system" was indeed linked to "national security," but not in the way supposed by the authors of NSC-68. If it was possible to carry out covert measures against the external enemy, why not against domestic opponents—finally, against anyone on a list of White House enemies?

And instead of "frustrating the Kremlin design," the process was making us enemies of ourselves.

One has to look deep for the source of this madness, into ourselves surely, but also into the empire we had built in the name of antiempire. "In the end," said Calhoun, "you put in the hands

286

of the Executive the power of conquering you." The bill of impeachment drawn up by the House of Representatives against Richard Nixon read almost like a modern addition to the list of particulars lodged against George III in the Declaration of Independence. It will be interesting indeed to see what follows and if the post-Watergate years prove finally whether Calhoun was right or wrong.

Notes

[1] Quoted in Theodore Sorenson, *Kennedy* (New York: Harper & Row, 1965), p. 640.

[2] Quoted in J. P. Morray, *The Second Revolution in Cuba* (New York: Monthly Review Press, 1962), p. 98.

[3] Quoted in Chalmers Roberts, *First Rough Draft* (New York: Praeger, 1973), p. 186.

[4] William Appleman Williams, *The United States, Cuba, and Castro* (New York: Monthly Review Press, 1962), pp. 107–09.

[5] Quoted in Morray, *Second Revolution,* p. 94.

[6] Quoted in the *New York Times,* July 31, 1975, p. 11.

[7] Quoted in Richard J. Walton, *Cold War and Counter-Revolution: The Foreign Policy of John F. Kennedy* (New York: Viking Press, 1972), p. 14.

[8] Quoted in Alain C. Enthoven and K. Wayne Smith, *How Much Is Enough?* (New York: Harper & Row, 1971), p. 124.

[9] Quoted in Ibid., p. 8.

[10] Speech at San Francisco, September 18, 1967, in U.S., Department of State, *American Foreign Policy: Current Documents, 1967* (Washington, D.C.: Government Printing Office, 1969), pp. 17–24.

[11] Arthur M. Schlesinger, Jr., *A Thousand Days: John F. Kennedy in the White House* (Boston: Houghton Mifflin, 1965), pp. 608–09.

[12] Quoted in Ibid., p. 782.

[13] Quoted in *The Winds of Freedom: Selections from the Speeches and Statements of Secretary of State Dean Rusk, June 1961–August 1962,* ed. with an introduction by Ernest K. Lindley (Boston: Beacon Press, 1963), p. 148.

[14] Quoted in Ibid., pp. 144–48.

[15] Quoted in Schlesinger, *Thousand Days,* p. 381.

[16] Harold Macmillan, *At the End of the Day, 1961–1963* (London: Macmillan, 1973), p. 193.

[17] Public Papers of the Presidents, 1962 (Washington, D.C.: Government Printing Office), pp. 897–98.

[18] Garry Wills, *Nixon Agonistes: The Crisis of the Self-Made Man* (Boston: Houghton Mifflin, 1970), p. 463.

[19] Quoted in Tom Wicker, *JFK and LBJ: The Influence of Personality Upon Politics* (Baltimore: Pelican Books, 1968), p. 205.

[20] Airgram to Washington, December 24, 1964, in *The Pentagon Papers,* New York *Times* edition (New York: Bantam Books, 1971), p. 379.

[21] Wicker, *JFK and LBJ,* p. 286.

22 U.S., Department of State, *American Foreign Policy: Current Documents, 1965* (Washington, D.C.: Government Printing Office, 1968), pp. 848–52.

23 Memorandum of off-the-record conversation with Johnson, June 24, 1965, from a copy in the Arthur Krock Papers, Princeton University Library, Princeton, N.J.

24 Memorandum of a conversation with McNamara, April 22, 1965, from a copy in the Krock Papers.

25 Quoted in Henry Graff, *The Tuesday Cabinet: Debate and Decision on Peace and War under Lyndon B. Johnson* (Englewood Cliffs, N.J.: Prentice-Hall, 1970), p. 134.

26 Quoted in Jim Heath, *John F. Kennedy and the Business Community* (Chicago: University of Chicago Press, 1969), p. 91.

27 U.S., Congress, Joint Economic Committee, Subcommittee on Foreign Economic Policy, *Hearings: A Foreign Economic Policy for the 1970s*, 91st Cong., 1st sess. (Washington, D.C.: Government Printing Office, 1970), p. 64.

28 Quoted in Peter Dale Scott, "The Vietnam War and the CIA—Financial Establishment," in Mark Selden, ed., *Remaking Asia: Essays on the American Uses of Power* (New York: Pantheon, 1974), p. 107.

29 Quoted in Richard Whalen, *Catch the Falling Flag: A Republican Challenge to His Own Party* (Boston: Houghton Mifflin, 1972), p. 86.

30 "Economic and Political Developments in the Far East," Report by Senator Charles Percy to the Senate Committee on Foreign Relations, March 30, 1973, 93rd Cong., 1st sess. (Washington, D.C.: Government Printing Office, 1973), p. 1.

31 Ibid.

32 Quoted in Wills, *Nixon Agonistes*, p. 20.

33 Quoted in the *International Herald Tribune*, November 22 and 23, 1975.

34 NSC-68, *A Report to the National Security Council by the Executive Secretary on United States Objectives and Programs for National Security, April 14, 1950* (declassified, February 27, 1975).

Bibliography

Ball, George. *The Discipline of Power.* Boston: Little, Brown, 1968. An insider's survey of how America neglected Europe in the Vietnam War.

Barnet, Richard J., and Muller, Ronald E. *Global Reach.* New York: Simon and Schuster, 1974. The role of multinational corporations in the making of one world.

Brandon, Henry. *The Retreat of Power.* New York: Doubleday, 1973. An excellent look at the Nixon-Kissinger strategy.

Halberstam, David. *The Best and the Brightest.* New York: Random House, 1972. How the best and the brightest got carried away, if they did.

Schurmann, Franz. *The Logic of World Power.* New York: Pantheon, 1974. Ideology and practice.

PICTURE CREDITS

289

Index

295

A 6
B 7
C 8
D 9
E 0
F 1
G 2
H 3
I 4
J 5